WHERE TO SKI

in Austria

Edited by
Chris Gill

Consultant Editor
Dave Watts

Guide
EDITORS

Contents

The resorts

The resort descriptions are arranged in chapters which may cover:
* ❄ a large ski area linking several resorts (eg Arlberg)
* ❄ a single resort (eg Obertauern)
* ❄ a group of resorts that share a lift pass (eg Ziller valley)

Foreword

by Martin Bell

Austrians live, breathe, eat, drink and dream skiing. They claim to be the 'Ski Nation Nummer Eins,' and with good reason: in Alpine racing, the Austrians have won the Nations Cup every season for the past 30 years – a team dominance that is unparalleled in any other sport.

My own skiing career is rooted in this culture. My first experience of it was on a family holiday to Fieberbrunn, aged 7. I still remember the jovial ski instructors, and the joyful lederhosen-clad antics of the Tiroler Abend. Two years later, my first serious race was at the British Junior Championships in idyllic Alpbach. And I spent four of my teenage years at the elite Stams Ski Gymnasium (also in Tirol) really learning to race, alongside the world's best.

The great temple of alpine ski-racing finds its home in Austria. Cricket has Lords, tennis has Wimbledon, golf has St Andrews; ski-racing has Kitzbühel. The very name still sends a shiver down my spine.

In 1986, I became the first British skier to finish in the top 15 in Kitzbühel's World Cup Hahnenkamm downhill race, on the infamous Streif. At the time, I was simply relieved to make it across the finish line in one piece. In 1994, my brother Graham repeated the feat; I'm proud to say that we are still the only Brits to have done it.

The Hahnenkamm downhill race is something every skier should witness: 50,000 juiced-up spectators, many of whom have had at least one *grosses Bier* for breakfast, scream encouragement as the racers hurtle past at up to 95mph.

That same passion permeates the whole Austrian ski industry. You'll find it in your instructor if you join an Austrian ski school, and quite possibly if you join a school on the far side of the world: wherever there's skiing, you'll find Austrian instructors – it's as if they are on a mission to share their love of skiing.

Austrians love to share other things too – including home-distilled Schnapps. Hospitality, and a down-to-earth sense of humour, run deep in their culture. I would go as far as to say: if you have not skied in Austria, you are not yet a true skier.

I have known Chris Gill for decades; he is one of the UK's most knowledgeable writers on ski resorts. What Chris and his fellow editor Dave Watts do best is to pin down what different British holiday skiers are looking for in a resort, and spell out to what extent each resort can provide it.

This isn't just a matter of sitting at a desk and gathering information. Chris and Dave have repeatedly visited all the resorts they write about. This is crucial. Take the matter of the difficulty of the runs, for example: the colour-coding varies notoriously between resorts; there is no substitute for personal observation.

Personal observation, with balanced judgements and clear conclusions, are exactly what you get with this guide. Enjoy it, and *'viel Spass beim Schifahren!'*

Martin Bell
Eagle, Colorado, 20 August 2017

◀ the finish of the Streif at Kitzbühel, before the crowds arrive

About this book

by the editor

If you're a skier, you probably know *Where to Ski and Snowboard* – the annual guide to all the resorts that matter to a British skier, published from 1994 to 2015.

Or maybe you don't. WTSS, edited by me and Dave Watts, set the standard for ski resort guides for those 20-odd years, seeing off various rival books (including *The Good Skiing Guide*, which I started back in the 1980s while editor of *Holiday Which?* magazine). WTSS was widely recognised as the British skier's bible.

Based on the same foundations of thorough research, impartial evaluation, warts-and-all text and reader-friendly layout, the book you're reading is the first in a new series of smaller resort guides, each dealing with a single country. *Where to Ski in Italy* is published alongside this book; France, Switzerland and other countries will follow. Various ebook versions are planned, too.

This book is all-new: it has been written from scratch, and has a new structure – an improved one, I hope. As you might expect, it covers more resorts in Austria than WTSS did – some resorts that had been squeezed out by cost pressures are back, and some resorts are covered in detail for the first time.

You might expect this book to cover the resorts in more detail, too. Well, it does and it doesn't. Some of the detail that seemed necessary in 1994 (or even 2004) is now made largely redundant by comprehensive resort websites and feedback sites such as TripAdvisor. So, some of that detail (on hotels, for example) has gone.

On the other hand, a book covering 80 resorts rather than 350 has room for more detailed analysis of the skiing. In these new books, beginners get more attention, and the broad church of intermediate skiers is split: the needs of cautious 'true blue' skiers are considered separately from those of confident intermediate skiers.

Much of the redundant detail that has disappeared was also quick to go out of date. With that detail gone, annual revision looks extravagant; so these new books will stay on sale for about three years before they are revised. Don't expect a revised edition before 2020.

Where to Ski and Snowboard started life as *Where to Ski*. The 'Snowboard' was added in year three, after Dave and I decided to get to grips with boarding, and sent ourselves off to Colorado to take a course strictly for grown-ups. Twenty years on, ski resorts are still called ski resorts; so the 'Snowboard' has gone.

My WTSS co-editor Dave Watts is acting as consultant editor to this series, which means he is making contributions to some chapters based on his resort visits, and bringing his vast experience to bear by reviewing others. But I carry the can: comments and contradictions to me, please – or compliments, if you like.

Creating this book has been hard work, but I've really enjoyed the process; I hope you enjoy reading the result, and find it helps you decide ... where to ski in Austria.

Chris Gill
Exeter, 23 August 2017
chris.g@wheretoski.co.uk

ON TOP OF THE WORLD

#GET MORE WINTER

Fresh tracks, steaming hot chocolate and fun with friends.

From first timers to old pros - it's your winter, so make the most of it.

Find your place on the mountain at crystalski.co.uk

ATOL protected. For more information please see our booking conditions.

CRYSTAL
SKI HOLIDAYS

Austria: an introduction

by the editor, Chris Gill

Austria and France are where most British skiers take their holidays – together, they have around 60% of the market, with France currently taking the slightly bigger share. Go back 30 or 40 years, though, and it was Austria that dominated – until France was propelled to the top of the league in the mid-1990s by the big lift systems and reliable snow of its high, purpose-built resorts.

But now the tide has turned again: in recent years Austria has steadily regained ground, and it's not hard to figure out why: outstanding snowmaking that compensates for low altitudes, world-class lift systems and competitive prices.

For many people wavering between France and Austria, day-to-day prices will often be the clincher: your morning coffee, lunchtime pasta, afternoon glühwein and après beers are going to be way cheaper in Austria than in France.

Austrian resorts now set the standard for slick lift systems, while France now lags behind. Austria still lacks ski areas to match the very biggest in France, such as the Trois Vallées, Paradiski and Portes du Soleil; but it now has a healthy number of linked areas scoring four stars for size in this book, which means offering at least 160km of pistes – enough to satisfy most keen piste bashers.

Perhaps even more impressive than Austria's progress on the lifts front is its achievement in improved snowmaking. The low altitude of many resorts is always going to affect snow quality on the home slopes, particularly later in the season. But Austria's snowmaking is now so powerful and heavily used that you can generally count on all the key pistes being open for a long season.

Although snowmaking has been a lifesaver for many Austrian resorts, it's also worth noting that the most snowy resorts in the Alps are in Austria – in Vorarlberg, in the north-west, where many Atlantic storms first hit the Alps. Little Warth is the snowiest, but the linked bigger resorts of Lech and Zürs are not far behind.

Enduring appeal

At the same time, some skiers have always preferred Austrian resorts because of their enduring qualities – attractive, traditional villages at the heart of long-standing rural communities, prettily wooded landscapes, and incomparably lively beer-fuelled après-ski and nightlife.

The classic Austrian resort is a village developed in traditional chalet style on the valley floor, with a church conspicuously at its heart; sometimes it will have skiing immediately above the village on gentle, wooded valley sides, sometimes all or most of the skiing will be on higher slopes above steeper woods.

Austria doesn't really do purpose-built high-altitude ski stations, in the way that arch-rival France does, though there are a few resorts high up on open slopes – Zürs, Obergurgl and Obertauern come to mind. But even these much-expanded old settlements have retained their traditional chalet style.

If there is one thing that defines the divide between Austria and France, it is the après-ski scene. Many Austrian resorts have mid-mountain restaurants where crowds of people abandon skiing for the day in mid-afternoon and congregate on the terraces to consume large quantities of beer to the sound of thumping music of various primitive kinds.

Even restaurants that don't attract such crowds are likely to carry on serving drinks and sometimes food to a surprisingly late hour, without intervention from the piste patrol. Restaurants on the lower slopes may carry on serving well into darkness.

A version of this phenomenon has been manufactured in some French resorts in recent years, chiefly in the form of the Folie Douce chain, but it's not the same –

Look after yourself

In these new guides I have tried to give direct guidance to specific groups of skiers about which resorts and which runs will suit them. In particular, I have tried to help a group that we perhaps neglected slightly in the many editions of *Where to Ski and Snowboard*: the inexperienced, not entirely competent or confident early intermediate skier.

Obviously, giving clear guidance of this kind is problematic. I don't know your individual abilities or how well equipped you are; I can't guess at the conditions you'll meet; I can't guarantee that the judgements Dave and I have made are absolutely consistent from day to day, or year to year, although after 30 years in this business it's reasonable to hope that they are.

So I feel bound to say that you should not decide what runs you ski on a particular day on the basis of what you read here. Treat this book as a starting point. If you haven't reached the stage where you can get down any slope (given enough time), you should ideally be skiing with others who know the slopes and understand the current conditions. This might mean joining a class or hiring a private instructor.

Skiing off-piste

At the other end of the scale, this book also spells out the opportunities in each resort for off-piste skiing – or freeriding, as it is now branded. Off-piste skiing is inherently dangerous; avalanches are the high-profile hazard, but there are others. Off-piste skiing requires specialised skills, equipment and – crucially – knowledge, some of it general and some of it very local. For most people, the only safe way to do it is with professional guidance.

more a display of conspicuous consumption (often of champagne) than a naturally boisterous party. And the piste patrol certainly does intervene as the lifts close.

I suspect a link between Austria's vibrant après-ski scene and a less attractive feature of Austria – the short skiing day. The lifts in many resorts close at 4pm, regardless of the hours of daylight. So (in spring, especially) you head for a hut for a couple of hours. Do the breweries perhaps control the lift companies?

Some Austrian resorts are very lively later in the evening, too. In places like Saalbach, Ischgl, St Anton and Sölden you can just carry on partying through the evening – you'll see people in ski boots and carrying skis at all hours – or resume after dinner.

Restaurant norms

Of course, the mountain restaurants do function as restaurants, too. Here, Austria has positives and negatives to weigh in the balance. Many resorts have countless small, traditional restaurants, with most offering table service. Large shared tables are the norm, which can lead to jolly exchanges with fellow lunchers if you find a language in common – but also means that reservations are rarely possible, and even bagging a few seats for chums who are running late can be a challenge.

More of a concern for those with any interest in food is that a great many Austrian huts serve a very limited range of drearily standard dishes, with spag and frankfurters featuring prominently. Spare ribs can seem like a special treat.

As the Gastein valley website puts it with some delicacy:

'… in this part of the world, there are certain dishes you expect to encounter whenever you stop in at a ski hut. Don't get us wrong, goulash soup and hot dogs still have their rightful role to play … but every now and then you also develop a yearning for something more refined.'

To tackle the problem, Gasteinertal has picked up an idea first developed in Alta Badia, in the Italian Dolomites. Here it's called Skihauben. Seven restaurants serve 'gourmet' dishes devised by top chefs from around Salzburger Land, using regional ingredients; the dishes cost no more than €15 a pop.

There is also a wider trend towards more civilised lunching. The Sonnbühel above Kitzbühel, for example, has been taken over by an Italian who serves a wide-ranging menu including lots of seafood – and takes bookings, even on the terrace.

Not that I'm against traditional Austrian nosh altogether. I consume a lot of the aforementioned *gulaschsuppe*. And all visitors to the Austrian Alps are required to try, at least once, the famous *Kaiserschmarrn*. This is a thick pancake chopped into chunks and served with fruity sauces. It carries a risk of addiction — and also a risk of over-ordering; portions can be large. You have been warned.

Sadly, Austria still hasn't got a grip on smoking in restaurants. There are rules, but they are either too complex or too slack — you never quite know whether a given establishment will or will not be smoke-free. (Actually, you can be pretty confident that it will not be.) In a world where the Italians managed to put a stop to smoking in restaurants overnight, the Austrian performance is pathetic.

Mountain management quirks

Many Austrian resorts show 'ski routes' on their mountain maps, but very few offer a definition of them. You can probably assume that such routes will be marked on the ground, and open only when the risk of avalanches has been dealt with. You can't assume, though, that they will be patrolled at the end of the day.

You might think all these routes would be ungroomed, but you'd be wrong: many are groomed occasionally, and some are groomed frequently because they form a key part of their ski area. The runs from Zürs to Zug and Lech are examples, forming part of the much advertised 'White Ring' circuit.

The best explanation I have had of this chaos is that the Austrian rules set a minimum width for pistes, and if a run falls below the minimum, it cannot be advertised as a piste, regardless of how it is operated.

The classic Madloch–Zug run – a ski route; but it's a key part of the Zürs skiing, and groomed – why is it not a piste?

Practicalities: getting to Austrian resorts

One neat feature of the standard valley-village Austrian resort is that it is easy to reach by car. Road access usually involves no hazardous hairpin roads and normally involves no snow to speak of. Lech and Zürs are the famous exception, accessed via the very snowy 1773m Flexenpass – though most of this is now protected by galleries. Nearby Warth is also reached over a pass – the 1675m Hochtannbergpass – which gets exceptional amounts of snow.

By road it's 1,060km/660mi from Calais to Innsbruck, and it takes over 10 hours – so for many people living in south-east England it's possible to drive out in a full day, but it takes appreciably longer than the drive to the nearer French resorts.

Two Austrian airports are very convenient for skiing – Salzburg (towards the eastern end of the skiing mountains, so perfect for the Salzburger Land resorts such as the Sportwelt and Schladming) and Innsbruck (centrally placed in the Tirol). But you'll often find more convenient flights to Munich (in Germany, but quite well placed for many resorts).

You might think Innsbruck, set in the deep, steep Inn valley, would be especially vulnerable to bad weather. On a bad day, it can of course be closed, but in general it seems a pretty reliable route. And on a good day it offers a spectacularly scenic approach.

Quite a few resorts are either on railway lines or quite close to them. The classic example is St Anton, which is on the main line from Zürich to Innsbruck. But the journey involves two changes of train in Paris and a third in Zürich, and takes a full day. And that's assuming you can get from home to the Eurostar terminal at London St Pancras by 7am (I certainly can't).

So, for many people, a flight plus hire car (or bus/minibus transfer) is much the slickest way to go skiing in Austria, particularly if you live near an airport but not near St Pancras. Get an early flight out, and you can be on the slopes of some resorts for lunch. Get a late flight back, and you can ski those same resorts until close of play.

Rules for drivers

Despite its usually snow-free access roads, Austria has stringent rules about winter equipment. These are a little bit complex, but in practice the only sensible course is to fit winter tyres (on all four wheels). It's not just a matter of conforming to the rules; winter tyres do work. Rental cars hired in Austria are fitted with winter tyres by default, and it is now easier than it once was to get them on cars hired in Munich.

Use of the motorways, which is more or less inescapable, requires the purchase and display of a windscreen sticker. Short-term ones are sold by gas stations (in Germany and Switzerland, as well as Austria), and they are not expensive – about £8 for 10 days – so it's just a bit of a nuisance.

The result is that ski routes in some resorts are essentially narrowish pistes with unreliable snow. In others, they are off-piste routes that are safe just as long as you don't injure yourself when you are on your own. If planning to ski a route alone late in the day, check that it is patrolled. Or, better, change your plan.

Another Austrian idiosyncrasy is that it is very common for multiple adjacent runs to share the same run number, creating the potential for all sorts of confusion in an emergency. What are they thinking of?

Size matters, to most of us

Followers of Austrian skiing will have noticed the ding-dong over ski area size that has gone on at the top of the market in recent years. For some time the SkiWelt and the Saalbach area vied to be recognised as Austria's biggest area.

Then, in 2015, the matter was settled by Saalbach's link to Fieberbrunn, putting the area ahead with 270km of runs (249km of pistes). But only a year later both of these areas were eclipsed by the Arlberg, where a new pisteless gondola replaced the buses linking St Anton to Lech-Zürs. By the unwritten rules of ski resort marketing, Austria's only area with over 300km of runs was thereby formed.

That's not the end of it, though. Saalbach is about to be linked to Zell am See. Ah, but then the long-discussed link between St Anton and Kappl now seems to be on the cards. And if Kitzbühel ever builds the short missing link to the slopes of Westendorf, the combined Kitzbühel/SkiWelt area will put the others in the shade. And it will take some beating.

A bit of complexity is added to comparisons of this kind by the fact that some resorts make exaggerated claims about the size of their ski areas. Faithful readers of *Where to Ski and Snowboard* will be aware of the campaign we ran about this.

You might think determining the length of an area's pistes would be simple – you run your surveyor's wheel gadget or its digital equivalent down the middle of each run, and add up the results. But apparently it's not: some resorts like to inflate their assets by applying a multiplier, on the basis that skiers don't go straight down the hill – they make turns, and therefore travel further than a simple measurement would suggest.

As *Where to Ski and Snowboard* said for years, this is nuts. Different skiers do different things, and even an individual skier does different things on different days and on different slopes. It makes no sense to apply arbitrary multipliers, unless perhaps all resorts agreed on the same multiplier. Some scrupulous resorts apply no multiplier. What we all need is a consistent approach, and the obvious one to adopt is the simple one: no multiplier.

This mess has been illuminated by the work of a dedicated German consultant, Christoph Schrahe, who has digitally measured the runs of the world's top 100 resorts (and more). He has published his findings, and you'll find many references to them in these pages. Naturally, he uses no multiplier.

As it happens, Austria's resorts are better behaved than most. Areas such as Kitzbühel and the Arlberg were publishing pretty accurate figures before *Where to Ski and Snowboard* and Christoph Schrahe got involved. And since Schrahe published his first report, a few other Austrian resorts have seen the error of their ways and reduced their stated run totals – or at least published a realistic figure alongside the inflated one they really want you to take in.

Beginners welcome here?

Is it a trend, or has it always been thus?

Working on a single volume on Austria has brought home the fact that many Austrian resorts make no special arrangements for beginners' use of their lifts. No free lifts; no cheap, limited lift passes, no points cards that allow you to pay by the ride. And the problem isn't confined to resorts where the nursery slopes are at mid-mountain. Obergurgl, for example, no longer sells a limited beginner pass for its village lifts.

This is a great shame. In their early days, beginners take very few, very short lift rides. What's more, beginners don't know, at the start of their scary first week on skis, whether they are going to like the whole thing or give up in tears on day four. So what do they do? Splash out €285 on a six-day pass, or buy day passes at €52 per day, and end up paying more than other skiers?

Indifference to the needs of beginners isn't universal. Sölden, down the valley from Obergurgl, and with a lift-pass sharing deal with the higher resort, sells special passes for its two nursery areas; one of them also covers the big access lift you need to get up to the mid-mountain beginner slopes. The Arlberg does the same. Even better, Kitzbühel has free drag-lifts, in addition to magic carpets, on the main nursery slopes and at the linked lift bases of Jochberg and Pass Thurn. Why can't the others do the same?

Choosing your resort

If you are a widely experienced skier, you'll know how different one resort can be from another, and you'll be practised in the craft of sifting out resorts that suit you. If you're not ... well, you've probably got a lot to learn. Even within one country, the variety of resorts is astonishing.

How big?

The introduction a few pages back touches on the important and controversial matter of the size of ski areas, and talks a bit about Austria's biggest – the Arlberg, Saalbach and the SkiWelt. They are all areas linking multiple resorts to offer well over 200km of interconnected, marked runs – that is, prepared pistes and ski routes. The Arlberg has (just) over 300km.

The intro doesn't discuss the opposite extreme, though. Several resorts that get a chapter to themselves in these pages have only 60km or 70km of pistes – Obergurgl, Obertauern, Ski Juwel (Alpbach etc) and Zell am See. We've also given a couple of pages to the seriously small area of Gargellen (in the Montafon valley chapter) with about 30km of pistes. If you're a confident, fast skier, to be happy spending a week in one of these small resorts you need to be in the right frame of mind, content with very little variation from day to day in what you do.

Or you need to be prepared to go on outings to other resorts. Austria is well set up for this, with various regional lift passes that are summarised in the 'Pass notes' section on the first page of each resort chapter. Some cover just the resorts in a particular valley, but in the eastern part of Austria's skiing mountains there are passes covering staggering amounts of skiing. Given a car, you can have a fabulous time visiting a resort a day.

How steep?

Ski mountains don't all come from the same mould. They all offer a mix of slopes, but in some cases the terrain limits what the resort can offer. If you're in the inexperienced category of skier that this chapter is aimed at, you're probably looking for friendly blue runs to ski. In this book we've made a determined attempt to help by reflecting in each chapter on how the piste network suits a 'true blue' skier – someone who is simply not comfortable, at present, on slopes that are even slightly challenging.

It's worth emphasising that you can't judge a resort in this respect on the basis of how much blue is visible on the piste map, or on numerical summaries of the skiing on offer – the number of blue runs, or the percentage of runs that are blue. First, you need to know how the blue runs connect (or not); second, you need to know whether the blue runs are truly of blue-run gradient; and you also are quite likely to want to know whether the blue runs available to you are 'proper' runs – broad, varying in gradient, maybe even with an inspiring view – or dreary cat-walks criss-crossing a mountain that is too steep to have 'proper' blue runs.

Look through the book, and in the sections headed 'The mountains in brief' you'll see a range of verdicts for true blue skiers, from 'Few better places' (Saalbach) to 'Limited options without tackling red runs' (Gastein valley).

How high?

Austria has plenty of extremely high mountains (Grossglockner, since you ask – 3798m) and happens to have the world's best glacier ski areas in Hintertux and Stubai, both of which have chapters here. But in general, Austria's mainstream resorts are unusually low: many villages are below 800m, and many mountains barely reach the 2000m mark.

Because Austria is at the eastern end of the Alps, far from the warm Atlantic, temperatures at a given altitude are lower than in France, for example. But even so, these low altitudes mean higher temperatures on the lower part of the mountain than you would expect in most French resorts. These days, Austrian snowmaking is so good that you generally don't have to worry about a lack of snow resulting in closed runs. But you may worry about the quality of the snow on the lower slopes: in warm weather it will be slushy in the afternoon and icy in the early morning, especially where the slopes are sunny.

So there is something to be said for aiming higher. Two kinds of resort will lift you above these concerns: places such as Mayrhofen, where the skiing is on higher slopes but does not extend down to the village; and resorts where the village itself is at a higher altitude. The classic example is Obergurgl, at 1930m, but there are quite a few at less extreme altitudes, including the Arlberg resorts and Ischgl.

The coin has another side, though: trees, lack of. Trees are the key to enjoyable skiing in bad weather – not so much because they provide shelter from the storm but because they give some direction to the light, which makes the ground and its contours easier to see. The treeline – the altitude at which forest gives way to open slopes – varies from place to place, but in general you don't get many trees

Kitzbühel: an ancient valley town (760m), seen here in party mode for its annual Hahnenkamm race weekend

above 1900m. So resorts such as Obergurgl, Obertauern and Ischgl (where very little of the skiing is below 2000m, although the village is at 1400m) are not good places to ski in a storm. If you go there, you are betting on mostly good weather.

Related to the matter of resort altitude is the matter of the character of the resort. Among the lowest resorts are Kitzbühel and Schladming, and these are both sizeable towns with town-like infrastructure including railway stations and proper shops meeting the needs of residents. Roughly speaking, the higher you go the more likely it is you are going to a village that has been developed for skiers.

How conveniently arranged?

Some skiers don't mind walking to the lifts and walking back to their lodgings from the end of the piste at the end of the day. For others, lodgings simply must be ski-in ski-out. Such lodgings are not easy to arrange except in purpose-designed resorts, which basically don't exist in Austria.

Ski-in ski-out accommodation has to be built on a skiable slope, with lift systems that have lower stations below your digs and top stations above. A very few mini-resorts, all outposts of lower resorts, consist almost entirely of such lodgings – Hochsölden, Hochgurgl, Oberlech.

But there are many more resorts where there are some slope-side lodgings slightly above the main village – examples include St Anton, Saalbach, Lech, Schladming. The online accommodation databases of resort websites are a great aid to finding such lodgings – specify what kind of accommodation you want, then go into map mode and look for establishments on the slopes. You can get a similar effect using Google maps.

St Anton – a classic example of a resort that doesn't work well for apprehensive 'true blue' skiers

Obergurgl (1930m) with its outpost Hochgurgl (2150m) in the distance, just above the unusually high treeline

Things get a whole lot easier if you relax the ski-out condition and look only for ski-in lodgings. In valley bottom resorts where there is no serious alternative to walking to a lift, many more lodgings come into the frame.

What sort of lodgings?

Practically all Austrian resorts offer a wide range of styles of accommodation – 4-star hotels, 3-star hotels, apartment buildings large and small, guest houses, private houses with rooms to rent. What is quite rare, though, is the style that is so common in France – the British-run catered chalet.

The Austrian chalet capital is St Anton, in the Arlberg, where you will find chalets at every level of the market, including chalet hotels aimed at young families. Other possibilities where you may find one or two British chalet operators (they tend to dip in and out of these places) include Ellmau, Ischgl, Kitzbühel, Lech, Mayrhofen, Obergurgl, St Christoph and Sölden.

How good for families?

As your editor can testify from parental experience, you can have good family holidays in all sorts of resorts, but you can improve your chances by choosing a resort with easy, safe access to good nursery slopes, and with activities to amuse the kids at the end of the day. We've tried to assess resorts in these respects.

You should also be aware that many British families gear their resort choice to the holidays offered by specialist tour operators who provide childcare and convey skiing kids to and from ski school. Esprit Ski is the clear market leader; it operates mainly in France, but does have chalets in Obergurgl and St Anton. (They also go to Kühtai, which we might look at in the next edition.)

Buying property in Austria

For keen skiers with some cash in the bank, buying a property in a ski resort is a powerfully attractive idea. And in Austria, at least, it isn't just a matter of fun for the family – with an average of 4% growth in property values over the last decade, it makes sound financial sense. And Austrian resorts enjoy very good summer business, which isn't the case in all French resorts.

But what's involved? What are the pitfalls? Jessica Delaney of specialist agents Alpine Marketing guides us through the maze.

Who can buy?

If you are an EU citizen, you can buy a holiday property in any of Austria's nine provinces, and the process is very straightforward. If you are not, you may have a problem: in the key provinces of Tirol, Salzburgerland and Vorarlberg, where most of the ski resorts are found, you'll be able to buy only a special type of property called a 'second home' property – and they're really hard to find.

Can I use a company to buy?

Yes – there are no restrictions if buying in the name of an EU company. This is a particularly good option if there are more than two of you involved – you can't have more than two individual names on the purchase deeds in Austria. Another advantage is that ownership can be transferred tax-free (to children or grandchildren, for example) by a transfer of shares.

The set-up costs for an EU company start from around €2,000. You will also be required to pay a yearly maintenance fee of around €1,000 and to attend to formalities such as holding an annual general meeting.

What is the purchase process?

It's very straightforward. The notary, who is a semi-public official, will act on behalf of both the purchaser and the vendor, and has a duty to protect the interests of both parties. The notary will draw up all the documents required to transfer the legal ownership.

The deed of sale must be signed in the presence of the notary by both the vendor and you – but if you don't want to attend, you can sign a power of attorney authorising one of the secretaries working in the notary's office to sign the deed on your behalf.

What are the purchase costs?

There are various costs – tax, registration of ownership, notary's fees etc – which work out at about 6.6% of the gross purchase price.

Can I buy with a mortgage?

Yes – it is possible to borrow up to 60% of the purchase price from an Austrian bank. Variable interest rates are currently around 2%, and it is also possible to take fixed-rate mortgages for up to 20 years.

Banks are happy to lend as long as you are buying a property in order to let it for holiday use through a tour operator. In this case your property would be classified like a small business, and the income you earn from your rentals may be used to cover the loan.

What will a mortgage cost?

Banks will charge a set-up fee, and this is usually around 2% of the value of the loan. They will also charge an appraisal fee of 0.5% and you will need to pay the notary a fee of 1.5% of the amount of the mortgage to register the mortgage lender in the land registry. So in all, about 4% of the loan amount.

How do I pay if I buy property that isn't yet built?

New-build properties bought 'off-plan' are paid for in stages; all payments are made through the notary, who acts as trustee and releases cash to the developer as an independent surveyor signs off each stage. Alpine weather limits building to the summer months, which focuses the minds of developers and builders very effectively – so normally properties are built in a single summer season.

Are there construction guarantees?

Yes – all new-build Austrian property is covered by a 30-year building guarantee against all building defects, and developers will usually guarantee building fixtures for two years.

Can I specify how a new-build property is fitted out?

Yes – most chalets and apartments bought through Alpine Marketing are either built to order or already constructed and remain 'unfitted', so you can choose from an extensive range of bathroom fittings, flooring and wall tiles etc. Many properties also have the furniture included in the price, so your property is completely ready to occupy when it is handed over.

Do I have to let my property?

You are likely to be obliged to make your holiday home available for rental when you are not using it. Tourism is very important to Austria, accounting for over 15%

High, reliably snowy Obergurgl: a new development of apartments at prices starting from €244,000

of its GDP, and it is important for the infrastructure of the villages to have a good flow of tourists. Of course, you get the benefit of rental income, and you may get tax advantages.

How much rental income can I expect?

Austrian gross rental yields tend to vary between 4% and 6% – higher than in Switzerland and France. Of course, there are also running costs to deduct from this income.

What are the running costs likely to be?

As well as your utility bills, you have to meet the cost of snow clearance, rubbish removal, water rates, building insurance, local property taxes, cleaning and lighting for any communal areas, and maintenance of the gardens etc.

The expenses of a development of chalets or an apartment building are usually divided up proportionately between the owners, according to the size of their properties. As a rough guide, the basic running costs for a property (including the costs of energy consumed by visitors but not by you) usually work out around €3–€5 per m² per month.

If you buy a property with extensive leisure facilities such as swimming pools and spas then these costs could increase to around €7–€11 per m² per month.

Are there tax breaks for letting my property?

Purchasing a new-build property can have tax advantages – it is possible to reclaim part or all of the VAT on your purchase, giving a discount of up to 20%. To be eligible for this VAT discount you would be expected to let your property through professional agents when you are not using it – and you will need to show an overall profit over a period of 20 years.

Historic, fashionable Kitzbühel: these fabulous Kaiser chalets are selling for €3,350,000

Arlberg

St Anton / St Christoph / Lech / Zürs / Warth

Austria's biggest ski area by far – and in most respects its best

Keen skiers recognised long ago that the best skiing in Austria was to be found on the slopes of St Anton, straddling the Arlberg pass that separates Tirol from Vorarlberg, and of Lech-Zürs just on the Vorarlberg side.

The two areas have operated a shared lift pass for many years, but have frustrated visitors by operating a miserably poor bus link between the two. All they needed was a few more buses, but in 2016 the resorts instead built a piste-free two-way gondola link and, by the unwritten rules of the resort marketing game, became the biggest area in Austria, edging ahead of Saalbach with a claimed 305km of pistes and ski routes.

Three years earlier, the Lech-Zürs area had been extended in the opposite direction. The slopes of Warth, with the reputation of getting the most snow in the Alps, had always been tantalisingly visible from the upper slopes of Lech, but were inaccessible until a gondola link was built – another piste-free two-way affair.

The area is so big that it makes sense to break it down and deal with it as three – just as if they were linked by buses.

St Anton

St Anton / St Christoph / Stuben

For keen, competent, energetic skiers with a taste for booze and bopping, St Anton is one of the top places. Its mountains are high and steep, with abundant off-piste opportunities, its bars (particularly those on the lower slopes) the stuff of legend. It's also an attractive, traditional village, with a lively pedestrian main street where you find everyday shops as well as those aimed at winter and summer visitors.

St Christoph and Stuben have in common very small size and limited diversions, but are different; Stuben is a tight little village, where you might enjoy wandering out to a hotel bar for a beer; St Christoph is a roadside cluster of hotels, where you're unlikely to find such excursions tempting.

The mountains in brief

Size Extensive local slopes, now part of Austria's biggest linked area

Slopes A good mix of terrain, but very little of it is naturally gentle

Snow A good snow record, even if no match for Lech; sunny, though

System, Lift Satisfactory, but with weaknesses, notably on neglected Rendl

Sustenance No more than adequate in number, but some good spots

For beginners Quite good arrangements – go to Nasserein, given a choice

For true blue skiers Far from ideal; ideally, seek guidance to easier runs

For the confident This area has everything you could want

For experts There aren't many better places – lots of routes, lots of snow

Fancy stuff A decent park on Rendl, and a funslope on Galzig

St Anton – the resort in brief

Convenience Mostly bearable walks to everything, and some ski-in options

Lodgings Austria's catered chalet capital, with the usual options too

Bars and restaurants Legendary après-ski leading seamlessly into the night

Off the slopes Excellent facilities for all kinds of activity, indoor and out

For families The suburb of Nasserein could have been made for families

Pass notes
The Arlberg pass covers the Sonnenkopf area above Klösterle, west of Stuben, as well as all the linked areas covered in this chapter.
You can buy cheap day passes or points cards for beginner lifts in all the resorts.

Key facts

Altitude	1305m
Range	1280–2646m
Slopes (claimed)	305km

Where to stay, ideally
Beginners and families in Nasserein. Others in central St Anton, a walk from the gondolas

Websites
stantonamarlberg.com
skiarlberg.at
abbag.com

Key ratings

Size (Arlberg)	*****
Snow	****
Fast lifts	****
Mountain rest's	****
Beginner	***
True blue	**
Confident	*****
Expert	*****
Convenience	***
Families	****
Village charm	****

The mountains in detail

St Anton essentially has skiing in four sectors. The simple bit first: Rendl is a small area, isolated on the south side of the village, reached by a gondola near the bus station. The other three sectors are to the north of the village.

From the sunny slopes running the length of the village, a chair-lift goes up to Gampen (1850m); 1km to the east, a gondola from the suburb of Nasserein does the same. From there a chair-lift goes to Kapall (2330m).

Runs and lifts from Gampen (and a big gondola from the village) access the next hill, Galzig, with runs on the front and on the back in the direction of St Christoph. From the shoulder of Galzig a long, high cable car shifting a modest 440 people an hour goes to the high-point of the Arlberg on the shoulder of Valluga (2646m), while from a lower point behind the hill a chair-lift goes up to the very slightly lower Schindler Spitze – the start of some of St Anton's best-known descents. There is a little cable car to the very top of Valluga, for sightseers or for experts with a guide.

A long piste from Schindler Spitze goes to Alpe Rauz, where a recently built gondola accesses the fourth sector, the previously neglected slopes of Albona, above Stuben; a second makes the link with the slopes of Zürs.

ARLBERG

26

Size

The slopes around St Anton and Stuben are extensive, with well over 100km of marked runs. More importantly, the linked Arlberg area is Austria's biggest, with runs claimed to total 305km. Christoph Schrahe (read the Intro) arrives at a slightly lower figure, but the difference is academic. You may also see references in the resorts' marketing material to a further 200km of 'deep powder' runs. This is a slightly weird attempt to quantify the area's proper off-piste terrain – Courmayeur in Italy is the only other resort that has tried this, as far as we know. Ultimately it is meaningless, but it does give you an idea of the scale of the off-piste terrain here.

Further expansion is possible before very long. The long-discussed plan to link the Rendl slopes to those of Kappl, near Ischgl in the Paznauntal, looks increasingly likely to go ahead eventually. From Schröcken to the top of St Anton's Rendl is about 23km as the eagle flies. With the Kappl link in place, the Arlberg would be over 30km across, overtaking the French Trois Vallées.

Slopes

The slopes around St Anton are basically of red steepness, with upper open areas that tend to blue and some direct descents on wooded lower slopes that reach black gradient. Much the best place to head in a storm is the long red home run from Rendl.

With the villages at a decent altitude, there are several top-to bottom runs of 1000m or more, but runs of 400–500m are more common. The on-piste descent from Schindler Spitze to the village is about 8km long and over 1300m vertical.

There are countless ski routes here, and these include some of the classic descents from Schindler Spitze, for example. The routes are coded red or black, the latter labelled 'extreme'.

The piste map says the routes are not patrolled and are groomed only occasionally or not at all. In fact, some of the most popular routes (notably the Schindlerkar from Schindler Spitze) are frequently groomed, creating the nutty situation of groomed runs that are not patrolled. Be careful late in the day.

It's worth noting that a very high proportion of the total extent is accounted for by these ski routes – much more than in most ski areas. Many of these may be off limits because of your own abilities or snow conditions (especially in warm weather), reducing greatly the quantity of skiing open to you.

The Arlberg piste map, in this chapter split into three bits, is a lesson in poor design. At various points you can't work out where the runs go. At one point in

Zürs the map is deliberately misleading because (we are told) otherwise it would be unclear. Lift names are in type 0.7mm high (x-height); restaurant names are 0.5mm high – six times the thickness of an average European human hair.

Snow

North-westerly weather has nothing much in its way until it hits the Arlberg and dumps snow. St Anton isn't quite in the same league as Warth, but does very well by normal standards. Almost 90% of the slopes have snowmaking.

Most of the slopes are sunny, which can lead to problems as you approach valley level, and means that later in the season you need to time your runs to get good conditions. The front of Stuben's Albona is shady, and Rendl partly so.

System, Lift

The lift system is adequate, with fast access lifts out of St Anton and St Christoph, and fast chairs in most of the key positions on the upper slopes. But there are still slow chairs at Stuben (including the famously cold double chair from the village), and Rendl is rather spoilt by its three slow doubles.

The high runs are reached by a cable car of modest capacity and a fast triple chair, which manages surprisingly well.

It's difficult to avoid the suspicion that saving up for the Lech link has put a stop to investment elsewhere.

Sustenance

Restaurants are not super-abundant, but there are quite a few worth seeking out – and there are more places than you would guess from the useless piste map, which marks many but not all, and names them in type that's invisibly small.

Good traditional places that are missing include Rodelalm, on the extreme skier's left of the Gampen slopes, and Bifang-Alm, quite close to the bottom of the Rendl home run.

In a different league is Verwallstube on Galzig – a proper restaurant (two toques from the Gault-Millau guide) that happens to be set at 2085m. The Gampen restaurant, rebuilt in 2015, is also worth noting – a long, low chalet with an impressive self-service food court, a cool bar and a spacious, relaxed table-service Himmeleck section (indoor and terrace) with small tables. Reservations are taken.

It's not really a mountain restaurant, but Hospiz Alm at St Christoph can't be ignored – a favourite lunch spot for decades, doing good food in a lovely traditional building. Among other features is an amazing wine cellar.

More on the slopes

For beginners

The beginner lift pass and points card cover several lifts spread widely along the fairly gentle slopes next to the village – the 200m Mulden drag near the village, the slightly longer Kindlisfeld drag further east, the 300m Nasserein drag further east still at Nasserein, with the gentlest slope. The pass/card also cover the much longer Fang fast quad chair-lift, which rises almost 300m and serves a long, winding blue run back to the base.

There are also beginner slopes at mid-mountain on Gampen, with a genuine blue winding run to the valley, and on Rendl; you need a lift pass to use these.

These are pretty good arrangements, but your options for further progression are limited – read on.

For true blue skiers

There are some gentle blue runs to be found here, but they are in a minority – most blues are tough, and some would be red in many other resorts; you can easily find yourself tackling moguls, particularly if the sun has led to soft, heavy snow or if there is fresh snowfall.

The main problem is that you can't get around the area without skiing reds or testing blues, or riding lifts to get from one place to another. Isolated easy runs that require detailed planning to reach don't make for a great holiday.

On Galzig, the best bets are the blue looping out wide on skier's right to the Tanzböden chair, and the meandering run 64 to St Christoph. Beware the blue home run from Galzig, the infamous Steissbachtal – usually very crowded and in the lower parts seriously mogulled.

Rendl has some good genuine blue runs, but no easy way back to the valley. Getting to Zürs and Lech is really viable only by bus – the long blue down to Alpe Rauz is steep enough to get mogulled for long, long stretches.

For confident intermediates

The combination of abundant genuine red pistes, blues that are tough enough to be well worth skiing and red ski routes that are not too tough makes this an excellent area for the keen, confident skier.

Wherever you go you'll find worthwhile runs; it's scarcely worth picking any

St Anton's interminable (well, 4km long) Valfagehr piste to Alpe Rauz, seen from the linking gondola to Zürs

out. But don't overlook Rendl, the lower slopes of Gampen, the back of Galzig down to the Arlenmähder chair, and Stuben – the reds on the front side often have the best piste conditions in the area. The run down to Stuben from Schindler Spitze can be a real blast, or a tiring three-mile stretch of messy little moguls.

The black runs are not super-steep – read the following section.

It's well worth asking about the snow conditions on the ski routes, or just checking them out by eye when you get the chance. If recently groomed, high runs like Schindlerkar are superb; if groomed and then dumped on, the stuff of dreams.

You'll obviously want to explore the rest of the huge Arlberg area. The Flexenbahn from Alpe Rauz up to Zürs arrives at the mid-station of another new gondola from Zürs up to Trittkopf.

Unfortunately it does not quite meet a piste – the Trittkopf piste is reached via a long, hilly cat-track. So many prefer to queue for spaces on the top stage of the gondola or to ride down to Zürs – the best option, unless you're heading for the ski route from Trittkopf, or you've hit a quiet time: now that it is served by a powerful gondola, the Trittkopf piste gets unpleasantly crowded.

For experts

The black pistes are few, and not seriously steep, but all worth a try. Run 34 Fang at the bottom of Gampen is the steepest. Their sunny orientation means that snow conditions can be variable. But for experts St Anton isn't about pistes: this is one of the Alps' great resorts for off-piste skiing – hence the lift company's claim of 200km of 'deep snow' runs.

Dotted all over the map (except over Albona) there are ski routes, red and black. Generally, the distinction is valid, although the black ones on Rendl scarcely deserve the distinction, while the Osthang red route underneath the Galzig gondola probably ought to be black.

Some of the best known routes are in the Valluga/Schindler Spitze sector. Schindlerkar is usually a straightforward groomed red run, whereas Mattunjoch has some black pitches. Appreciably steeper than this, though, is Kapall, which joins it from, er, Kapall.

There are off-piste opportunities all over the place reachable by traversing from pistes and ski routes, but also many more serious descents. On Rendl, the Gampberg chair accesses the north face of Gampberg above the resort, and the Riffel chairs open up the big bowl of

Dorfstrasse: snowy, traditional, slightly rustic, traffic-free, animated, with everyday shops; practically ideal

Hinter Rendl also leading down to the town or to St Jakob. From the top of Valluga there are very definitely experts-only descents to Zürs. From Galzig and Kapall there are shorter descents in various directions – from Kapall you can head east, away from the ski routes, down to Nasserein. From Albona there are descents to Stuben, St Christoph or down the back into the Maroital, ending with a walk out. All of this requires guidance.

Fancy stuff

The Stanton Park is in a great location on Rendl – in full view of the RendlBeach restaurant terrace, and served by a short drag-lift and a long chair-lift. It's not huge, but has a serious Proline, a medium Kickerline and a Jibline. Its website seemed to be defunct when we tried it, in summer 2017, and maybe has been usurped by its Facebook page.

There's a 500m funslope on Galzig, with small jumps, waves and banked turns, served by the Tanzböden chair-lift.

St Anton – the resort

St Anton combines the vitality of a sporty ski resort with the charm of traditional Tirolean style and the grounded feel of a real community. Strolling down its animated, traffic-free main street, with the slopes only a short walk away and (probably) with snow underfoot, it's difficult to imagine how it might be improved.

In the land of resorts known for après-ski, this is one of the most lively examples, well up with Sölden, Saalbach and Ischgl – the bars on the lower slopes, within sight of the village, are the stuff of legend.

Convenience

If you pick the right spot at the top of the village, you can be a short stroll from both access gondolas, from the bus station (for easy access to Lech) and from the railway station. The pedestrian core of the village is about 400m long, the major part of the village twice that.

The suburb of Nasserein is 1km east of the main lifts (but of course has its own gondola to Gampen). In the opposite direction, west of the lifts, the village spreads a similar distance up the hill above the road towards the Arlberg pass, through areas called Oberdorf and Gastig. Further out, above a patch of forest, are Dengert and Moos, with some slope-side lodgings.

With a row of lifts along the north side of the village, nowhere in the central area is more than a walk from a lift. There are a few slope-side lodgings in several areas, though they are mainly ski-in, not ski-out.

Ski-buses operate on several lines linking the outlying parts of the St Anton, but for St Christoph, Zürs and Lech you need a post bus; these are not super-frequent, but are free as far as St Christoph. To get to Stuben you would have to go via Zürs, changing there.

Lodgings

As well as having the predictable range of apartments (hundreds), guest houses (scores) and hotels, St Anton has Austria's main concentration of catered chalets run by UK tour operators. There are lots of firms with chalets here, but good starting points are Ski Total, Skiworld, Inghams, Crystal and Supertravel.

There are two 5-star hotels; for those with the budget, the Tannenhof looks difficult to resist – just seven suites, and a three-toque restaurant. The 4-star places outnumber the 3-stars 2:1. The Schwarzer Adler is a fine old inn in the centre, with a small rooftop pool. Among several stylishly modern places is the Mooser, on the slopes and attached to the famous Mooserwirt (read on).

Bars and restaurants

Après-ski here is all about the lower slopes, within (or almost within) sight of the lift base. There's a series of very lively places as you approach the village – the Heustadl, with bands on the terrace, the Sennhütte, the no-longer-shabby Taps and Krazy Kanguruh, and the famous Mooserwirt, with longstanding DJ Gerhard in operation from 3.30. Good luck.

The bars around the lift base and in the main street are throbbing from late afternoon, too – notably the Piccadilly. But there are also places for the legendary quiet drink.

Bodega is good for early evening drinks and tapas. For a proper meal there are plenty of options; the cool basement Hazienda is our regular haunt. For a more serious meal, consider the village museum's restaurant, with its lovely panelled rooms. Top rated by the critics, though, is the hotel Tannenhof.

Off the slopes

There's lots to do, set out in an excellent downloadable leaflet on 'Something other than skiing' (covering plentiful walks and cross-country trails as well as the stuff mentioned here). Highlights include the excellent but pricey Arlberg-well.com leisure centre, with indoor and outdoor pools and spa, skating and curling; tennis,

bowling and climbing at arl.rock; and a good museum in a lovely old building.

Gampen is the start of a 4km/500m vertical toboggan run to Nasserein. It's open in the afternoons, with uplift on the gondola covered by the lift pass, and two evenings a week when the pass is not valid. Or if 200m vertical will suffice you can walk up to the Rodelalm restaurant and hire a sledge there.

For families

Surprisingly, perhaps, this is an excellent resort for families if you head for Nasserein, where there are the resort's most gentle nursery slopes plus a kids' practice area. (There is another near the main lifts if you have a pressing need to be in the heart of things.) What's more, specialist family tour operator Esprit Ski has several catered chalets here, all a short walk from the Gampen gondola; handy for that toboggan run.

Alternatives to St Anton

St Christoph is set a few miles out of St Anton, on the road over the Arlberg pass; it's just on the Tirol side, a chair-lift ride or good blue piste from Galzig. It's a tiny place, and its location doesn't convey any particular advantages, but you may be attracted by the lodgings on offer there. Stuben is more isolated, well down on the Vorarlberg side of the pass, with the drawback of a slow, old, cold chair-lift on to its red pistes.

St Christoph 1800m

St Christoph consists of a handful of hotels either side of the Arlberg pass road, plus the rather industrial-looking Ski Austria Academy and a couple of ski shops. The road is emphatically a road, not a street – there are no pavements. There are drag-lifts for beginners on the lower slopes, and with the genuine blue run from Galzig it's a viable place to start skiing.

Convenience No one has to walk more than a few yards. Ironically, residents of the Arlberg Hospiz have to walk further than most.

Lodgings Inghams has a big chalet hotel here, right next to a drag-lift; well-run, with excellent food when we stayed. The Arlberg Hospiz is a huge 5-star hotel, and the centrepiece of what is called the Arlberg1800 Resort, which includes a small concert hall. The Maiensee is a very good 4-star hotel next to the chair-lift.

Bars and restaurants The Hospiz Alm (read 'Sustenance') is the main option, other than your lodgings, for a post-piste beer or for a meal out. But it is way more expensive for dinner than for lunch.
Off the slopes It's all down to your hotel.
Families Immediate access to snow is about the only attraction; this is no winter wonderland.

Stuben 1405m

Stuben is a proper little village, huddled around its church, at the foot of the Arlberg pass road. Snowy paths separate the chalets, with cars parked at the edge.

There are beginner slopes on the sunny side of the valley, but it makes no sense as a place to start skiing – the Albona slopes above the village are genuinely red.

There are several hotels, guest houses and apartment buildings, and some contain bars and à la carte restaurants.

Lech

Lech / Zürs / Oberlech / Zug

Lech and its linked neighbour Zürs are Austria's most glamorous and expensive resorts. Lech has seven 5-star hotels. Like Kitzbühel, Zürs has four – but, unlike Kitzbühel, Zürs is a tiny place.

But don't be put off; these are not resorts for posers. The skiing is excellent, as is the snow, and Lech is an attractive village without much conspicuous consumption. It has only three jewellers, for example.

Zürs offers immediate access to the best red pistes but is a charmless place, recommendable only if you plan to closet yourself in your swanky hotel. Above Lech, the more attractive slope-side outpost of Oberlech may be just the ticket for beginners and true blue intermediates – and families.

The mountains in brief

Size Extensive local slopes, now part of Austria's biggest linked area

Slopes A good mix of gentle and challenging slopes – mainly short, though

Snow The snowiest major resorts in the Alps – though beaten by tiny Warth

System, Lift Generally OK, but with some non-trivial flaws and queues

Sustenance Now a good range of options, with one or two standout places

For beginners Pretty good; given a choice, consider staying at Oberlech

For true blue skiers Not quite deal, but lots to do all over the area

For the confident Great if you're happy to spend a lot of time on ski routes

For experts Good ski routes, lots of off-piste, great snow; a top place

Fancy stuff A fair-sized park and, for once, it is right above the resort

Lech – the resort in brief

Convenience A few ski-in locations, and bearable walks for most

Lodgings Plenty of budget guest houses alongside the 5-stars

Bars and restaurants Lively at close of play, with the usual options later

Off the slopes Lots to do, much of it in and on water (or ice)

For families Oberlech could have been made for families

Pass notes	Key facts		Key ratings	
The Arlberg pass covers the Sonnenkopf area near Klösterle, west of Stuben, as well as all the linked areas covered in this chapter.	Altitude	1450m	Size (Arlberg)	*****
	Range	1280–2646m	Snow	*****
	Slopes (claimed)	305km	Fast lifts	****
	Where to stay, ideally		Mountain rest's	****
You can buy cheap day passes or points cards for beginner lifts in all the resorts.	In Lech, at the foot of the slopes – or, with kids, up at Oberlech.		Beginner	****
			True blue	****
			Confident	****
	Websites		Expert	*****
	lechzuers.com		Convenience	***
	zuersamarlberg.at		Families	****
	skiarlberg.at		Village charm	****
	abbag.com			

The mountains in detail

The slopes of Lech and Zürs are connected at two points by lifts and ski routes, but you can ski a circuit of the area only one way – clockwise.

The Lech slopes are quite complicated to navigate, partly because of the poor piste map, but are in essence quite simple. Beyond the quite steep slope above the village is a broad, undulating mountainside beneath Zuger Hochlicht, served by a handful of chair-lifts. The Hasensprung chair accesses a bowl on the south side of that peak. The chair to Kriegerhorn does the same, and serves ski routes back to mid-mountain. On skier's left of the sector is the gondola link to the Warth slopes, visible in the distance.

In the opposite direction, twin cable cars from the centre of Lech to Rüfikopf are the start of the clockwise circuit. Long intermediate runs with no return lifts take you to the afternoon-sun side of Zürs, partly shown in the photo over the page. At the far end of that mountainside is the gondola link to Stuben and St Anton. There are further runs on the morning-sun side, including the beautiful Muggengrat-Täli, away from all lifts back to the village. Alternatively, a slow double chair takes you to Madloch-Joch for the ski routes to Zug, where another slow chair goes up to the Lech slopes.

Size

With 305km of pistes and ski routes, the Arlberg is Austria's largest ski area, for the moment. There's more on this under St Anton, and in the book's introduction. The local Lech-Zürs slopes amount to a respectable area, in excess of 100km.

Slopes

This sector has a good mix of easy and more challenging intermediate gradients. There are no steeps to speak of. Although there is a band of forest reaching up into the slopes above Lech, practically all the skiing is on open slopes.

With high villages and modest top heights, long runs aren't a feature of this area. At Lech the main lifts are around 1km long, with very limited verticals – the only real exception is the Steinmähder chair on Zuger Hochlicht, and even that vertical is under 500m. But you can ski on-piste from Zuger Hochlicht to the village, a descent of about 6km and 870m vertical. The ski route from Rüfikopf to Lech drops over 900m, but requires the use of a short drag-lift part way down.

The Zürs lifts and runs are generally a bit longer, with bigger verticals. Trittkopf above offers about 700m on-piste. The big descent is via the ski routes from Madloch-Joch to Zug – 950m.

There are countless ski routes here. The piste map clearly explains that the routes are not patrolled and are groomed either occasionally or not at all. In fact, some of the most popular routes (notably the runs from Madloch-Joch and the Zuger Tobel to Zug) are frequently groomed. This creates the lunatic situation of groomed runs that are not patrolled. Be careful.

There are some observations on the poor Arlberg piste map under St Anton.

Snow

North-westerly weather, of which western Europe gets quite a bit, dumps snow when it hits the Arlberg – which is why Warth-Schröcken gets more snow than anywhere else in the Alps. Zürs is close behind; Lech doesn't do quite so well, but is still among the snowiest major resorts in the Alps. Snowmaking covers only about 60% of the slopes overall.

System, Lift

The lift system is generally good, with fast chairs at most of the key points. But when doing the circuit you have to put up with slow chairs to Madloch-Joch and then out of Zug to the Lech slopes. Possibly more irritating than those is the eight-minute ride on the slow Rotschrofen chair at the top of the Lech slopes, a lift on which you might like to do laps. If you're planning on staying at the far end of Lech, note that the Schlosskopf chair is slow, too.

There are plans to rectify all these problems, but not in the immediate future.

There are some bottlenecks. The circuit is popular enough to create queues for the Madloch-Joch slow chair. And there are regular morning queues for the twin Rüfikopf cable cars out of Lech, which have a joint capacity of a miserable 1,300 people an hour; a slow double chair would shift the queue more quickly.

Sustenance

Mountain restaurants have improved in number and quality over recent years, and good lunches can now be found without resorting to the hotels in Oberlech.

Rud-Alpe, not far above Lech, is a lovely place built of old timbers, with excellent food. Kriegeralpe is a cosy place strictly for snowy days – the terrace, perhaps uniquely in the Alps, has no worthwhile view. Massive Kaiserschmarren is served only late in the afternoon. The steel-and-glass Schlegelkopf offers style, space and comfort, and its glass-sided little dining room has fabulous views. The food is out of the ordinary too – sushi and steaks as well as more routine stuff. Seekopf, above Zürs, manages to serve good food efficiently on its huge terrace.

More on the slopes

For beginners

Behind the Rüfikopf cable car station in the main street are the village nursery slopes – an admirably gentle, quiet area served by a 160m drag-lift and a longer slope, steeper at the top, served by two 400m drags. If one of these was cut to 300m, the setup would be perfect. There is also a gentle slope between the two parts of Oberlech, with a 450m drag-lift.

The beginner pass and points cards cover all these lifts, the Oberlech cable car and the rather steep Hinterwies drag on the left of the main lower slopes.

There are plenty of easy blue runs to progress to above Oberlech. Sadly, the runs to the village are not easy; but you can always resort to the cable car.

For true blue skiers

Lech is a great place to enjoy cruising on good snow without having to worry about moguls or other unpleasantness. Pretty much all the blue runs that criss-cross the mountainside above Oberlech are genuinely easy. The same can't be said for the home slopes immediately above Lech. Even the otherwise easy

The Trittalp chair on Hexenboden, above Zürs; note the off-piste slopes from the further Hexenboden chair

run through the woods from Oberlech delivers you to the red-gradient home slopes. Why has the resort not created a winding alternative?

You can get around pretty much the whole area, including Zuger Hochlicht, the link to Warth (where there is further easy terrain) and the pistes above Zürs reached by the Rüfikopf cable car. If starting to spread your wings, don't be tempted by the Trittkopfbahn, or the Madloch-Joch ski routes. And don't mess with St Anton.

For confident intermediates

Although the pistes directly above Lech are a bit tame for a confident skier, there is such a lot to do a bit further afield that Lech makes a great choice for the keen intermediate.

Beyond those tame blues is Zuger Hochlicht, with some good, long, red pistes on both flanks and two or three ski routes down to its lift base. This is a fabulous mountain when snow is good, but it's very sunny, unfortunately. And it doesn't take long to get to the slopes above Zürs, with multiple satisfying reds on both the morning-sun and afternoon-sun sides. Try to miss the crowds on the otherwise excellent piste from Trittkopf by doing it early or late, or at lunchtime. On the morning-sun side you won't want to miss the highlights mentioned in the introduction – Muggengrat-Täli back to Zürs and the ski routes from Madloch-Joch to Zug (or Lech when conditions permit).

From Zürs it takes three quick gondola stages to be skiing the lovely, shady front side of Albona above Stuben, with St Anton a further fast chair away.

In the opposite direction, a gondola from beyond Oberlech opens up a day or two on the super-snowy slopes of Warth.

The distinction between red and black ski routes is generally worth observing – the blacks to Zug and from Kriegerhorn, for example, have steep pitches, as do the routes from Rüfikopf to Lech.

For experts

Essentially there is no steep piste skiing – the one black piste above Zürs is great fun in the morning sun, but not steep – but there are some very rewarding ski routes and a huge amount of lift-served off-piste (for which guidance is advised),

covered with more snow than just about anywhere else in the Alps, on average. Basically, all the high-points of the lift system offer opportunities.

For example ...

From Zuger Hochlicht you can descend to skier's right of the pistes to the chair-lift base. Or in the opposite direction you can traverse north under Mohnenfluh then down to the line of the linking Warth gondola and run out to the Warth lifts.

From Madloch-Joch there are multiple variations on the Zug ski routes, and separate, steeper off-piste routes further west, down the Stierlochalpe valley to Zug. Or you can turn back towards Zürs, traversing to skier's left under the Omeshorn to access excellent steep snowfields above the Lech-Zürs road. Shorter versions can be accessed from Zürsersee.

The Muggengrat chair-lift accesses several routes starting with long traverses, either on skier's right of the chair-lift or on each side of the Muggengrat-Täli, all ending in good slopes above Zürs or the road through it.

From Hexenboden you can traverse beyond the lift and then curl round to the Trittalp lift (visible in the photo).

There are more routes opened up by a bit of hiking – for example to the ridge of Trittkopf, or the col beyond Zuger Hochlicht.

And if all that is not enough, this is the only area in Austria where heli-skiing is permitted. (What a coincidence! It is also an area where lots of people can afford it!) There are only two drop points: beneath Orgelspitze, west of the Lech pistes, for an easy descent of a sunny valley to Zug; and Mehlsack, where there is a choice of more difficult routes – north towards the Zug valley (where you face the indignity of a 20-minute walk) or south to Spullersee. Naturally, the sunny routes are favourites for spring snow.

Fancy stuff

Snowpark Lech is on the lower slopes, close to the village, beside the Schlegelkopf chair-lifts – a sizeable park with Fun Run, Rail and Pro lines. But the lack of information about the park on the resort websites raises the suspicion that it's not a high priority in this rather grown-up resort.

Lech – the resort

Although Lech is a traditional-style Austrian village, it is not super-cute and it is spoiled, to a degree, by traffic on the through road (even though that road doesn't go far beyond Lech). But its riverside setting is lovely, the paths are pretty much always snowy, and the place has a lively atmosphere, in the early evening at least. Later on it's pretty quiet, but there are places to go.

Convenience

The hotels and guest-houses at the foot of the slopes are more or less ski-in, and the walks to the lifts from such places are not long. A few are ski-out as well, being slightly above the chair-lift base. The far end of the main village is about 600m from the cable car station, and there are lodgings further afield, so some visitors need to use the ski buses. These link Lech to Oberlech, Zug and the far end of Zürs, among other destinations. There's an hourly bus service to St Anton via St Christoph, not covered by the lift pass.

Lodgings

Catered chalets are nowhere near as numerous here as in St Anton, but Ski Total has a well-established programme with a large chalet and two chalet hotels, and Skiworld has a couple of places in Zug. The Oxford Ski Company has some very swanky places of the kind that you rent wholesale with chauffeur (for a sum well into five figures).

In addition to the Austrian Alps' widest choice of 5-star hotels there are dozens of 4-stars and a few 3-stars – plus plenty of simpler guest houses, and countless apartments.

If the budget will stand it and you favour cool over trad, the case for the 5-star hotel Aurelio is strong: a private-house feel, possibly the best restaurant in town, and an ace ski-in ski-out position a few yards up the slopes.

For self-caterers, there are some food shops, including a butcher's.

Lech is a traditional village in a high valley setting – sunny but very snowy; Zürs is up the valley in the centre

Bars and restaurants

Lech is not St Anton, but it is lively enough. As the lifts close the bars in Oberlech are popular, and crowds build in the village on the terraces of the hotels Krone, Tannbergerhof and Pfefferkorn. In midwinter, you might want to follow us indoors to savour the smoke-free atmosphere of the stylishly welcoming, wood-built Schneggarei.

The serious gourmet restaurants are in the top hotels, but there are some good mid-market alternatives elsewhere. The Schneggarei does good food, including but not limited to pizza. Fux is another cool bar-restaurant, and it gets a toque from the Gault-Millau guide – choose between Asian-fusion cuisine or charcoal-grilled steaks. Rud-Alpe (read 'Sustenance') is open for dinner – the walk up is said to take 15 minutes.

Of course there are disco-clubs open until the early hours – the Archiv and K.Club among them.

Between 8pm and 3am a bus service called James operates around the village and satellites; you pay a few quid for an evening's use of it.

Off the slopes

There's a decent range of things to do, although swimming seems to be a matter for your hotel (over 20 4-stars have pools). Sport.park.lech offers a range of activities including tennis, climbing and 10-pin bowling, plus fitness rooms. The hotel Monzabon has an indoor ice rink, normally for skating but curling can be arranged in advance.

The toboggan run from Oberlech to Lech is open daily until 10pm and serviced by the cable car, but is only a modest 1.2km long.

There are quite a few walking paths, and cross-country skiing trails up the valley to Zug and beyond.

For families

There's an excellent kids' practice area with magic carpets on the nursery slopes, but the obvious place to head with a family is Oberlech.

Alternatives to Lech

Zürs is a collection of deeply comfortable hotels, 300m higher than Lech, straddling the road to St Anton and Stuben. Oberlech, on the slopes above Lech and reached by cable car or bus, is the best of the Austrian mid-mountain mini-resorts. Zug is a cute hamlet, reachable only by ski routes.

Zürs 1720m

Zürs has a fabulous location from the skiing point of view, in its high valley with good red slopes on both sides. That apart, its main attraction is its hotels. It needs a tunnel to remove the through-road, and a central focus to make it an appealing place to spend time.
Convenience There are lifts at each end of the village, 400m apart, so there are no long walks. Several hotels can be reached on skis, and one or two can be left on skis.
Lodgings 4-star hotels dominate, but there are four 5-stars, and a solitary 3-star b&b place.
Bars and restaurants Zürs has never been a lively après-ski spot but, with St Anton residents zipping home by gondola instead of waiting for a bus, it is now quieter than ever. There are of course excellent restaurants in the best hotels.

Off the slopes There's a natural ice rink. The hotel Enzian has a squash court.
Families There's a kids' practice area with three magic carpets, and plenty of snow. But it's a bleak place.

Oberlech 1630m

If you like the idea of staying up on the slopes without compromising on creature comforts, this is just the spot. Oberlech's 4-star hotels (and one 5-star) are set on gentle slopes, with trees around to complete the winter wonderland effect, and have some of the resort's best restaurants. It's a two-part hamlet, with a nursery slope between the parts.

Zug 1500m

Zug won't appeal to many people as a base, with a slow chair-lift to the Zug slopes and sunny ski routes to get home. But the little hotel Rote Wand has one of the best restaurants around.

Warth 1495m

Warth / Schröcken

Exceptionally snowy Warth and Schröcken offer a radically different alternative to Lech and Zürs – tiny, low-key villages, with more economical lodgings. Until its planned (read 'wished for') lift link into the slopes is built, you're not likely to favour staying in Schröcken.

The mountains

The Arlberg piste map is not a great aid to comprehension of the area. The central feature is the low peak of Saloberkopf, with runs south towards the linking gondola from Lech and north to a big car park at Hochtannbergpass on the Schröcken–Warth road – and north-east towards another roadside lift base at Hochkrumbach. Above that point and Warth is another area of runs. And west of Saloberkopf are runs around the lower peak of Falkenkopf, including a run to Schröcken.

Size Warth's local area is much smaller than those of its big-name partners – about half the size. But the linking lift to Lech takes only eight minutes.

Slopes The terrain is a bit steeper than in Lech – generally of red gradient. Most of the blacks don't justify the label. The runs are on the short side – less than 400m vertical on Saloberkopf, around 500m down to Warth or Schröcken. There are patches of woodland, but essentially the slopes are open.

Within the lift network there are some short ski routes, usually just offering shortcuts from one piste to another.

Snow Although there is some debate over the claims of other areas between here and Bregenz, for practical purposes this area gets the most snow in the Alps – slightly more than Zürs, with almost 11m at resort level. That's twice as much as Val d'Isère, for example.

System, Lift You can enjoy most of the slopes using only fast chair-lifts, the main exceptions being a small central area served by the slow Karhorn double chair and the peripheral Falkenkopf.

Sustenance There aren't many huts, but probably enough – and you can always pop down to the Warth lift base. Hochalpe is a cosy spot with cheerful and efficient service of satisfying traditional dishes.

More on the slopes

For beginners In the village there is a gentle nursery slope with a 100m drag-lift and nearby the Wannenkopf slow quad chair serves a 400m blue run. There are similar lifts out at the Saloberjet lift base, aimed at skiers arriving by car. Points cards and cheap day passes are available, valid on all four of these lifts.

For true blue skiers It's a good area, with genuine blue runs to every lift, including the vital Lech gondola. The cross-mountain runs to the Hochkrumbach lift base are a bit tedious, but the higher blues and the run to Warth are more rewarding.

For confident intermediates There are some worthwhile red slopes on Saloberkopf and above Warth, and the shady groomed blacks from Saloberkopf are a great blast. But you'll soon be wanting to jump on the gondola to Lech, and wondering whether you'd have been better off coughing up for a bed there.

For experts You'll enjoy carving down the crowd-free groomed black pistes down the Saloberjet chair; for more of a challenge, take the one away from the lift, on skier's left, Ochsakopf. Some of the short blacks over towards Warth are more challenging too, as is the ski route down the Jägeralp chair. There's plenty of off-piste terrain between the pistes or just outside the network, some of it quite steep; but the runs are short.

An obvious first thought for a more serious adventure would be the route from Lech's Zuger Hochlicht to Warth's Sonnenjet lift – a glorious slope of 550m vertical, beneath Juppenspitze.

Fancy stuff The Wannenkopf chair-lift at the main lift base serves the Funslope Steffisalp, with 'boxes, jibs and more'.

The resort

Warth isn't just small, it is positively minute – a half-dozen hotels and guest houses at the lift base, and a larger cluster around the church, a walk away. 156 inhabitants, they say. It has a splendid snowy setting, with good mountain views.

Convenience That walk is only 500m, but at the time of writing, in 2017, an eight-seat gondola is under construction to save your legs in future. In any event, there is ski-in lodging at the lift base.

Lodgings There are three 4-star hotels around the lift base, all with pools, and it's difficult to see why you would want to stay anywhere else. The 'boutique' Lechtaler Hof has a good spa, and a bar that is lively at close of play.

Bars and restaurants The bar of the Lechtaler Hof isn't the only drinking hole in town – other hotels compete.

Off the slopes There's a toboggan run a walk above Warth, daily to 10pm, with snowcat lifts two nights a week.

For families Provided you don't have great demands for ready-made diversions, it's a good place for a family holiday, with easy access to snow.

The Schröcken option

For years, the Arlberg piste map has shown a planned link from Schröcken (1280m) to Falkenkopf on the edge of the Warth slopes. But, for the moment, access still depends on driving or bussing a few km up the Warth road to the lifts at Hochtannbergpass. At least there is now a piste from Falkenkopf. But you're unlikely to be staying right at the arrival point, given how diffuse the place is.

Schröcken is not so much small as barely detectable – a scattering of hotels and guest houses along the road up to the pass. Next to the church is a nursery slope, the tourist office, the ski school and a mini-market. And that's about it.

No, not a mid-mountain satellite of Warth – this is Warth; it really is tiny, although it's about 1km end to end

Gastein valley

Bad Hofgastein / Bad Gastein / Dorfgastein / Grossarl

The Gastein valley doesn't come from any of the standard Austrian moulds. Its mountains are a bit higher than most, without reaching glacial heights, and its main resorts are spa towns – not at all your standard ski resort villages. If radioactive waters turn you on, there's nowhere like it. The slopes are a bit fragmented – in two main sectors and two minor ones, widely spread and linked by buses – and are not the best for near-beginners, but for confident skiers are excellent.

Bad Hofgastein is the best base – less city-like than Bad Gastein, with much more going on than Dorfgastein. And in a valley with no perfect location, it's the best compromise for accessing all areas.

The mountains in brief

Size Classic mid-sized area, but multiple sectors make it seem bigger

Slopes Basically of red gradient, partly wooded; some good long runs

Snow A tad higher than most local rivals, so not at all bad

System, Lift Some inadequate access lifts, and some slow lifts higher up

Sustenance Some good spots, but they're crowded at peak times

For beginners Progression from the nursery slopes is problematic

For true blue skiers Suitable runs are few, and far between

For the confident Lots to do in every sector of slopes in the valley

For experts Few blacks, none steep, but plenty of off-piste

Fancy stuff A decent three-line park, and a family-oriented funslope

Bad Hofgastein – the resort in brief

Convenience The main weakness: be prepared to bus around the valley

Lodgings A reasonable range, with more 4-star than 3-star hotels

Bars and restaurants A better-than-usual choice, from trad to cool

Off the slopes Quite a bit to do; pity the tobogganing is daytime only

For families Good ski/play area by the nursery slopes at Angertal

Pass notes	Key facts		Key ratings	
The standard weekly pass is the Ski Amadé one, also covering the Sportwelt, Schladming and Hochkönig. Cheap day and half-day passes and points cards are sold for the beginner lifts at Angertal and Bad Gastein, and something similar operates at Dorfgastein.	Altitude	860m	Slopes extent	****
	Range	860–2686m	Snow	***
	Slopes (claimed)	208km	Fast lifts	***
			Mountain rest's	****
	Where to stay, ideally		Beginner	**
	In the heart of downtown Bad Hofgastein, close to a ski-bus stop.		True blue	**
			Confident	****
	More info		Expert	****
	www.gastein.com		Convenience	*
	www.skigastein.com		Families	***
	www.grossarltal.info		Village charm	***

The mountains in detail

The valley has four ski areas. Much the largest consists of the peak of Stubnerkogel, reached from the upper fringes of Bad Gastein by a gondola, and the undulating bowl of Schlossalm, reached from a point beyond the fringes of Bad Hofgastein by a funicular and then cable car. These two hills meet at a major lift station in the Angertal.

The residents of the two resorts naturally spend most of their time in that area, but all the other sectors are well worth exploring. On the opposite side of Bad Gastein, Graukogel is a much smaller but higher area, neglected but worth a visit despite its slow chair-lifts. Higher still and also quite small, but served by a gondola, Sportgastein lies 10km up the valley from Bad Gastein.

Down the valley, 8km beyond Bad Hofgastein, is Dorfgastein, sharing a fair-sized area with Grossarl, in the next valley to the east. A gondola goes up from Dorfgastein to the high-point of Fulseck. Grossarl has two access gondolas, and the upper mountain has a quite complex network of chair-lifts. This sector lacks a handy name; we're calling it Fulseck.

It has to be said that the valley piste map is about the most poorly designed on the planet. It is reproduced here in two parts to give you a fighting chance of deciphering some of it, but you'll struggle.

GASTEIN VALLEY

44

Size

There is plenty to do here, provided you are willing to get on a bus occasionally. For the valley as a whole, the resort claims a total of 208km of pistes. It publishes individual run lengths, and they seem fairly accurate. This puts the valley comfortably into the ✳✳✳✳ category. Each of the main areas would get ✳✳ if rated individually.

Slopes

The mountains here are essentially of red steepness, but Sportgastein, Schlossalm and Dorfgastein have plenty of blue terrain too, whereas on Stubnerkogel and Graukogel the blue runs have to take roundabout routes.

There are some good long runs – in all sectors you can ski around 1000m vertical, and the famous away-from-all-lifts red run to the valley from Hohe Scharte on Schlossalm offers almost 1450m. But the piste map is misleading: it marks the top of Graukogel as 2492m, the height of the peak; the lift goes only to 2007m.

The km figures are quite impressive, too: the Hohe Scharte run is over 10km, while top to bottom at Dorfgastein is almost 8km – and again it's a red run, not a winding blue.

There's a good mix of open and wooded slopes. Sportgastein is almost entirely open – it has trees on just the bottom fifth of the hill. Graukogel, on the other hand, is trees top to bottom. Fulseck is largely wooded on the Dorfgastein side, but there are large open areas over the ridge, above Grossarl.

Stubnerkogel and Schlossalm have a lower treeline, and quite a bit of skiing above it – especially Schlossalm, essentially a broad, open bowl. The lower slopes of Stubnerkogel into Angertal would be more useful in a storm if the Angertal chair 11 stopped at the treeline.

The piste map is admirably clear about ski routes – they are 'marked, not laid out, not prepared, not patrolled, avalanche protection'. Well, clear in the key respects – 'not laid out' seems to mean not shaped by bulldozers. There aren't many routes – none on Stubnerkogel (surprisingly), a short one low down on Schlossalm (good in a storm, they say), one good long one and three shorter ones on Fulseck, two decent ones and a short one on Sportgastein. The map marks one on Graukogel, but when we last visited it seemed to have become a piste.

This area is covered by the Ski Amadé regional lift pass. There's an excellent 3D interactive piste map at skiamade.com.

Ski

höchster Punkt in Ski amadé

Kreuzkogel 2.686 m

Sportgastein 1.590 m

Stubnerkogel 2.251 m

Graukogel 2.492 m

Skischaukel Schlossalm-Angertal-Stubnerkogel

Skizentrum Angertal 1.175 m

Bad Gastein 1.002 m

Bad Hofgastein 857 m

Hohe Scharte 2.300 m

Schlossalm 2.050 m

Kleine Scharte

Kitzstein 1.302 m

Autoschleuse Richtung Mallnitz

Sportgastein

Heilstollen

Maustelle

Bad Bruck

Kötschachdorf

Kötschachtal

...027 m

chaukel n-Großarital

Goldbergstub'n

Weitblick

Kugelbahl

Jungerstube

Stubikogel
Gipfelrestaurant

Stubneralm

Stubnalm

Ahornhütte

Bergstadl

Rossalm

Belespe Alm

Felsentherme

Graukogelhütte

Graukogelalm

Weitmoser Schlossalm

Hamburger Skihütte

Hofgasteinerhaus

Haitzingalm

Kleine Scharte Bergrestaurant

Angertal-Tóle

Angerblick-Hütte
Feldingalm

Hirschkarhütte
Waldgasthof

Wallnerhof

Bärentherm

Alpentherme

Das Goldberg

Brandnerbauer

Snow

Our standard warning about the low resorts in this part of the world applies: these days, snowmaking may be good enough to keep runs to the valley reliably open; but with lift bases below 900m you can't expect great snow conditions on the lower slopes, especially later in the season. Be prepared for ice and/or slush, and count yourself lucky if you find packed powder.

But in other respects this area has more going for it. With top heights in the main area of 2200–2300m and Angertal between those heights going not much below 1200m, you can be fairly confident of good snow on most of the slopes – and you have the fallback of Sportgastein rising from 1600m to 2650m.

Sportgastein has snowmaking on only one run on the lower mountain, and Graukogel is all natural, but the other sectors have pretty thorough coverage.

System, Lift

The lift system is adequate rather than impressive. The slow chairs on Graukogel are part of its charm, you could say, but there are other slow lifts dotted around the other sectors, Schlossalm in particular.

The access gondola at Bad Gastein can build queues at peak times in high season. And there are greater problems at Bad Hofgastein, leading many people based there to take buses to the Angertal lifts instead of queuing for the Schlossalm funicular. This shifts only 1,660 people an hour and is followed by a cable car shifting 820 an hour (or a slow double chair).

But all this is changing. All being well, December 2018 will see the replacement of the funicular and the cable car by a 10-seat gondola shifting 3,000 an hour and starting from a new base station on the resort side of the valley road – so closer to the car parks. (The piste bridge over the road is already in operation.) The top station will be a bit higher than the existing cable car station. The double chair and the queue-prone Kleine Scharte quad chair 4 will be removed, as well as the cable car.

The Sendleiten fast quad chair 6 nearby will also be replaced, by a very powerful eight-pack, but not before 2019.

Sustenance

There are lots of restaurants in the main sectors, a couple in each of the minor sectors, and few duds. The restaurants are named, in tiny type, on the piste map.

Schlossalm consists mainly of this broad, open, rolling bowl, but has one or two steep descents into Angertal

Close to the bottom of Stubnerkogel in the Angertal (ski the black or walk from the blue) is the excellent woody Hirschenhütte. On Schlossalm, Aeroplanstadl is another lovely spot – mainly efficient self-service, but there is table service of a limited menu at the back of the place. The standout place on Fulseck (and possibly in the whole valley) is Wengeralm – ticks all the boxes. One of the simple pleasures of Graukogel, a place of simple pleasures, is the cosy little Graukogelhütte, near the top.

The resort operates a scheme of the kind invented in Alta Badia some years ago, where well-known chefs from the region create dishes that selected mountain restaurants then offer. Wengeralm is one of seven restaurants in the scheme.

More on the slopes

For beginners

There are excellent, gentle beginner slopes a bus-ride away at Angertal, where the Schlossalm slopes meet those of Stubnerkogel. Cheap short-term passes and points card are available. So far, so good. The problem is where you go from there – read the next section.

For true blue skiers

This is not natural blue run territory. Many blues are little more than cat tracks traversing the mountain, while others are quite tough – the blues on the Weitmoser chair on Schlossalm, for example.

Ironically, Stubnerkogel, the steepest hill, is the only one with a blue run to the valley, and that is largely a path. Or it was the only one: on the latest map, the bottom red run on Fulseck at Dorfgastein has become blue. No doubt it has been improved in some respects, but it will still be a tricky blue, particularly in the afternoons late in the season.

In other respects, Fulseck is actually a good bet for the cautious intermediate, with genuine and interesting blues on both the front and back of the hill. Sportgastein has arguably the single best blue run in the valley, S1 on the upper mountain; the upper reds here are on the soft side, too. But you really don't want to spend your week schlepping out there every day.

For confident intermediates

The Gastein valley was made for confident, competent intermediates. Every sector has rewarding runs – including long ones, given good snow on the lower slopes.

Runs worth noting include those to skier's left of the Sender gondola on Stubnerkogel, down into Angertal; on the opposite side of Angertal, the tough red H32 Käferstall; the main red slopes on Schlossalm; from Schlossalm, the varied, away-from-all-lifts Hohe Scharte red to the valley; the top to bottom reds on both sides of Fulseck.

Graukogel's runs are excellent, and deliciously quiet unless everything else is closed. Sportgastein is not steep – only the lowest red is really red – but worth a visit to enjoy the snow; if the snow in the main area is good, it will be quiet. If not …

For experts

There is no seriously steep piste skiing – the few black runs dotted around the valley are not greatly steeper than the nearby reds. But there is a lot of satisfaction to be had from the more testing reds, especially the longer ones. The longer ski routes are worth a try.

Happily, there is lots to do off-piste. On Stubnerkogel, there are routes from the top in several directions and an excellent wide area served by the Jungeralm chair-lift on the Angertal side. There are lots of options from the top lifts on Schlossalm – from Hohe Scharte, for example, going beyond the famous piste, or down the line of the cable car. But the big opportunities are from Kreuzkogel, at the top of Sportgastein – south into Weissenbachtal and back to the lift base, or north down to the access road for a vertical of 1400m.

Fancy stuff

The QParks snow park on Stubnerkogel, just above the Stubneralm restaurant and served by the Burgstall drag, is a fair size, and has beginner, intermediate and advanced lines, with 30 features in total. It has a good website at www.snowpark-gastein.com.

On Schlossalm, by the Senderleiten chair-lift, is a family-oriented funslope, with easy obstacles as well as banks, waves and tunnels. Fulseck also has a park and a funslope, on skier's right of the Grossarl slopes.

Bad Hofgastein – the resort

Bad Hofgastein, like Bad Gastein, is a spa resort first, a ski resort second. Its pedestrianised centre is pleasantly neat but town-like, and from there the resort spreads into spacious suburbs, complete with parkland. The Schlossalm funicular base is some way off, across the valley.

Convenience

The resort's main flaw. It's not a huge village, but it does spread quite widely, and the valley's skiing is very widely fragmented. Most of the lodgings are 500m to 1km from the Schlossalm funicular lift base. There are buses every 10 minutes, not only to the funicular but also to Angertal, for direct access to Stubnerkogel. Of course, access to the other sectors requires buses, too.

Lodgings

There are scores of apartment houses and plenty of guest houses in the valley. Bad Hofgastein has almost 30 hotels, with rather more 4-stars than 3-stars. Arguably the best located is the Carinthia, 400m from the lift base, less from the centre.

Bars and restaurants

On-mountain après – pleasantly lively, rather than riotous – starts mainly at the lovely, woody Aeroplanstadl, from which point you have the choice of descending the remaining 400m vertical on skis or by toboggan. At the base there's an umbrella bar, and nearby the popular Gastein Alm.

The village has quite a range of bars and restaurants, from the cosily traditional to the glass-walled Ice Cube on the roof of the Alpentherme. Zum Boten is a wine bar notable for its lack of smoke. The Almrausch appears to be the late-night venue of choice.

There are more independent restaurants than you find in many Austrian resorts, including several Italians and a Japanese place. Rudi's Klause Stüberl does good pizza.

Off the slopes

The valley is famous for its thermal spas (and mildly radioactive rock and water). The Alpentherme Gastein is a huge and impressive place close to the centre with

It's a towny resort in a broad, flat-bottomed valley; note the huge spa complex, below the church

mineral-rich water throughout. It offers saunas, massage and a fitness centre as well as various pools. It's not cheap, but a dozen hotels in the resort are members of a partnership scheme that gives guests free entry.

There's a big skating rink with several Bavarian curling lanes. And a 3.3km toboggan run starts from the Aeroplanstadl restaurant, a short walk from the Schlossalm funicular top station. It ends about a mile north of the Schlossalm lift base, with the return presumably by taxi. It's daytime-only,

open only during the funicular operating hours.

The tourist office has a comprehensive guide-map to the many cleared walking paths in the valley and the not-so-many cross-country skiing loops.

For families

If you're not put off by the inconvenience of bussing around, this could be quite a good place for a family trip, with excellent facilities at the Angertal nursery slopes – not only a kids' skiing practice area with moving carpets but a small tubing hill.

Alternatives to Bad Hofgastein

These days the valley's bus services are pretty efficient, so you can explore it fully from more or less any base. Bad Gastein is livelier than Bad Hofgastein, Dorfgastein quieter and more rustic. For most people, Grossarl is of academic interest.

Bad Gastein 1090m

About the only thing Bad Hofgastein and Bad Gastein have in common is spa-hood. Central Bad Gastein is crammed into a horseshoe of steep slopes with a torrent plunging through the middle. With its narrow streets lined by grand Belle Epoque buildings, it has a very urban feel. Above the centre, a more conventionally Alpine area spreads away from the railway, spa and gondola station. There's a beginner slope near the main lift station, along with a kids' snow garden.

Convenience The upper level of the resort is convenient for the gondola. Distant parts of the lower town are far from that – but may be handy for Graukogel.

Lodgings A wide range of options. The Miramonte is a small, funky hotel with good food. The Grüner Baum cannot go unmentioned – a lovely collection of traditional buildings, a bit out of town, best suited to motorists.

Bars and restaurants Bad Gastein has quite a vibrant après scene.

Off the slopes Bad Gastein's thermal spa is a match for the one in Bad Hofgastein. There is also skating here, and a 2.5km toboggan run from Bellevue Alm, served by its own chair-lift and open daytime and evenings.

Dorfgastein 865m

Lacking a supply of radioactive hot water, Dorfgastein is a normal Alpine village, and a pleasantly rustic one at that. It spreads down a gentle 500m from the lift station to the valley road. There is a nursery slope with a 200m button lift, and a kids' practice area with magic carpets.

There are half a dozen hotels. The 4-star Römerhof takes some beating. It's a relatively quiet place, but not devoid of life. At the base is the Thomaselli bar, with attached umbrella bar. S'Einkehr Schluckerl is another. The Römerhof has a pleasant bar in a medieval stone 'tower', Die Turm.

Grossarl 885m

Grossarl, over the hill from Dorfgastein and quite some way up its valley from Alpendorf (at the west end of the Sportwelt north area) is a low-key village, unremarkable but pleasant enough. Maybe it attracts visitors who want to ski the slopes shared with Dorfgastein at minimum cost, but for skiing the rest of Gasteinertal it makes no sense as a base.

According to the Grossarltal website, the lifts on the Grossarl side of the hill run until 4.30, half an hour after the Dorfgastein lifts have closed. A mistake, or a rare outbreak of common sense?

Hochkönig – Dienten

Dienten / Mühlbach / Maria Alm / Hinterthal

Like the Salzburger Sportwelt, Hochkönig is a multi-valley ski area that is hardly visible on the UK ski market, and well worth getting to know.

Its chain of lifts extends over roughly five valleys, and is an impressive 15km across, from the western lift base near Maria Alm to the eastern lift base near Mühlbach. Dienten is the third main village, in the middle, and way the best base for making the most of the area. Another village, Hinterthal, lies on an offshoot of the lift system, west of Dienten.

It's a thin network, and the quantity of skiing isn't huge; the altitudes are modest, too. But the red-run skiing is good, the views are great, the villages pleasant and non-commercial.

The mountains in brief

Size On the small side, despite its impressive overall width of 15km

Slopes Mostly red-gradient, mostly wooded, on the short side

Snow Worryingly low altitudes, but very effective snowmaking

System, Lift Generally impressive, with one major flaw at Dienten

Sustenance Plenty of good spots – one a bit special

For beginners The slopes are good but inconvenient, the lift pass pricey

For true blue skiers Far from ideal, with suitable runs scattered around

For the confident Good red slopes in every sector, but little choice of route

For experts Some challenges, but you're likely to end up wanting guidance

Fancy stuff An impressive park at Mühlbach, and a funslope at Maria Alm

Dienten – the resort in brief

Convenience The walks are bearable; beginners need the bus, though

Lodgings Only a handful of hotels; but how many do you need?

Bars and restaurants They exist, in very small quantities, mainly in hotels

Off the slopes When a man is tired of tobogganing, he is tired of life

For families Not a bad choice for a family trip; one very attractive hotel

Pass notes	Key facts		Key ratings	
The standard weekly pass is the Ski Amadé one, also covering the Sportwelt, Schladming and Gastein valley. It seems there are no special payment arrangements for beginners, so you need a full lift pass from day one.	Altitude	1070m	Size	**
	Range	800–1900m	Snow	***
	Slopes	80km	Fast lifts	****
			Mountain rest's	****
	Where to stay, ideally		Beginner	***
	In the village of Dienten, within walking distance of the lift base; or out at Übergossene Alm.		True blue	**
			Confident	****
			Expert	***
	Websites		Convenience	***
	hochkoenig.at		Families	***
			Village charm	****

The mountains in detail

The Hochkönig area has a simple structure. Whether you head east or west from Dienten, you have very little choice of route: go up one side of a hill and ski down the far side; repeat.

Going east, you ride a fast chair then a drag to Wastlhöhe, ski down to the roadside lift station of Hochkönigalm, ride another fast chair up to a ridge below Kollmansegg, and finally take a long blue down to the Mühlbach lift base – or take one more fast chair to Schneeberg with the option of reaching Mühlbach on a final black run down.

Going west, you ride a slow double chair-lift out of Dienten to Gabühel – the only real impediment to progress in the area – then ski a long red run to the roadside lift station of Hintermoos, then take a six-pack to the shoulder of the pretty bowl of Abergalm. At Gabühel there is the option of a worthwhile side-trip down to Hinterthal, to another six-pack.

Size

The ski area claims to offer 120km of pistes, but this presumably includes the small detached areas of Hinterreit (at Maria Alm) and Hochkeil (near Mühlbach), which are on the piste map. It also publishes individual piste lengths, and some quick checks using Google maps suggest they are accurate, although a bit of cheating goes on where two pistes merge. Putting that aside and totting up those figures gives a total of 80km. This puts Hochkönig firmly in the ** category.

The piste map identifies the lifts and runs to take for a tour of the whole area – scarcely necessary, given the lack of options. Interestingly, the press office puts the distance skied at a modest 32km.

Slopes

The slopes are almost all wooded, with various exceptions, including the upper part of Langeck at Maria Alm.

Hochkönig is basically an area of red steepness, with some marked exceptions. The runs are not notably long – typically around 2km, with verticals no more than 400m or 500m. The top-to-bottom blue run 10 on Langeck is exceptional – just short of 6km, and over 1000m vertical.

Apart from some valley-level links, the only ski routes are two short ones and a third longer one on the top of Langeck. They are not groomed or patrolled.

This area is covered by the Ski Amadé regional lift pass. There's an excellent 3D interactive piste map at skiamade.com.

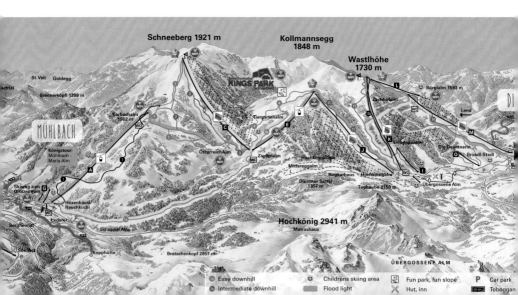

Snow

The altitudes here are typical of this region, which means low – so snow quality on the lower slopes will always be a concern, especially late in the season. But snowmaking is impressively effective, and most of the slopes face close to north, so you can be confident of being able to ski. Last time we visited, in late March, with hardly any natural snow on the ground, only the black run to Mühlbach was closed. It apparently has snowmaking, but keeping it open in spring would be a big expense. The piste from Gabühel to Dienten, facing south-east, is much the sunniest run in the area; it was entirely slush.

System, Lift

The lift system is now impressive, with gondolas and fast chairs in all the key places except Dienten, where a slow old double chair goes up Gabühel in the direction of Maria Alm. This is the only point where queues are likely to be a problem. There is also a drag-lift on the right side of the Abergalm bowl.

Sustenance

Our visits to this area have been rather rushed affairs, but it's clear that there are some good spots among the roughly 20 huts. The standout is Steinbock Alm at Gabühel, a spectacular combination of traditional woody interiors and cutting edge design – the panoramic glazed bar-lounge is fab. The menu is wide-ranging and the cooking first class.

More on the slopes

For beginners

Dienten's main beginner lift is the Zachhof drag, about 500m outside the village. The Schischule Top, however, is based out at the Liebenau drag, near Hochkönigalm. These are good slopes, and there is a further good slope at the top of Wastlhöhe, with a long, winding 'skiweg' back to the village. But all of these lifts require the purchase of a full lift pass on day one of your holiday. Shame.

For true blue skiers

There is quite a bit of skiing to suit the cautious intermediate, but it is dotted about the area. And the area as a whole is mainly of genuine red gradient.

At Dienten, there is a nice slope at the top of Wastlhöhe served by a drag that is about 1km long, but the 5km blue back to the village is a cat-track to get you home, not a run to enjoy.

To judge by the map, the best sector is at Mühlbach, where there are longish blue slopes at altitude and a long blue back to the base. Blue run 4 down the Kings Cab gondola is excellent after its steep start – and there is a way round that.

But getting to this run presents difficulties. From Dienten you would have to ski the genuine red run 13. From Mühlbach access is not simple either: emerging from the gondola you find yourself on a bit of blue run 1 that is of distinctly red gradient. It soon softens, but

there are other red pitches on the way to Kings Cab.

Then at Maria Alm there is the long blue run 10 from top to bottom. Make sure you're confident on the lower part to the valley before tackling the top part of the same piste, from the peak of Langeck – it has some tricky pitches.

For confident intermediates

Most of the skiing in this area is on rewarding red pistes – great fun at first. The long, thin nature of the network means your options are limited, but from Dienten you at least have the choice of heading east or west.

All the red pistes east of Dienten are satisfying runs. Pistes 13 and 3 are about the best – both nicely varied, slightly winding affairs.

At Abergalm, the reds served by the Kar drag-lift are short but sweet. The reds down lifts 6 and 16, above Hintermoos and Hinterthal, are good slopes and easily reached from Dienten even if it is by slow chair-lift; so you may spend quite a bit of time doing laps here. Red 30 connecting them is quite unusual – first, a long but unusually wide traversing track, followed by a lovely proper red descent. The track part makes it over 4km long.

For experts

There are some genuine black pistes – two short, sharp ones from the eastern lip of the Aberg bowl, and the much longer Osthang down the Mühlbach gondola – sadly closed when we last visited (read 'Snow'). Run 13a on Wastlhöhe is little steeper than the next-door red.

The ski routes were also closed when we visited, but we're told they are well worthwhile, especially the longer run 17 on skier's left, which dips outside the Aberg bowl. There are proper off-piste opportunities in several parts of the area – for example, from both Langeck and Gabühel to Hintermoos.

Fancy stuff

The main park is Blue Tomato Kings Park on the slope served by the Kings Cab gondola in the Mühlbach sector. At 1.8km long it is claimed to be Austria's longest, with a huge number of features. It has a website (kingspark.at); in a curious German/English mix, but with photos.

On the Aberg slopes at Maria Alm is an 850m funslope served by the Schönanger six-pack – waves, small jumps, banked curves and a tunnel. Maria Alm also has a beginners' park on its little Natrun hill, which is floodlit three evenings a week.

The red Bürglalm piste to Dienten – a typical run, although some are more interestingly twisty than this

Dienten – the resort

Dienten is a small, quiet, traditional village squeezed into the narrow bottom of the valley lying at the heart of the Hochkönig area. The quiet minor road through, coming up that valley from the south, winds between the chalet-style buildings, including a handful of hotels and guest houses. It's hardly picture-postcard stuff, but does have character and a relaxed air.

Convenience

It's a small village, the furthest hotel a walkable 500m from the main lift base. From the easterly sector towards Mühlbach you may be able to ski back almost to your door.

There is a ski-bus linking the village and the various lift bases, but it runs only seven times a day. Most affected by this are beginners wanting to use the drag-lifts which have their bases some way up the valley road.

Lodgings

The choice is basically between apartments, private rooms and a handful of hotels – two 3-stars and three 4-stars. The 4-star Vital Hotel Post is very close to the Gabühel chair-lift station, not so close to the chair for Wastlhöhe. A quite different option is out near the Hochkönigalm lift base – Übergossene Alm is a big, self-contained 'resort' at the bottom of the Liebenau drag and its blue slope. In-house ski shop and ski school, two tennis courts.

Bars and restaurants

There are several huts on the lower slopes of Wastlhöhe where you might find a bit of après action. Later on, it's largely hotel bars; we're told a highlight is the weekly live music session in the Hotel Post's Postalm bar, fronted by the boss. But there are a couple of other bars and simple restaurants.

Off the slopes

There's a 1.5km floodlit toboggan run from Grüneggalm to the south end of the village. The hotels mentioned have pools, and doubtless others do, too; and out at Übergossene Alm there's tennis. Shopping? There's a bakery ...

For families

The hotel Übergossene Alm would be a great place to take young children, with its own snow garden and immediate access to easy skiing. There is also a snow garden on the main nursery slope near the Zachhof drag-lift.

Alternatives to Dienten

Although Dienten is the best all-round location from the skiing point of view, you might have reasons to prefer the bigger village of Maria Alm, at the western end of the ski area – and Hinterthal has its attractions too. It's not so easy to see why you would prefer Mühlbach.

Maria Alm 800m

Maria Alm of course shares Dienten's traditional style of building, but in other respects could hardly be more different – away from the pleasantly random core it spreads widely along spacious avenues.

It's an appealing place for families. A pivotal feature is the little local ski hill, Natrun, where there is a kids' snow garden. It has gentle slopes served by a very short absolute beginner drag and a longer one, and the main ski school meets here or mid-mountain on Aberg. There is also a gondola serving longer red runs. Natrun also has a beginner terrain park, and a 2.5km toboggan run from the cosy gasthof Jufenalm to the fringe of the village (it's a 2km walk from the top of the gondola, though).

The main Aberg lift base is 2km from the village. When snow conditions are good you can ski there from Natrun on a red run. If not, there is a reasonable ski-bus service, with some services running on to the next lift station at Hintermoos.

There are about a dozen hotels in the village, a couple near the Aberg lift base and others further afield. There are quite a few guest houses, and lots of apartments.

Maria Alm is not without life in the evenings, at least the early evenings. There are jolly traditional bars, one or two with live music.

Mühlbach 855m

Mühlbach is a quiet little village with a gondola to the shoulder of Schneeberg at the eastern end of the Hochkönig network. It is not at all like a ski resort, with its few hotels and guest houses dotted along the road passing through from Bischofshofen to Maria Alm and Saalfelden. It has nursery slopes at village level, and two toboggan runs. Possessing neither Dienten's central position nor Maria Alm's fuller facilities, it makes little sense as a base.

Hinterthal 990m

Hinterthal is an unusual village, spreading widely on either side of the stream running through it, with no real focus other than the junction between its main street and the Hochkönigstrasse. It feels more like a rustic suburb than a village.

Hinterthal sits on a branch of the main Hochkönig network, with a six-pack going up to Gabühel. There are nursery slopes on both sides of the village, with links to the main lift base. The shorter, gentler slope has a kids' snow garden. The home piste from Gabühel is a genuine red run, so progression from the nursery slopes would mean getting the ski-bus to Maria Alm's Aberg lift station.

There are half a dozen 3-star and 4-star hotels. The starless Jagdgut Wachtelhof stands out: a lovely place with panelled rooms giving something of the feel of a modern hunting lodge; a member of the Small Luxury Hotels group. Its Zirbelstube restaurant gets a toque from the Gault-Millau guide. Mind you, the nearby 4-star Almhof gets two toques.

There are a couple of bars where you can find a bit of après atmosphere.

Abergalm at mid-mountain on Maria Alm's main mountain, Langeck – Hochkönig's one multi-lift mountainside

Ischgl

Ischgl / Galtür / Kappl / See

Ischgl offers an extensive, high ski area (spreading over the Swiss border to duty-free Samnaun) with a top-notch lift system above a village built in traditional style. It sounds great, and it is; but it does have flaws.

One is that the high slopes are virtually treeless. More importantly, the village has been very intensively developed, and has a rather brash, urban feel. And Ischgl is famous for its raunchy après-ski and nightlife. It represents recreational downhill skiing at its most glitzy.

The other, smaller resorts in the valley are interesting for a change of scene, but don't make much sense as bases for skiing Ischgl – the lift pass upgrade is pricey. Read the 'Outings' section.

The mountains in brief

Size A good-sized area, although not in the premier league

Slopes Nearly all treeless, offering a good variety of terrain

Snow At these altitudes, pretty reliable, with extensive snowmaking

System, Lift Fast lifts wherever you look, and few queues – one of the best

Sustenance Some excellent spots both sides of the border

For beginners Good slopes, but you'll pay through the nose to use them

For true blue skiers A good area, though there are no blues to the village

For the confident A great range of reds, plus encouragingly soft blacks

For experts A few serious blacks and ski routes, and plenty of off-piste

Fancy stuff The Jeep Snowpark at Idalp is world-class, with easy bits

Ischgl – the resort in brief

Convenience Adequate, provided you stay within the village

Lodgings A good range of options, including a couple of catered chalets

Bars and restaurants The liveliest bars in the Alps, plus some great food

Off the slopes Lots to do, indoors and out, with a good leisure centre

For families There are many better places for a family trip

Pass notes	Key facts		Key ratings	
The standard 'VIP' pass covers only Ischgl-Samnaun. For a further £10 or so you get two days in other valley resorts. The Silvretta valley pass costs much more; few people would find it worthwhile. Beginners need a full lift pass from day one – read 'For beginners'.	Altitude	1400m	Size	★★★★
	Range	1400–2872m	Snow	★★★★
	Slopes	172km	Fast lifts	★★★★★
			Mountain rest's	★★★★
	Where to stay, ideally In downtown Ischgl, on the main pedestrian street, within walking distance of one of the access gondolas.		Beginner	★★
			True blue	★★★
			Confident	★★★★
			Expert	★★★★
			Convenience	★★★
	Websites www.ischgl.com		Families	★★
			Village charm	★★★

The mountains in detail

The Swiss border divides the ski area into more or less equal halves in terms of area, but with many more lifts and pistes on the Austrian side. The border is crossed, in one direction or both, at five points. Passports should be carried, they say.

At the heart of the Austrian slopes is Idalp (2320m), a major hub including several big restaurants, ski schools, shops and nursery slopes, reached by gondolas starting on opposite sides of the village. The Idalp bowl is blue-run territory, with runs towards Höllboden and lifts rising 300m to the minor peak of Pardatschgrat – also served directly by a third big gondola out of the village – and towards the Swiss border.

From Höllboden, lifts in the Höllkar valley take you on to Greitspitze (2872m), another border crossing and the high-point of the whole area, and to the very slightly lower Palinkopf.

Palinkopf is the start of long, away-from-lifts runs on both sides of the border – the gloriously long and lovely 'Duty Free' red run 80 to Samnaun and, on the Austrian side, runs accessing the jumbo cable car up Piz Val Gronda (2812m). This is yet another point where a lift reaches the Swiss border, but the one piste from the top of the cable car turns back into Austrian Fimbatal.

On the Swiss side, most of the skiing is above the focal points of Salaas (2456m) and Alp Trida (2263m). To the east of Alp Trida is an area of gentle red runs beneath Visnitzkopf.

Another 'Duty Free' run (red in the past but now classified blue) goes down from Alp Trida to the Samnaun valley. A bus is required to get to the two parallel cable cars (one a giant double-decker) that take you from Ravaisch back up to Alp Trida Sattel – or to get to the duty-free shops in Samnaun itself.

Size

Ischgl was one of the first resorts to respond to the inflated piste km scandal that broke a few years back – but did so by publishing a choice of figures for its slopes, calculated in different ways; happily, these include the real, non-inflated figures of 163km as measured on a map or 172km as measured down the slopes. These are good figures, and the area will satisfy most one-week holiday visitors.

There are some worthwhile smaller resorts within reach, too – Galtür, Kappl and See. For reasons it's difficult to fathom, the Silvretta pass covering all of these resorts is rather pricey – about £40 more than an Ischgl/Samnaun six-day pass; a more attractive option is to pay about £10 extra for an extension to cover day trips to two of them.

Ski-buses covered by the lift pass run to these places – more frequently up the valley to the Galtür lift base at Wirl than down the valley to Kappl and on to See.

Slopes

Ischgl sits on the bottom of a steep-sided, heavily wooded valley. Although there are red runs to the village, the skiing is essentially on gentler open slopes, above the trees. The short Bodenalpbahn chair-lift in the Fimbatal is the best bet in a storm.

The mountain offers a good range of terrain, from near-motorways in the main Austrian and Swiss bowls to a few genuinely steep slopes, although most of the challenge in the area comes from the 800m–1000m verticals that you can achieve around Pardatsch and Palinkopf than from serious gradients.

The runs back to the village add the challenge of tricky snow and crowds,

including a distressingly high incidence of young lunatics. At busy times, the alternative of riding a gondola down can be very attractive.

If you really want a descent on skis, you can make something special of it by starting from the area high-point at Greitspitze and skiing, via Idalp, down what the resort calls Route Eleven (on account of its 11km length); the vertical is about 1470m – pretty impressive.

There are ski routes, of course, although perhaps not as many as you might expect, given the number of lift-served high-points – nine at the last count. They are clearly explained on the piste map as 'not monitored' and 'only partially groomed'; they come in red and black flavours, the latter labelled 'extreme'.

Ischgl persists in the nutty practice of applying the same run number to multiple runs with different starting points or different destinations. Why?

Snow

The snow here is pretty reliable. More than most Tirolean resorts, Ischgl can count on natural snow through a long season, thanks to the altitude of its slopes; but snowmaking is now claimed to cover almost 80% of the pistes, too. The Austrian slopes are mainly west or north-west facing, the Swiss slopes much sunnier – in late season the runs to the Samnaun valley can suffer, but they end at respectable altitudes (1700m–1800m) so it's not a serious concern.

System, Lift

These days Ischgl can't match the Saalbach area in the race to eliminate slow old lifts – there are still a few here – but by any other standard the lift system is seriously impressive, and constantly upgraded. At the last count (in late 2017) it included four eight-seat chair-lifts and no less than 15 six-packs. You can avoid the few drags and stick to fast chairs if you want to. Bottlenecks are not unknown, but queues are rarely a serious problem.

Beginners should note that they will need to get up to Idalp for all their lessons, so will need a full lift pass from day one. Pedestrians can buy one-trip return tickets, or a pack of five.

Sustenance

Lunch is taken seriously here: there are several table-service places with attractive menus that take reservations – far from the norm in Austria. But this is not one of those Tirolean areas where there is a cosy hut halfway down every run: restaurants are nearly all located at lift bases, and the upper slopes are virtually hut-free. The piste map marks the restaurants, with notes on what they offer.

Pardatschgrat is the only high-point hosting a hostelry, the impressively transparent steel-and-glass Pardorama; ground-floor self-service and a proper table-service restaurant above it, with wide-ranging menu.

Down at Idalp, another designer place is a favourite – the Alpenhaus. Again, table service is on the top floor above the self-service below, with excellent food from a wide-ranging menu, and a relaxed ambience; there's a good elevated terrace, too.

For something more traditionally Tirolean, head down into the Fimbatal to join the party outside the proper wooden chalet of Paznauner Thaya and munch pizza, or retreat to the table-service restaurant inside.

On the Swiss side, the table-service Marmottes in the Alp Trida building (not to be confused with the Skihaus Alp Trida) is in a bit of a time warp decorwise, but does excellent food.

More on the slopes

For beginners

There are excellent, gentle nursery slopes at the mid-mountain hub of Idalp, with a range of lifts from magic carpets to fast chair-lifts. At 2320m the slopes can be relied on to provide good soft snow, and there are excellent long blues to progress to (though they are often crowded). So Ischgl is fundamentally a good place to start skiing, unless you want to ski from your door.

But you have to go up the gondolas along with everyone else, and there are no special payment deals for beginners – so you face the cost of a full lift pass from day one. Evidently, Ischgl isn't really interested in encouraging beginners.

For true blue skiers

This is a good area for building confidence, with the slight caveat that many of the most attractive runs get very busy – oh, and the other one that skiing to the village is off the agenda.

The Idalp bowl has lovely wide blue runs above and below the main lift stations – and having skied down to Höllboden you can ride two chairs to Palinkopf for a lovely long descent of over 700m vertical.

Then, from Viderjoch and Idjoch there are good blues down into Switzerland, where there are several chairs serving other runs you'll enjoy exploring.

The run from Alp Trida down into the Samnaun valley was re-classified from red to blue in about 2015. We haven't skied it since then, but in its red days it was a bit tricky in parts. Take advice before embarking on it.

The step up to red runs is not a big one – there are lots of broad cruising runs to progress to.

For confident intermediates

Wherever you look, you'll find worthwhile red runs – broad pistes great for fast carving, or more challenging runs, mostly higher up. And many of the blacks (generally groomed) are quite tame.

Palinkopf and Piz Val Gronda have lovely wide, open descents of 800m to 900m vertical to Gampenalp; and Palinkopf is the start of the beautiful run 80 to Samnaun. Don't overlook the reds from the Höllspitz chair. Greitspitze offers a more rewarding, less crowded run into Switzerland than the standard blues from Idjoch or Viderjoch – though it is of red gradient only at the start. Both of those cols offer good descents back towards Idalp. Pardatschgrat has good testing runs (4 and 5) on the front face, and the lovely away-from-lifts run 7 down Velilltal – steep at the start then an easy cruise until it gets a bit tricky in the forest.

Over on the Swiss side, don't neglect the Visnitz chair-lift and the two chairs above it, serving relatively quiet slopes with grand views.

The runs back to the resort are tricky: the lower sections are quite steep, relatively narrow, inclined to become icy and, at the end of the day, unpleasantly crowded – the crowds including hooligans skiing way too fast. The final part of run 1a is especially challenging, and probably should be classified black. Note that taking run 7/7a does not avoid this stretch of 1a.

The bowl of Idalp, with the lift hub on the right; the roughly central peak with avalanche barriers is Palinkopf

For experts

There's a lot to do, on- and off-piste, although the resort's claim of 11 black pistes may give an exaggerated impression – many are quite short, or are of black gradient for only short stretches. Greitspitze offer a range of options including piste 14a, which is promoted as the steepest, with a gradient of 70% – 35°, which is certainly black steepness. The Höllspitz chair serves two good black slopes, one of which is a designated mogul slope. Piste 4 from Pardatschgrat is another good black, dropping 735m.

The ski routes from Palinkopf, Höllspitze and Viderjoch are all worth exploring – and when you are in the Velilltal give the short run down the double Velilleck chair a whirl.

There is lots of off-piste terrain close to the pistes, notably on the runs from Piz Val Gronda and down the Velilltal.

And there are more serious off-piste opportunities from many of the lift-served peaks – for example from Greitspitze and Palinkopf towards Samnaun, from Piz Val Gronda into the Fimbatal, from Pardatschgrat into the Velilltal. There are several specialist guiding outfits, as well as the ski school.

Fancy stuff

There are terrain parks on both sides of the border. The Jeep Snowpark above Idalp on the Austrian side is mightily impressive. There are two parts, reached by lifts B1 and B2, including the longest pro line in Europe, a more approachable 'public' park and a beginners' park including a fun crossline with banked turns. At Alp Trida on the Swiss side is the Obstacle Park, aimed particularly at expert snowboarders.

Ischgl – the resort

Ischgl is built almost entirely in traditional style, has the regulation church with pointy spire at its heart, is bypassed by traffic up the valley to Galtür, and is traffic-free in the centre. Excellent: all boxes ticked. But it is no idyllic rustic backwater – a combination of very intensive development and a certain brashness about the place make it seem very commercial, and difficult to warm to.

The steepness of the valley sides means that the village gets very little sun in midwinter – something that non-skiing visitors have been known to complain about.

Convenience

It's a fairly compact village, no more than 2km end to end and much less than 1km across. The two gondola base stations are about 500m apart, with a tunnel under the low hill separating the Pardatsch and Fimba lifts from the main street. The home pistes reach the fringes of the village, so a very few properties can even be called ski-in, although not ski-out. More importantly, few lodgings are more than five minutes from a lift.

Lodgings

Four-star hotels form the backbone of the lodgings scene, though there are plenty of 3-stars too. At opposite ends of the resort, the 5-star Trofana Royal and Elisabeth are the best in town.

Ski Total kick-started the catered

chalet department In Ischgl with its purpose-built chalet-hotel Abendrot – in an excellent position with short walks to the lifts – and has since expanded its programme here.

Bars and restaurants

Ischgl's après-ski and nightlife are legendary. In mountain restaurants such as Paznauner Thaya, lunch morphs into après in mid-afternoon. Then hundreds of people congregate in or outside bars at the end of the two home pistes, the Trofana Alm and the Schatzi bar of the hotel Elisabeth (with scantily clad girls gyrating on the bars). Other places nearby absorb the overflow. Meanwhile, those in search of the legendary quiet drink head for the Kiwi bar.

Some of these places function as decent restaurants too, notably the

Trofana Alm and the Kitzloch. Other recommended non-extravagant places include La Nona, Allegra and the hotel Nevada.

There are some serious restaurants in hotels. The Trofana Royal has a well-known chef overseeing at least two, and Benjamin Parth at the Yscla now runs a close second. In the hotel Christine is an offshoot of the Innsbruck institution Lucy Wang, doing polished French/Japanese cuisine.

Some of the bars are packed throughout the evening, and stay open late, and then there is another raft of serious nightclubs that are open until the early hours.

Off the slopes

There's a 7km toboggan run dropping 950m from Idalp – impressive statistics, though the website claim of 'one of the longest toboggan runs in the Alps' is optimistic. Medium difficulty, they say. But it's open only two nights a week, for 90 minutes. It's not cheap, but kids under 16 with parents in tow go free.

Other diversions include a 2km-long zipwire – or rather a pair of zipwires, which allows two to fly in parallel – dropping 280m from the mid-station of the Silvretta gondola; it's open daily.

There is skating and Bavarian curling on an open-air ice rink just outside the village, across the valley road. The Silvretta Center has a good leisure pool, and bowling. If you plan to use it a lot, get the cheap optional extension to the lift pass. There is a tennis centre with four courts.

There are cross-country trails up the valley to Mathon and beyond, and cleared paths both up and down the valley and up the sunny mountainside facing the ski area. It's not a great resort for these purposes.

For families

The ski school has a kindergarten with an 'adventure course' at Idalp, and older children in ski school can have lunch provided. Children under 8 get a free lift pass. But wouldn't you rather go to a quieter resort with village-level slopes?

There's little space to spare in central Ischgl; this snowy plot surely can't escape development much longer

Outings

There are several other, smaller resorts in the Paznaun valley. You could stay in these resorts and make day trips to ski Ischgl, but the lift passes that make this possible are a lot more expensive than the resorts' local passes. So really they make most sense as day trips from Ischgl.

Galtür 1585m

Galtür is appreciably higher than Ischgl; its top heights are appreciably lower, but the whole vertical of over 700m is usable. The claimed extent of the pistes is a modest 40km. There are basically six main lifts, of which two are drags. The two access lifts – a fast quad and a gondola – depart a little way out of the village. In 2016 a powerful new gondola was built at the far end of the system, replacing the old Breitspitz double chair.

The pistes are mainly red and black, with just one long blue run accessible from either of the main lifts from the village; not surprisingly, this can get rather busy. But many of the red runs are relatively easy.

The most challenging skiing is from the two highest lifts. The Ballunspitz chair serves genuine reds and a black, and one of the three or four ski routes in the area. And it accesses an off-piste area to skier's left of that route. The sector served by the new Breitspitz gondola offers some of the best off-piste in the area, as well as good red and black pistes and another ski route.

There are 73km of cross-country trails around the resort.

Kappl 1260m

Kappl is about 15min down the Paznaun valley from Ischgl. The village sits on an elevated shelf on the sunny side of the valley, but the access gondola starts in the valley bottom at roadside car parks.

The resort claims 42km of pistes. There is a red run to the valley station, which offers some shelter in bad weather, but most of the skiing is above a mid-

mountain hub about on the treeline at 1800m, where the nursery slopes are set.

Two fast quad chairs go up to Alblittköpfe at 2720m, with two drags and a double chair supplementing them. The sunny slopes suit confident skiers best. The pistes are mainly genuine reds, with a couple of blacks and one or two winding blues. A highlight is the red Latten piste, down a deserted valley to a point just below the hub, where the double chair-lift awaits. There are several ski routes, and considerable off-piste terrain.

Plans to link this area to St Anton's Rendl slopes have apparently been approved, and a linking gondola is slated for construction in 2019. The top lifts are only 4km apart.

See 1050m

See is a bit further down the valley from Kappl, but on the shady side. It claims 41km of pistes. A gondola goes up from roadside car parks to a restaurant and nursery slopes at 1900m, just below the treeline. A red run goes back to the valley, but most of the skiing is on the open slopes above, served by a six-pack and a slow quad, plus a couple of drags.

A red piste and black ski route 'Adrenalin' go off the back of the hill and swing round back to the base, passing on the way the base station of an eight-seat gondola built in 2014, going up to the top height of 2456m and serving a further area of good red-gradient skiing, on- and off-piste.

See's lift company has the domain name bergbahn.com, which must annoy various larger lift companies in the German-speaking Alps.

Kitzbühel

Kitzbühel / Kirchberg / Jochberg / Pass Thurn

Kitzbühel is one of the great names of Alpine skiing. It hosts the most famous ski race in the world – the Hahnenkamm downhill, plunging to its finish about 200m from the town centre. That centre, dating from the middle ages, is a key attraction – a lovely assembly of grand houses lining traffic-free cobbled streets. Of course, your budget may lead you to stay in more ordinary surroundings. Or in other places with lifts into the skiing – smaller, unremarkable Kirchberg, or much, much smaller Jochberg.

The slopes are extensive and satisfying, particularly for competent intermediates – at least in midwinter, or in the wake of a blizzard. In warmer weather, though, you might wish you were somewhere higher.

The mountains in brief

Size It's big, with lots more mileage easily accessible nearby

Slopes Classic intermediate terrain, partly wooded, long valley runs

Snow Great snowmaking keeps things open, but low slopes suffer in spring

System, Lift Transformed in recent years, though not without its flaws

Sustenance Plenty of good spots with table service – a highlight

For beginners There are many better places to start, but you'll get by

For true blue skiers A lot to do, but few blues are motorway cruises

For the confident Enjoy the whole area, almost – blues, reds and blacks

For experts Pray for powder, and prepare to pay for guidance

Fancy stuff The park looks OK; bit of a schlep from town, though

Kitzbühel – the resort in brief

Convenience Could be better, but could be a lot worse; just pick your spot

Lodgings Something for everyone, including the budget-conscious

Bars and restaurants A wide choice of lively spots, from trad to cool

Off the slopes Lots to do, but tobogganing means travelling

For families Not an obvious candidate for a family trip; pick your spot

Pass notes	Key facts		Key ratings	
For a small premium, the AllStarCard covers a huge range of resorts including two of the largest areas in Austria: SkiWelt (Söll, Ellmau etc) and the Saalbach area reachable via nearby Fieberbrunn. There are free beginner drag-lifts on the valley nursery slopes at Kitzbühel, Jochberg and Pass Thurn.	Altitude	760m	Size	★★★★
	Range	800–2000m	Snow	★★★
	Slopes	215km	Fast lifts	★★★★
	Where to stay, ideally		Mountain rest's	★★★★
	In Kitzbühel, near the Hahnenkamm gondola. Or maybe at the Jochberg Kempinski, if you like that kind of thing.		Beginner	★★
			True blue	★★★
			Confident	★★★★★
			Expert	★★★
	Websites kitzbuehel.com kitzski.at		Convenience	★★
			Families	★★★
			Village charm	★★★★

The mountains in detail

Kitzbühel's home mountain is the famous Hahnenkamm, reached by a gondola starting close to the centre of the resort. The slopes spread from there via Ehrenbachhöhe (arrival point of two gondolas from the fringes of Kirchberg) and Steinbergkogel (see photo – at 1970m, high-point of this sector) to Pengelstein, start of long runs going east to the outskirts of Jochberg and west to the hamlet of Aschau and the lift station of Skirast.

From Pengelstein a big cross-valley gondola goes to Wurzhöhe, arriving above the gondola up from Jochberg. A chain of lifts and runs then takes you to the high-point of the whole KitzSki area, Zweitausender (2004m), at one end of the broad, quite complex mountainside of Resterhöhe. There is another lift into the Resterhöhe slopes from the roadside at Pass Thurn.

There are three separate minor sectors. Kitzbüheler Horn is a sizeable hill, with its access gondola starting across town from the Hahnenkamm gondola; up a side road east of the town is the one-lift Bichlalm area; the very small Gaisberg slopes are close to the centre of Kirchberg.

Size

KitzSki's stated piste extent figures are verified by the esteemed Christoph Schrahe, so they are reliable. The total (including ski routes) is 215km, which makes it the fourth-largest area in Austria. The area is an impressive 17km across from north to south. It's pretty big.

The linked sectors where most people spend their time amount to 179km. As an alternative to the cross-valley gondola – effectively an elevated bus service – you can take a long ski route, with a short walk to the Jochberg lifts at the end of it.

At the opposite, western extremity of the lift system at Skirast, a two-minute terrestrial bus service will deliver you to the Ki West gondola taking you via Westendorf into the even larger SkiWelt area. The two areas together offer over 400km of pistes; but the unwritten rules of ski resort marketing mean that areas linked by buses remain separate.

Slopes

Despite the fearsome reputation of the Hahnenkamm downhill race course, the Streif, most of the KitzSki slopes are blues and none-too-serious reds.

The valley runs offer satisfying length and vertical (the longest is over 8km, and over 1000m vertical) – but bear in mind the remarks below on snow conditions.

The lower slopes of the main sector are quite heavily wooded, the upper slopes largely open. The north-facing slopes of the Resterhöhe sector are almost entirely above the trees.

The map is dotted with ski routes. These are not only marked and safe for avalanches but are generally groomed; they may be a bit narrow in places, and they may be kept open when conditions would require a piste to be closed.

Snow

Our standard warning about the low resorts in this part of the world applies: these days, snowmaking (with no less than 1,100 machines) may be good enough to keep runs to the valley reliably open; but with lift bases below 900m you can't expect great snow conditions on the lower slopes, especially later in the season. Be prepared for ice and/or slush, and count yourself lucky if you find packed powder.

Naturally, the Resterhöhe slopes, almost entirely above 1300m, usually offer the best snow. Kitzbüheler Horn faces mainly south, which is bad news.

System, Lift

Not long ago, this area was a byword for shockingly long lift queues. Until 1996 the main cable car out of Kitzbühel had a capacity of under 400 people per hour, with predictable results.

The improvements since then, and particularly in the last decade, have been very impressive, and the lift system is now very respectable, including no less than seven eight-seat chair-lifts and seven

The Legend. **Kitzbühel**®

Kitzbühel, 365 days of pure pleasure
Experience your perfect winter in Kitzbühel.

www.kitzbuehel.com

six-packs. But there are still some slow chair-lifts and T-bars, and some of them build queues – notably on the way back to Kitzbühel from Resterhöhe. Pressure on the key lifts out of Ehrenbachgraben will be relieved by the upgrade of the Jufenalm chair to an 8-seater for 2018.

As in so many big-name resorts, increasingly efficient lifts mean that the central parts of the main slope sector can be uncomfortably busy.

Sustenance

The piste map marks and names about 60 huts, most of which charming traditional chalets doing table service.

Panorama Alm up at Resterhöhe offers a characterful and cosy interior, and a fine terrace looking south to the high Alps, with a jolly bar to sit at if you get there early. And Bärenbadalm, which you pass on the way to Resterhöhe, is a newish wood-built chalet with a cool bar, a cosy lounge with sofas and open fire, and rustic dining rooms. The food includes welcome departures from the Austrian norm, some making use of Angus beef that grazes the pastures here in summer.

Top of the agenda for our next visit is Sonnbühel, behind the Hahnenkamm, where the recently installed Italian owner is offering serious food and table reservations, even on the terrace.

More on the slopes

For beginners

In Kitzbühel there is an adequate nursery slope at village level, close to the Hahnenkamm gondola, with three free lifts – two magic carpets and a 400m-long drag-lift. These days, snowmaking can generally keep this valley slope in operation when nature falls short, but the condition of the snow may be less than ideal. For very warm weather there are nursery slopes up on Kitzbüheler Horn, reachable by gondola. The main concern for beginners is progression from the nursery slopes. Read on.

For true blue skiers

Despite the preponderance of blue runs, this is not a resort where there is a lot of motorway skiing, and the timid early intermediate will find some of the blues a bit challenging. On the other hand, many

of the reds are not appreciably steeper.

Heavy traffic and the wrong type of weather can reduce some key slopes to boilerplate at times. Quite apart from how this sounds to a nervous intermediate, it is bad news for a beginner who wants to get off the nursery slopes after a day or two.

On the main Hahnenkamm/ Pengelstein sector there is a row of four lovely long blues dropping 900m/1000m, two to Kirchberg and two to Skirast. But they are not super-easy. In the distant past, all but one of these long valley runs were actually classified red. No doubt they have had surgery over the years to remove wrinkles, but at least one of them (27 Brunn to Skirast) remains a bit tough for a blue. If in doubt, start with 30 Pengelstein II towards Skirast, and take it from there.

If the snow on the lower slopes is a bit challenging, you'll do well to stay on the upper mountain. Three of the valley runs can be truncated at mid-mountain lift stations, and there are a couple of very short runs into an east-facing bowl below Pengelstein.

On Wurzhöhe there is some good blue skiing at a decent altitude, and at Resterhöhe there is a nice mixture of very easy linking blues, more direct blues and easy reds. The snow here is the best around – you're mostly above 1500m. But getting to this sector from Kitzbühel on skis involves testing red runs, so you'll have to take a bus to and from Pass Thurn. There is a blue run back down to Pass Thurn, but it's a pretty tedious path.

On the Kitzbüheler Horn, reds dominate the map. They are in fact fairly gentle, but they mostly get a lot of direct sun, spoiling the snow conditions, which may be why they are classified red. If snow conditions are good, think about trying these reds – and the blue run to the valley.

The Horn has the attraction that it is less crowded than the main area; but to really relax head for the new slow chair-lift at Bichlalm, which serves one deserted and genuinely blue run.

For confident intermediates

Very little of the terrain here is so gentle that your practically perfect parallel turns become redundant, and even less of it is too steep to be manageable. Most of the blues described above are worth skiing,

KitzSki

www.kitzski.at

GEPRÜFT
215 Km
VERIFIED
by Christoph Schrahe

and most have red variations along all or part of their length.

If it's open, you'll want to tick off the famous Streif – the race course from the Hahnenkamm to Kitzbühel. The regular red piste 21 skirts the serious bits at the start, but they are often accessible to the public.

Other red highlights include the descent from Wurzhöhe to Jochberg, the link between Wurzhöhe and Resterhöhe, and the longish runs from that sector to Pass Thurn and on the back of the hill to Breitmoos – mid-station on the gondola up from Hollersbach.

When you're riding lift G8 to Zweitausender, pay attention to the state of the return piste 75. If it looks and sounds hard, it will be harder still when you are on your way back to Kitzbühel, and the bus back from Pass Thurn may be an alluring alternative.

You'll see numerous ski routes dotted around the map. These are generally of nothing more than red gradient; snow conditions are unpredictable, but they can be great (and safe) fun after a dump, before the groomers get to them – and they get you away from lifts and crowds. Run 33 Giggling from Steinbergkogel to Hechenmoos offers fine views on the top

half, but becomes a bit dreary once it hits the forest. Run 56 Schwarzkogel from Pengelstein to Aschau is a lovely way to end the day. These and several other routes require the use of buses to get back to the lifts – get the timetable.

For experts

There is very little steep piste skiing; it mainly consists of quite short runs around the Steinbergkogel chair-lift, which climbs 500m vertical out of the bowl of Ehrenbachgraben. These are genuine blacks; piste 38 is aptly named Direttissima, and is worth avoiding if there is any trace of ice. The slow Hochsaukaser quad at the far end of the main sector also serves a worthwhile short black. Read about the many ski routes above.

There is a lot of off-piste to be explored, some of it close to the pistes and relatively safe, much of it more adventurous and requiring guidance – not least to make sure you end up in a sensible spot, and not in super-tight trees miles from anywhere. Naturally, a lot of it is below the treeline, making this a great place to ski in a blizzard.

In the main sector, the places to head for are the two lifts serving black runs

The only seriously steep mountain in Kitzbühel – Steinbergkogel; a typical restaurant, though – Sonnenrast

already mentioned – Steinbergkogel and Hochsaukaser. Both offer multiple long descents, as well as piste-side playgrounds.

Little Bichlalm has something of a name for off-piste. After a period offering only snowcat access, it now has a chair-lift again. This serves a single blue piste back down to the lift station, but also accesses a continuing snowcat service, carrying up to 25 people beyond the chair-lift up to Stuckkogel – a minor peak, but opening up routes in several directions, including a long run off the back to Fieberbrunn.

And, yes, Resterhöhe and the Kitzbüheler Horn have off-piste opportunities, too. At Resterhöhe the Zweitausender chair-lift accesses the steepest and longest slopes, and the snow is as good as it gets in this area.

There are nine avalanche transceiver checkpoints dotted around the slopes.

Fancy stuff

There is a fair-sized terrain park at Hanglalm in the Resterhöhe sector, with a fast chair-lift nearby. It has a German website at www.snowpark-kitzbuehel.at and a Facebook page at www.facebook.com/snowpark.kitzbuehel. It seems a pity that the main park is so far out. Why not on the Horn?

Kitzbühel – the resort

Kitzbühel isn't perfect – what resort is? – but it is special. It's unique among ski resorts: a lovely town dating to the middle ages right at the foot of its main mountains, with massive stone buildings lining its largely car-free central streets. Of course, most of the resort consists of more ordinary, pleasant but unremarkable Tirolean chalet-style development, but you can stay in the centre if you can afford it.

The town has a bit of life in the evening but it is not in the Ischgl/Sölden/St Anton league (for which some visitors may be grateful). On the other hand, the off-slope activities are top-notch, including Austria's only proper curling rink.

Convenience

Kitzbühel's heart is an almost car-free central area of handsome, solid, ancient buildings, about 500m end to end. The town as whole is much bigger – about 2km long and 1km broad, and mostly enclosed in a loop from the railway from Innsbruck via Wörgl to all points east.

So it is not a small resort, and if you care about convenient access to the lifts without using buses, you need to choose your location with care.

The gondolas to the main mountains are on opposite fringes of the town, 900m apart. The major Hahnenkamm lift is a bearable uphill walk from the centre, much closer than the Kitzbüheler Horn gondola, out by the railway station.

It's possible to find lodgings within easy walking distance of one or other of the main lifts, and even lodgings that are ski-in and roughly ski-out. But for many people life revolves around the ski-bus service circling the town.

Lodgings

Most of the lodgings are in hotels and guest houses, although quite a few of those offer apartments as well as standard hotel rooms. There are plenty of small apartment buildings and chalets to rent, some close to the centre and the main lifts. Inghams added a mid-sized catered chalet to its programme in 2017.

There are several 5-star hotels, but the classic Kitzbühel hotel is the long-established 4-star. Two particularly appealing and distinctive 'boutique' places in quite different styles are: the warmly welcoming ski-in, skate-out Rasmushof, right on the nursery slopes at the foot of the Streif piste; and the cool, swanky Schwarzer Adler, with rooftop pool and top-notch restaurant, on the eastern edge of the old town (and therefore not well placed for the lifts).

Of the roughly central 3-stars, the Resch is best positioned for the Hahnenkamm and is reported to be well run; but the historic Eggerwirt, just the far side of the old town, may be more appealing for those prepared to use the ski-bus.

Bars and restaurants

At close of play you have a choice of tea rooms doing wicked cakes or lively bars at the foot of the slopes and in the town – notably the terrace of the Stamperl and the long-established Londoner, across the road (with a live band at weekends). Both of these are popular through the evening and in to the night. There are plenty of other bars to explore. And yes, there are discos – two, at least.

You can slide from après into eating schnitzel or ribs at the Stamperl, but there are plenty of other options. If no expense is to be spared, there is a handful of restaurants the tourist office puts in the 'gourmet' category. Among the most interesting is Lois Stern, on the fringe of the old town.

Our more modest regular haunt is Chizzo, in a fine old building close to the centre – an unusual blend of traditional and modern food, reasonable prices, with cheerful, youthful service. Other very popular central places on the agenda for the next visit: Huberbräu Stüberl (plain, vaulted rooms, plain trad menu), Centro (cool, stylish Italian place), Hillinger (edgy wine bar).

Off the slopes

The Aquarena pool complex is excellent, offering a leisure pool with waterfall, a 25m sports pool, an adventure slide, children's area and spa facilities. Massages are available. The lift pass gets you a 50% discount on the hefty entry charges.

The Sportpark ice rinks offer skating and curling (proper curling, with an instructor, as well as the less serious Bavarian form), and the local hockey team is highly competitive. There's bowling and climbing, too. Check out www.sportpark-kitzbuehel.com. When the ice is up to it, there's also skating on a bigger scale on the sizeable Schwarzsee.

For tobogganing, you basically have to get on a bus to Kirchberg's floodlit run on Gaisberg – not far, but a bit of a drag. There are also long, unlit runs from two mountain restaurants on the way to Pass Thurn, but apparently you have to walk up to slide down.

There are lots of footpaths up into the hills, and cross-country loops in various parts of the valleys, with a good map available showing both.

Unique in skiing – a handsome town dating from the 13th century (though shaped by a later mining boom)

For families

It's possible to have an excellent family holiday here if you pick your location with care. Stay at the Rasmushof, for example, and you'll be able to lounge on the hotel terrace while watching your kids work on their snowploughs. More generally, a sprawling towny resort like this doesn't seem ideal for young children. Some of the ski schools will take infants.

Oh, and one more thing

A plaque In the 'Legends' park reveals that in the first ever Hahnenkamm races, in 1931, the combined downhill/slalom was won by a Brit – one Gordon Cleaver, later awarded the DFC for his bravery defending RAF Tangmere in August 1940: almost blinded by a shell, he succeeded in landing his Hurricane rather than bailing out. Cleaver died in 1994.

Alternatives to Kitzbühel

Kirchberg is set on the north-western side of the KitzSki area; it markets itself under the Kitzbüheler Alpen brand alongside Brixen and Westendorf (both in the SkiWelt area). Confusing, eh? And a bit cheeky.

The highest sector of the KitzSki slopes, Resterhöhe, has its own micro-resort at Pass Thurn. Halfway along the road to the pass, Jochberg doesn't amount to much, but is worth considering as a quiet base.

Kirchberg 850m

Kirchberg is a pleasant, bustling little town, bypassed by the busy Brixental road, with some life in the evening. That apart, its main attraction is lower prices than Kitzbühel – and quite quick access to the SkiWelt slopes too, especially if you take a car. There is a 300m beginner drag-lift close to town – not super-gentle.

Convenience Strangely poor – both lifts into the Ehrenbachhöhe slopes are a bus ride out of town (though there are some lodgings near each of them).

Lodgings Plenty of choice, especially of 3-star places; like-for-like prices are lower than in Kitzbühel.

Bars and restaurants A good range of bars both on the home slopes – the final run home can be a lengthy affair – and in the town. Restaurants are mainly in hotels, although there are a few alternatives.

Off the slopes Quite a bit to do, including a good floodlit toboggan run on Gaisberg.

Families The schlepping about to lifts may not appeal – but on the other hand there is that toboggan run.

Jochberg 925m

Jochberg is a small village spreading for some distance along the valley road going south to Pass Thurn, with a powerful gondola up to Wurzhöhe – a good launchpad for skiing both Resterhöhe and Pengelstein. Lodgings consist mainly of simple guest houses, plus a couple of smarter hotels, including the uncompromisingly modern 5-star Kempinski Hotel das Tirol, set just outside the village (and thus a T-bar ride from the gondola).

Pass Thurn 1275m

If you require the most direct access to the highest slopes (or to the terrain park), the roadside Berghotel Holzer will do the trick. There is little else here, though.

Montafon valley

Silvretta Montafon – Gaschurn / Gargellen / Golm

One fair-sized area and two smaller ones, sharing a lift pass

The Montafon valley, in Vorarlberg near the Swiss border, persists in having
a low profile on the UK market, despite a history of British visitors to one
or two of its resorts in the early days of holiday skiing. It lacks big resorts
and big hotels, and 20 years ago its skiing offered a rather fragmented
picture; but since 2011 the major Silvretta Nova area above St Gallenkirch
and Gaschurn has been linked to the Hochjoch slopes above Schruns by
the Grasjoch gondola, forming the fair-sized area called Silvretta Montafon
(not to be confused with Ischgl's Silvretta Arena). This link, like some other
more recent and more prominent ones elsewhere in Vorarlberg, has no
pistes – though you can ski down the gondola off-piste.

It wouldn't be impossible to link Silvretta Montafon to little Gargellen,
tucked away in its high side-valley; but few of its devotees or residents
would be likely to favour such a development – it's a lovely little backwater,
and probably should stay that way.

The other main sector – Golm – may be bigger than Gargellen but has
no special appeal, and is probably of interest mainly as a day-trip change of
scene, although there is accommodation to be had in Vandans.

Dotted around are other bits and pieces of skiing that are covered by
the lift pass, as is another quite serious ski area next door – Brandnertal.
That will have to wait for another edition.

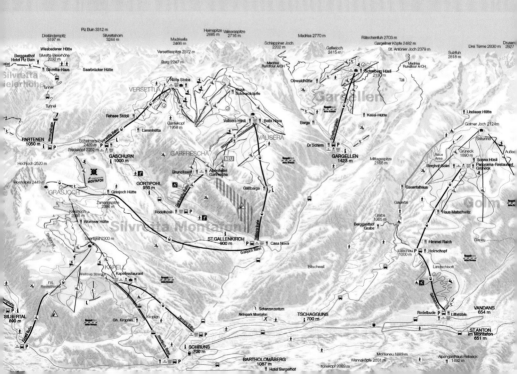

Silvretta Montafon

Gaschurn / St Gallenkirch / Schruns

This area was formed by the linking of Silvretta Nova and Hochjoch via the valley lift station at Galgenul, near St Gallenkirch and about equidistant from Gaschurn (at the far south-east end of the Nova area) and Schruns (at the far north-west end of Hochjoch).

Pleasantly traditional Gaschurn has direct gondola access to the major Nova sector of slopes and is a bearable bus ride from Galgenul, and so is the location of choice – except for groups of blue-run skiers, who might be better off in towny Schruns.

The skiing here has something for everyone, and is mostly at reasonable altitudes, above mid-stations in the 1500m–1700m range.

The mountains in brief

Size A middling area, with a couple of options for day-trip supplements

Slopes A good mix of terrain, mainly above the trees; mainly short runs

Snow Decent altitudes, not too much sun, adequate snowmaking

System, Lift Not a highlight: key lifts are fine, but lots of options are slow

Sustenance Few memorable spots, but you won't starve

For beginners A good valley slope, but progression is not straightforward

For true blue skiers Excellent slopes on Hochjoch, but Nova is trickier

For the confident Challenging short runs, and one distinctive long one

For experts Some demanding ski routes, and short off-piste shots

Fancy stuff A decent park and a kind of funslope, high on Hochjoch

Gaschurn – the resort in brief

Convenience It's a small village, but it's far from ski-in ski-out

Lodgings The usual range; one captivating central 4-star hotel

Bars and restaurants They exist, but don't expect a riot

Off the slopes Not a highlight, but a good floodlit toboggan run nearby

For families Good facilities at the lift base; but think about language

Pass notes	Key facts		Key ratings	
Like the other valley ski areas, Silvretta Montafon sells its own part-day, day and 2-day passes. Longer passes cover all the Montafon areas plus the Brandnertal next door and some other bits and pieces. Beginners can buy points cards for the 150m Vallüla T-bar next to the main Gaschurn lift station.	Altitude	980m	Size	★★★
	Range	690–2430m	Snow	★★★★
	Slopes	209km	Fast lifts	★★★
			Mountain rest's	★★★
	Where to stay, ideally In the middle of Gaschurn, a walk from the Versettla gondola.		Beginner	★★★
			True blue	★★★
			Confident	★★★★
	Websites montafon.at silvretta-montafon.at gargellen.at bergbahnen-gargellen.at		Expert	★★★★
			Convenience	★★★
			Families	★★★
			Village charm	★★★★

The mountains in detail

The major sector of slopes, Nova, has two parts – an M-shaped system spreading over two ridges above Gaschurn, separated by the Novatal, and a similar but smaller and lower system above St Gallenkirch. The two meet on the westerly ridge. Gondolas access the slopes from two points, one a walk from central Gaschurn the other a short bus ride from central St Gallenkirch; between the two is the slow old Garfrescha double chair-lift.

Hochjoch is less neatly arranged. A cable car from Schruns (and a gondola nearby) to the treeline access an open area of runs at Kapellalpe. From there another gondola goes on to another set of runs from Kreuzjoch, also accessing a third set of runs above Grasjoch, at the top of the gondola link from Nova. The blue run back involves skiing an exceptionally long tunnel.

Size

The area claims over 140km of pistes; Christoph Schrahe puts the total a bit lower, but in any event the area falls in the middle of the range with a ✳✳✳ extent rating. With the option of days at Gargellen and Golm, there's enough to satisfy most visitors.

The area as a whole measures over 13km across from north to south, so there is serious travel on offer, though there is a yawning 6km gap in the middle, where you're not skiing but riding two gondolas down then up – a great shame.

Slopes

There's a good range of terrain, from broad easy-intermediate slopes to very challenging mountainsides.

The skiing is mainly above the treeline, and reasonably high, though there are runs through the forest to the valley at three points. Top heights are in the range 2100m to 2430m – so yes, the runs are generally on the short side, typically 300–400m vertical. But there are exceptions, and one is notable – the Hochjoch Totale.

This is touted as the longest descent in Vorarlberg – around 10km and 1700m vertical from 2430m (at the top of the Hochalpila gondola) to Schruns. One day a week you can get fresh tracks on it by joining a group of up to 100 riding the Grasjochbahn at about 7.20am. After the run you get an excellent breakfast at mid-mountain. The whole deal cost €35 when we did it on a Wednesday in 2017; good fun, but do it in good weather.

There are other first tracks options too. One is a guided tour of the Nova sector in small groups. And on Saturdays the Zamang gondola and the Panorama gondola beyond it open at 7.30; for this, all you need is a lift pass.

If you are desperate to get out of the Montafon, you can have a day in Galtür, in the Ischgl valley, starting out by riding the cable car at Partenen.

There are lots of ski routes, particularly in the Nova sector; these are unexplained on the piste map, but the lift company tells us they are not groomed and not patrolled. Four of the black routes and three black pistes are given the tag 'Scorpion', identifying the steepest runs.

Snow

The altitudes here are respectable, and most of the skiing is quite shady – though the gentle bowl at Grasjoch, at the top of the linking gondola from the Nova sector, faces south-east. But even that is at over 2000m. Snowmaking isn't comprehensive but it does cover the key pistes.

System, Lift

All the key lifts are fast, but you do encounter the occasional slow irritant – there are several double chairs on Hochjoch that you might want to ride, and a couple of slow lifts at Nova Stoba in the Nova sector. Sunny weekend invasions might lead to some queues in places.

Sustenance

The restaurants on Hochjoch are adequate; the main one, Kapell, has table- and self-service sections. Seek out Wormser Hütte for Alpine atmosphere and views. Nova is better equipped,

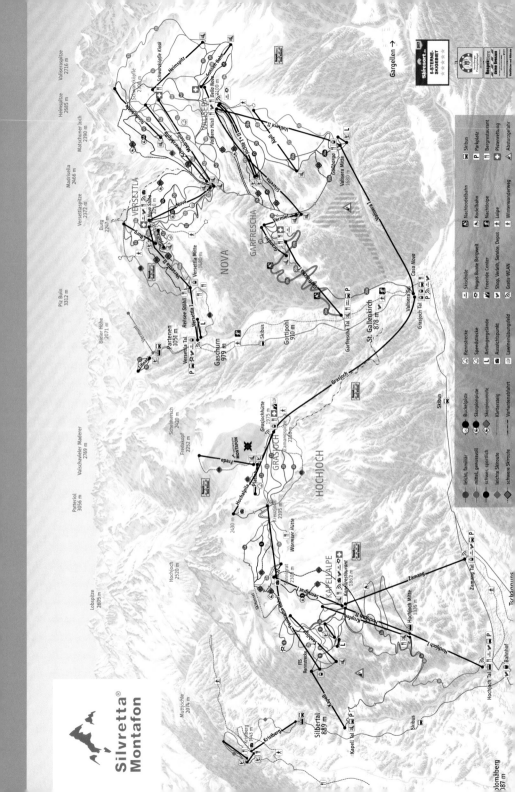

Silvretta®
Montafon

but standards vary. Valisera Hüsli is the pick – a lovely log-built place doing good traditional food.

More on the slopes

For beginners

Gaschurn has a nursery slope at valley level – a gentle one next to the gondola station, served by the 150m Vallüla T-bar. You can buy a points card for this lift. At the top of the gondola there are longer easy blue runs. So it's a not a bad spot to start. But read on.

For true blue skiers

It's a game of two halves. Hochjoch has two areas of excellent, high, easy blue slopes at Grasjoch and Kapellalpe, and the ideal way to find your ski legs would be to ride the Grasjoch gondola to explore those slopes. Nova is different.

The Novatal has plenty of blue pistes, but the sides of the valley are essentially of red or black gradient, and the blue runs vary widely in steepness, some little different from nearby reds. Happily, genuine blues have been created down into the Novatal, and from there the Madrisella fast chair accesses a blue

linking to a broad area of easy skiing served by the top stage of the Valisera gondola (the link to/from Hochjoch).

There is no easy piste down to Gaschurn; but since the only way down is an ungroomed ski route, many other non-expert skiers will be with you on the gondola at the end of the day. (There is a blue run to valley level at the Garfrescha chair, along the valley, but it is a path by the toboggan run, so not much fun – and you then need a bus back to Gaschurn.)

For confident intermediates

There's quite a bit to amuse you here, and plenty to challenge you. But you need to be satisfied with skiing many short runs down increasingly familiar mountainsides, with just the occasional treat of the leg-testing long descent to Schruns (read 'Slopes'). Few pistes other than that stick in the memory; you might guess that red piste 33, curling away from the lifts from the Rinderhütte chair, would be one, but you'd be wrong – it's just a dull easy piste.

On Nova, the ski routes really divide into the pretty stiff and the pretty easy – the second group including the two stages of the descent to Gaschurn. But there are some good middle-of-the-road routes on Hochjoch.

A fine panorama from the 2430m high-point of Hochjoch, start of the famously long descent to Schruns

For experts

You'll find quite a lot to do without requiring guidance. The black pistes generally have stretches of genuine black gradient, and those with the scary Scorpion label are definitely the genuine black article. The Scorpion ski routes offer some sustained challenges – for example the routes 44 and 55 from the two top lifts of the Nova system, the Rinderhütte chair and the Burg drag. The steepest Scorpion runs have gradients up to 81%, they say, which is a very serious 39°. Happily, on our visits we haven't encountered anything quite that steep.

There is a lot of off-piste terrain on the steep sides of the central valley of the Nova sector, notably from the two top lifts mentioned above, down into the Novatal. Strangely, there is even one route from the Burg drag marked on the piste map.

Hochjoch has off-piste waiting to be exploited, too, at Grasjoch for example. And there is another route marked on the map here, from the edge of the Grasjoch slopes down to the valley lift station – an epic 1200m vertical, at least.

The top of the valley is a famous ski touring area, with lifts and high-altitude buses to get you on your way. At a less ambitious level, there is a famous short tour into Switzerland from the top of Gargellen, around Madrisa.

Fancy stuff

The Freda chair-lift at the top of Hochjoch has on one side the valley's snow park – 40 obstacles, something for everybody, current set-up shown on the Silvretta site – and on the other a 'freeridecross'. This has waves, banks, drops and a tunnel, but the connection with freeriding is not clear.

Gaschurn – the resort

The Montafon doesn't really do chocolate-box-pretty, but Gaschurn is as close as it gets – a pleasant, traditional village bypassed by the valley traffic, with a neat church and a characterful old hotel in the middle.

Convenience

Gaschurn is a small village, and development is so limited that it's difficult to say where the village ends and the countryside starts. But it's about 400m end to end, and the Versettla lift and the nursery slope are about the same distance from the church. So everything is walkable, but nothing is on your doorstep.

Lodgings

There is the usual range of rooms, apartments, guest houses and hotels – half a dozen 3-stars, rather more 4-stars. In the centre, a walkable distance from the lifts, is the fine old shingle-clad Posthotel Rössle.

Bars and restaurants

In the afternoon the big terrace bar of the gigantic Nova Stoba restaurant at the top of the Gaschurn gondola gets very lively.

In the village, activity seems to centre (as it has for years) on two lively disco bars not far apart in the centre – Heuboda and Ausrutscher, but there are several other options, including quieter ones. The Ausrutscher also operates as a simple restaurant. There are several other places

to eat, other than in hotels, including a couple of pizzerias.

Off the slopes

In a village this size, it's not surprising that the options are limited. The hotel Saladina has a curling rink. Down the valley at Schruns, the Aktivpark offers skating and curling (it's home to a hockey team).

The nearest toboggan run goes from the top of the Garfrescha double chair-lift 4km down the valley; at 5.5km, it is Vorarlberg's longest floodlit run. Alternatives are down the upper stage of the cable car at Schruns, and down the bottom stage of the gondola at Golm (floodlit twice a week). The hotels Adler and Zamangspitze in St Gallenkirch have pools open to the public.

There's a lot of cross-country skiing in the valley, and plenty of cleared paths – plus marked snowshoe routes.

For families

The ski school has an excellent kids' practice area at the main lift base. But in this valley don't count on a ready supply of English-speaking chums, or for that matter English-speaking staff.

Alternatives to Gaschurn

There are two main options for access to the Silvretta Montafon slopes – the town of Schruns, at the north-west extremity of the Hochjoch sector, and the roadside village of St Gallenkirch, nominally the point at which the lift system of Hochjoch meets that of the major Nova sector.

Schruns 690m

Schruns together with its close neighbour Tschagguns is the major population centre of the Montafon, and definitely a town rather than a village. It is at the north-west extremity of the Hochjoch slopes, accessed by a small cable car on the edge of town, a 400m walk or bus ride from the centre. There is also a gondola 1.5km out, aimed at motorists.

Beginners here must buy a full lift pass and ride a lift to a nursery slope at mid-mountain.

There are countless apartments and rooms to let, and about a dozen hotels more or less equally split into 3-star and 4-star (plus the starless Taube where Hemingway famously scribbled). The elegant 4-star Löwen is best placed for the cable car. It has a pool, which is open to the public. The Aktivpark is nearby (read Gaschurn 'Off the slopes').

St Gallenkirch 880m

St Gallenkirch is arguably the village best positioned for exploration of both halves of the Silvretta Montafon area; but is that the key factor? You'll be using the ski-bus anyway: the lift station is 750m from the middle of the village. It's a very ordinary place spread along the main valley road, which carries a fair amount of traffic.

Beginners here must buy a full lift pass and ride the gondola to the mid-mountain nursery slope.

The village has a handful of hotels, pensions and apartments. The Zamangspitze has a good pool. There is simple accommodation dotted around both lift stations, but not much.

Other bars and restaurants exist, but there is little ski-resort atmosphere here.

The Zamangspitze's pool is open to the public. The Garfrescha toboggan run is nearby (read Gaschurn 'Off the slopes').

Gaschurn is a quiet, traditional village, bypassed by the valley traffic, blending into the surrounding farmland

Gargellen 1430m

Gargellen, tucked away on the Swiss border, is a real backwater, deliciously crowd-free and relaxed, with an unusual mix of easy and stiff skiing. Both the village and the ski area are tiny, but buses will get you to other parts of the Montafon for more variety.

The mountains

At 1430m Gargellen is way higher than the other Montafon resorts, but its hill peaks at 2260m – typical of the valley. A gondola goes up to Schafberg Hüsli at 2130m, in the middle of the skiing; chair-lifts take you a bit higher, and there are other lifts on the slopes below mid-mountain.

Size The stated run lengths (which seem reasonable) add up to 31km, of which about half is down to the four longish runs to the valley. At the furthest, highest point you are no more than 3km from the base.

Slopes The skiing divides into a small network of lifts and pistes above the treeline and the runs to the valley below it. The pistes are generally gentle, and short – the main lifts have verticals in the order of 200m. But the valley runs, in contrast, offer descents of up to 7km, and 800m vertical. Four ski routes are marked, three of them labelled 'extreme'. The piste map says clearly that these routes are not prepared or patrolled.

Snow Most of the skiing is above 1800m, and the slopes face east to north-east, which is quite helpful. Snowmaking is limited, and covers only one of the long valley runs (the red).

System, Lift Most of the lifts are slow, the exceptions being the access gondola and one six-pack on the upper slopes. But queues are not a problem.

Sustenance Adequate options. Kessl Hütte is an atmospheric wooden chalet doing good food, on the blue Täli run.

More on the slopes

For beginners The village nursery slope is on the steep side – you can see it in the photo, if you look closely – but happily

Tiny Gargellen has a fine mountain setting, in the shadow (in the early morning) of the steep Schmalzberg

there is a longer and gentler slope about 700m further up the valley, at Vergalda. It gets more morning sun, too.

For true blue skiers This area is made for those needing to build confidence. As well as the main open slopes at the top of the gondola there are lovely long runs away from all the lifts to the valley. And the red runs are barely distinguishable from the blues.

For the confident Gargellen doesn't make a lot of sense for you unless you're wanting to use your time to progress to more challenging stuff in deep snow. If you're going to Gargellen to pander to a bunch of true blue skiers in your group, you'll probably want to plan some bus trips to other resorts.

For experts The 'extreme' ski routes down the line of the gondola go over genuine black terrain – particularly route 11 on skier's left. There is lots of proper off-piste, too; the piste map marks three named off-piste routes, even. All very sweet, but short. And then there is the Madrisa Rundtour – an easy ski-touring expedition to Switzerland involving no more than 300m climbing.

Fancy stuff There is a funslope on the upper mountain.

The resort

Again, the village is not the stuff of picture postcards, but it is small and uncommercialised, and in a beautiful mountain setting.

Convenience It's a tiny place, but the gondola is 400m from what amounts to the centre, and overall the village spreads for almost 1.5km along the valley.

Lodgings Surprisingly, hotels number about ten, including four 4-stars, among them the lovely old hotel Madrisa. A conspicuous feature these days is the Landal holiday park – 12 chalets with 90+ apartments, with shared swimming pool.

Bars and restaurants On the hill, Obwaldhütte and Kessl Hütte are obvious pit stops on the way home. There is an umbrella bar at the base, and several other bars dotted around the village. Some hotels operate à la carte restaurants, and there are others.

Off the slopes There are cleared walking paths, including a short one up on the slopes. Curiously, there is apparently no proper toboggan run.

For families The ski school has a good kids' practice area in the village. But few fellow pupils will be speaking English.

Golm 655m–2124m

Golm is the Montafon's third ski area, above the small town of Vandans. You're unlikely to consider spending a holiday here, but the mountain is worth bearing in mind for a day-trip change of scene.

The area claims 27km of pistes, plus 17km of ski routes – this includes two long routes to Vandans and Tschagguns. You can ski the pistes in a couple of hours. The pistes are properly classified blue and red, though the reds are not difficult.

It's very much a family-oriented, easy-skiing area. A very long three-stage gondola rises over 1200m from the edge of Vandans (655m) to Grüneck at 1890m where there is a big kids' practice area. There are three fast chair-lifts on the slopes here, with one of the two six-packs going up to 2124m.

On a second flank of the hill, reached by a tunnel, a blue run or a ski route, is the one black run served by a fourth fast chair. Both the black and the ski route

have a seriously steep pitch, then mellow out. The blue run goes on to take you back to the front side. This blue run is the main gap in the otherwise comprehensive snowmaking coverage.

There is a winding blue run down the gondola as far as Latschau at 1000m, but the run down the bottom stage to Vandans is red.

There is a nursery slope with long rope tow at the lift base, and a longer button lift for beginners at mid-mountain. Cheap passes and points cards are available.

Golm has a toboggan run from Latschau, plus an Alpine Coaster – a sled-on-rails coaster, 2.6km long. The sleds are automatically braked to limit speed to 40km/hr. Gott im Himmel!

Obertauern

Obertauern is the nearest thing in Austria to a high-altitude French ski station. It's high up, about on the treeline, and therefore not liable to the slush/ice cycle that plagues many lower Austrian resorts later in the season. You do your skiing on open slopes surrounding the village, and may be able to ski to your door (though you're unlikely to be able to ski from it).

But it's mainly traditional in design, although some of its chalets are largish apartment blocks. Oh, and it's in Austria, which means plenty of woody mountain restaurants with service at big shared tables, a vibrant après-ski scene starting in mid-afternoon and similarly lively nightlife – not at all like a high-altitude French ski station.

The mountains in brief

Size There are smaller resorts in these pages, but not many

Slopes Generally gentle; short runs when you are doing the circuit

Snow A strong point, thanks to the village altitude and pass location

System, Lift Not quite in the premier league, but queues are few

Sustenance Hardly a highlight, but a reasonable choice of places

For beginners Several excellent nursery slopes, and easy progression

For true blue skiers Quite a lot to do, but in defined sectors of the area

For the confident Great, if you can live with the limited size and verticals

For experts Some steeps, but you'll soon need to think about a guide

Fancy stuff The park looks OK, but don't expect anything huge

Obertauern – the resort in brief

Convenience Pick your spot, and it can be ski-in, ski-out

Lodgings A good range, with some distinctive 4-star places

Bars and restaurants Vibrant après, and some attractive restaurants

Off the slopes There are diversions, but the range isn't great

For families There are facilities, but they're a bit unconvincing

Pass notes	Key facts		Key ratings	
The local pass is also valid in the Grosseck-Speiereck ski area at Mauterndorf, 15km south-east (infrequent ski-buses). The Salzburg Super Card costs about 15% more and covers countless ski areas over a broad region. Beginners can buy points cards – beginner lifts work out at about 60p a ride.	Altitude	1740m	Size	**
	Range	1630–2313m	Snow	****
	Slopes (claim)	100km	Fast lifts	****
	Where to stay, ideally		Mountain rest's	****
	Near the Gamsleiten chair-lift, which is a good starting point for circuits in either direction, and puts you close to most of the evening action.		Beginner	****
			True blue	***
			Confident	****
			Expert	***
	Websites		Convenience	****
	obertauern.com		Families	***
			Village charm	***

The mountains in detail

Obertauern's lift system has a simple structure. The resort sits on the south side of a bowl ringed by minor peaks, and lifts serve about seven high-points, forming a circuit that can be skied clockwise or anticlockwise.

You can start from several points – the Gamsleiten chair heading up the southern slopes from the effective centre of the village; the Zentral chair heading north from the northern fringes; or lifts up either side from the western and eastern extremities of the area.

Size

It's not a big area. The resort's claim of 100km of pistes feels like an exaggeration – the clockwise or anticlockwise circuit can be skied quite easily in a couple of hours. And Christoph Schrahe's measurements put it at about 70km.

Slopes

With a village at 1740m and top heights in the range 2000–2200m, naturally the runs are generally short. Most of the major lifts have verticals in the range 200–400m, the Zehnerkar gondola being a prominent exception with over 500m.

There are lightly wooded lower slopes at the western and eastern ends of the area, but most of the skiing is on open slopes – very unpleasant in bad weather.

Although there is a lot of easy skiing in the centre of the bowl and along the axis of the through-road, the upper lifts serve mainly genuine reds and blacks.

There is a ski route from one of the high-points of the circuit, Hundskogel. It is not explained on the piste map. At first glance the map seems to show countless other ski routes, but the diamond symbols are actually marking runs 'for skilled skiers' from the 'Super Seven' high-points.

Snow

Obertauern gets more snow than all the big-name resorts except Zürs; add in extensive snowmaking and you can be confident of good conditions.

System, Lift

Most of the important lifts are fast – Seekareck is about the only high-point served by a slow chair – and queues are few. The Sonnenlift double chair from the lower part of the resort into the middle of the bowl, serving several easy blue runs, can be a bit of a bottleneck at ski school departure time.

Sustenance

The distinction between mountain restaurants is a bit blurred, but there are about a dozen above resort level dotted around the bowl. That sounds quite a few for a small area, but at peak times it isn't enough. All but one are low on the mountain, perhaps with an eye on the après trade. The exception is Gamsmilchbar, at the top of Zehnerkar, which isn't quite as grim as it sounds, but does have a very, very limited menu.

You can't miss Hochalm and Kringsalm, with their popular terraces. Kringsalm now has a modern table-service section doing proper food. The little Flubachalm at the west end of the area is worth finding – a cosy, traditional spot with good food.

Note that a few of the hotels offer full-board deals – and going back to the village for lunch is no trouble.

More on the slopes

For beginners

There is an excellent, gentle beginner slope at the eastern extremity of the resort, served by its own drag-lift, an area in the heart of the village served by the shorter, steeper Perner drag, and at the western end a nice long, gentle blue run served by the Kirchbühel drag. Then, further west, outside the village, are very gentle slopes served by the Schrotteralm drag. The half-dozen ski schools have different meeting points, marked on the village plan in the downloadable accommodation guide. There is also an excellent longer slope up at 2000m, at the top of the Schaidberg chair-lift.

You can buy cheap points cards to use the lifts, delaying purchase of a lift pass until you are ready to progress to longer blue runs. That progression is easy from either end of the village.

For true blue skiers

There is a lot for cautious skiers to do, but only two of the high-points on the circuit have blue pistes from them. The easy skiing is basically in four sectors.

The main bowl has a gentle bump on its north-west side, with four lifts at various points accessing its blue pistes. Further west is the little Monte Flu, with three lifts. At the opposite east end of the area is the delightful, lightly wooded Schaidberg sector. And finally, one of the highlights is that the dramatic-looking east face of Zehnerkar, looming up on the south side of the village, is a blue piste of over 500m vertical – not the easiest blue in the world, but definitely a blue. Enjoy!

For confident intermediates

Putting aside (if you can) the small scale of the place discussed above, and the limited vertical of the runs, it is an excellent area for confident skiers. All the high-points have worthwhile red and/or black pistes. It's hardly worth picking any out, given that you can ski them all in a morning, but the two fast lifts on Seekarspitz are a good place to head if in doubt. The question is, are you happy to ski the same runs every day of the week?

For experts

You'll soon exhaust the on-piste challenges, but there is plenty to do off-piste. Some of the schools run guided groups.

Some of the black pistes are genuinely steep – notably those from the Gamsleiten chair – and those from Seekarspitz and the Plattenkar chair are worth a try. The ski route from Hundskogel starts gently but offers steep moguls lower down.

There are plenty of short off-piste slopes to be enjoyed within the bowl, for example under lifts such as the Seekarspitz chair, and from Gamsleitenspitz and Zehnerkarspitze. And there are more adventurous routes outside the bowl, from Gamsleitenspitz and Zehnerkarspitze south into the deserted valley leading down to Tweng and from Seekareck west to the main road at Gnadenalm.

Fancy stuff

There is an adequate-looking terrain park next to the Kehrkopf chair-lift, above the Almrauschhütte, at the extreme western end of the area. There are 40 elements in three lines, they say.

An open, snowy bowl with just a few trees; the bowl extends quite a way out of shot on the sunny side

Obertauern – the resort

Obertauern sits at the top of the Radstädter Tauern pass – historically an important route through the Alps, but now rendered largely redundant by the Tauern motorway tunnel a little way to the west. Nevertheless, the through-road does carry traffic. Much of the accommodation is spread along the road.

The main drawback of the resort's linear development is that there is no real centre, but there is a bit of a concentration of smart shops and bars in Ringstrasse, which goes off the main road opposite the Gamsleiten chair-lift. All in all, the place is lacking in charm, even though it mostly is built in traditional chalet style.

Convenience

The main part of the village is quite small – just over 1km long. But there are outposts of lifts and lodgings outside that central core, and the main easterly and westerly lift bases are about 2.5km apart. It's not difficult to find ski-in lodgings, and if you really set about it, you can find places that are ski-out too.

Lodgings

Accommodation comes in all the standard Austrian forms – as usual, no catered chalets. The majority of hotels are 4-star, though there are plenty of 3-star places – and some simpler places, too.

Two hotels stand out from the 4-star crowd. The Seekarhaus is on the slopes, a mile out of town and 70m higher, at the foot of the Seekarspitz chair and two others – next to the Kringsalm restaurant (they both belong to the Krings family). It has a swanky spa, and a restaurant that gets a toque from the Gault-Millau guide. The Manggei is a cool b&b-only 'designhotel', opened in 2009 by the Perner family and linked underground to the hotel Perner, where you can dine if you wish.

Bars and restaurants

Lots of places on the lower slopes and mountain-style places in the village get busy and lively from mid-afternoon. On the hill, Hochalm is popular.

In the village, the focus is Ringstrasse where you'll find the woody Latsch'n Alm and similar Lürzer Alm throbbing – but there are several alternatives elsewhere. At dinner time, these places transform themselves into quite civilised restaurants.

Most of the serious restaurants are in hotels. Apart from the Seekarhaus mentioned above, the hotel Panorama's restaurant is highly regarded.

For a quiet drink and a pizza, head for the central plate-glass Mundwerk. It's open until 2am. Of course, there are places open later, with dancing.

Off the slopes

The diversions off the slopes are somewhat limited. There is no ice rink or public swimming pool – you would have to go down the road to Altenmarkt for that. Many of the 4-star hotels have their own pools, of course. The nearest toboggan runs are not quite so far away, but they are 5km down the road, at Gnadenalm (1.5km floodlit run, skidoo/trailer uplift) and Südwiener Hütte (5km run, details elusive).

There are cross-country loops in the bowl, and longer ones at lower altitude a few miles down the road, in both directions.

There is a sports centre with pool tables, bowling, tennis and fitness kit. Oh, and darts. Darts without beer?

For families

There is a crèche over the tourist office in the centre of the village, the ski schools all seem to operate snow gardens (marked on the village plan in the downloadable accommodation guide), and there is a Bibo Bär 'family ski park' accessed via the Edelweiss chair-lift.

The village as a whole doesn't seem very child-friendly, but there are parts where there is easy access to snow, for improvised sledging etc. Thorough investigation of your proposed lodgings seems key.

Ötz valley

Sölden / Obergurgl

Contrasting resorts with one key feature in common: altitude

Sölden has regular slopes going up to over 3000m and two glaciers going even higher. Obergurgl is about as high as non-glacial resorts get – again, its top lifts go over 3000m, while the village (at 1930m) is reputed to be Austria's highest parish, whatever that means.

In other respects the two resorts could scarcely be more different – Sölden a valley town with its brash centre choked with traffic, Obergurgl a remote village where the road to Italy terminates in winter.

The two resorts are some miles apart, but worth considering jointly because their weekly lift passes are now valid in both resorts. The short bus trip is well worthwhile for keen skiers (especially those opting to stay in Obergurgl, with its more limited slopes).

There are other skiing opportunities in the valley, too. Down-valley there are slopes near Ötz itself, while west of Obergurgl, in the next side-valley, is tiny Vent, better known as a ski-touring launchpad than as a resort. But there are no interchangeable lift passes.

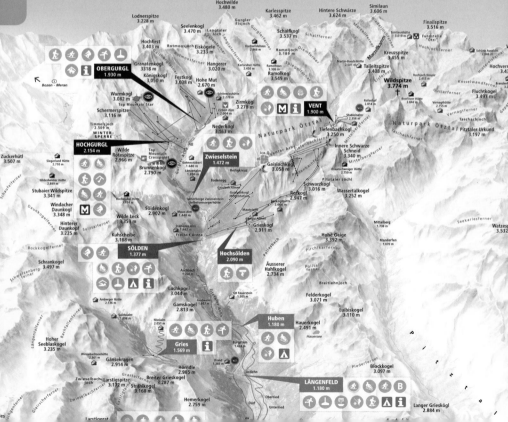

Sölden

Sölden / Hochsölden

Sölden's progress towards prominence on the UK package holiday market is slow, which is strange, given its USP: it is the only resort in Austria to combine a glacier area with an extensive conventional 'winter' ski area. Together, they form a quite compelling destination, though mileage-hungry keen intermediates may find it a bit tame.

One possible explanation for the continuing low profile is that the village is hard to like, and therefore hard to sell. It is very commercial, and traffic on the Ötz valley road through the centre is intrusive. But you can stay well away from the main drag if you want to, or retreat to a mountain hideaway in tiny Hochsölden.

The mountains in brief

Size On the small side; but you do have the option of day trips to Obergurgl

Slopes A good range of gradients, and some excellent long descents

Snow Few worries, given the altitudes and the glaciers

System, Lift Some problems, but morning queues have been sorted

Sustenance Futuristic or highly traditional – the choice is yours

For beginners Good slopes, good passes available, good progression runs

For true blue skiers Lack of a home piste from Giggijoch the only flaw

For the confident Some long, leg-testing reds and easy blacks

For experts Relish the long red descents, or head off-piste

Fancy stuff Park and funslope conveniently located at Giggijoch

Sölden – the resort in brief

Convenience Depends on where you stay, but OK overall

Lodgings A wide range, including a good Ski Total chalet hotel

Bars and restaurants A famously vibrant après/nightlife scene

Off the slopes A good but pricey leisure centre/pool

For families Not an obvious candidate for a family trip

Pass notes	Key facts		Key ratings	
For 2017/18, at least, passes for 3+ days are also valid in Obergurgl, 20min away by bus (covered by the pass). Beginners can buy day passes for the drag-lifts at Innerwald, reached by a short funicular from the village, or for two lifts at mid-mountain Giggijoch, plus the access gondola.	Altitude	1350m	Size	**
	Range	1350–3249m	Snow	*****
	Slopes (claim)	146km	Fast lifts	****
	Where to stay, ideally		Mountain rest's	***
	Within easy walking distance of a gondola – or the Zentrumshuttle if you plan to use the Innerwald nursery slope.		Beginner	****
			True blue	****
			Confident	***
			Expert	***
	Websites		Convenience	***
	soelden.com		Families	**
	oetztal.com		Village charm	**

The mountains in detail

The skiing is in three distinct sectors. Powerful gondolas at each end of the village go up to the peak of Gaislachkogl and to the mid-mountain lift base of Giggijoch. A chain of lifts and runs links the latter to the glacier area.

Both the Gaislachkogl and Giggijoch sectors offer a good range of slopes. They are linked by lifts and pistes via the intervening Rettenbachtal.

Most of the Gaislachkogl skiing is around mid-mountain. There is essentially one run from the top station, and three ways down to the valley.

The Giggijoch skiing is mainly above the gondola station, with the exception of the aforementioned link to Gaislachkogl and black and red pistes which go down past the mini-resort of Hochsölden to the valley.

The glacier area consists of two halves – the gentle Rettenbach, where you arrive, and the more varied Tiefenbach beyond it. You can access the latter at three points, by blue, red and black pistes; on your return there is just one way back, by a blue piste. From the base of the Rettenbach you can return to Giggijoch by lift and piste, or ski down the Rettenbachtal to ride lifts to either of the lower sectors. Or carry on down to the valley.

Size

The resort claims 144km of pistes plus a further 2km of ski route, which seems optimistic; it's not a big area. Christoph Schrahe (read the introduction to the book) puts it at about 90km, which seems more realistic – so it rates only ✱✱ for piste extent. For a bit more variety, the lift pass now gives you the option of spending as much time as you like up the valley in Obergurgl.

As the crow flies, the top of the Tiefenbach glacier is over 9km from the Giggijoch gondola base station down in Sölden, so there is some sensation of travel to be had here.

Rettenbach Gletscher: easy blue runs at the top (and off to the left) and a short, sharp black to the lift base

Slopes

Both of the lower 'winter' sectors offer a good range of slopes from blue cruising to some genuine black pistes.

Even the non-glacial slopes are mainly above the treeline. But there are some long descents through the woods to the valley that are worth skiing for fun, not just to get home at the end of the day – and, with the resort sitting at 1350m, these are pretty reliable for snow.

The resort likes to claim a biggest descent of 1980m from the Schwarze Schneide viewing platform to the valley, glossing over the fact that you have to hike up for 15min to that platform. For most of us, the longest run is the slightly reduced 1884m vertical from the Schwarze Schneide gondola to the valley, still about 15km long.

That descent has a long stretch in the middle along the road in the Rettenbachtal. Of more interest in skiing terms is the red run from Gaislachkogl which racks up 1678m/10km. There are descents of 1300/1400m from the high-points above Giggijoch, too.

The resort has one identified ski route, and a couple of unidentified ones that access restaurants around Gaislachalm, on the extreme left of the map. The tourist office says they are operated just like pistes – groomed and patrolled; weird.

Sölden is one of the many Austrian resorts to employ the insane practice of using the same number for multiple runs. On Gaislachkogl, for examples, there are three black runs with the number 3.

Snow

With a very healthy altitude range, snowmaking on over 75% of the pistes and extensive glacial backup, you could expect to be confident of good snow here. Generally you can, but on a recent December visit we found many pistes in less than perfect condition.

System, Lift

Pretty well all the key lifts in the lower sectors are fast, though there are still some slow lifts in annoying spots. Drag-lifts on the glaciers are excusable. The system has a structural flaw, which is that the chair-lifts to Rotkogljoch form the route to the glacier area as well as serving the main Giggijoch intermediate slopes. These get a lot of traffic. Morning queues can result.

In the past there have been big queues during the morning peak to get out of the village via the Giggijoch gondola, but in 2016 it was replaced by a new one (said to be the world's most powerful) with an astonishing capacity of 4,500 people an hour. The problem is presumably sorted, at least for the moment.

The Gaislachkogl gondola is less in demand, but shifts a pretty impressive 3,600 an hour, too.

Sustenance

Restaurants are marked and named on the piste map; supposedly there are 33 of them, which sounds a lot for a modest area – but many are concentrated in clusters on the lower slopes, and the higher slopes are not super-well equipped. On the glacier slopes, for example, the only restaurants are at the lift bases.

At the Gaislachkogl top station is a spectacular glass construction (featured in the Bond movie Spectre) containing the most gastro restaurant on the mountain, the Ice Q. No serious mountain luncher should fail to give it a try.

There are plenty of more traditional options. One of the best is Hühnersteign, famous for its eponymous chicken but serving lots of other good stuff too. It's the first place you get to when skiing down Rettenbachtal from the glacier, and quickly gets packed. Below Hochsölden (but happily above the Rotkogl chair-lift station), Eugen's Obstlerhütte is a cosy place doing substantial dishes – a great place to retreat to in bad weather.

More on the slopes

For beginners

It's not a bad place to learn to ski, though it's some way from ideal.

The best place to start, given good snow, is the drag-lifts at Innerwald, a short shuttle lift ride up the mountain from the centre – relatively quiet, with a cheap day pass for the lifts.

At Giggijoch there is another beginner drag, but the day pass here is twice the price because it also covers the Giggijoch gondola from the village and the Hainbachkar fast quad serving the long blue run 13 – good for progression, except that this slope can get fiendishly busy.

The pass also covers the Rotkogl

double chair-lift that links Hochsölden to Giggijoch, but getting back to Hochsölden means skiing red run 19.

For true blue skiers

There is a huge amount for the cautious intermediate to do. All sectors of the skiing have something to offer, and there are fairly easy blue-run links meaning that you can get around the whole area (though run 6 from Gaislachkogl towards Giggijoch is at the tough end of the blue range).

The one obvious flaw is that there is no easy way home from Giggijoch – so you either contrive to end your day on Gaislachkogl or you ride the gondola down.

The place to find your ski legs is Giggijoch, with a choice of longish, wide, gentle (but busy) blues served by fast chairs. From here it is no problem to proceed to the Rettenbach glacier and on to the Tiefenbach. Both offer fabulous easy skiing on excellent snow.

You can return from the glaciers by skiing blue run 30 down the Rettenbachtal, and then ride one of the chairs out of the valley, either back to the Giggijoch slopes or on to the slopes of Gaislachkogl.

The Gaislachkogl blues include some that are a bit steeper than those on Giggijoch, but on the other hand they are much less crowded. Head for the Heidebahn chair on the extreme left of the map, above Gaislachalm; run 2 offers lovely quiet cruising. This is despite the fact that it is one of several blue runs here that once were red; no doubt wrinkles have been smoothed out.

Another is run 10 from the mid-station through the woods towards the village – an excellent, varied trail, but with one or two challenges along the way. An easier way back is from Gaislachalm – the lovely blue run 8; the main challenge here is that in parts it becomes virtually flat.

For confident intermediates

There are no great networks of red runs here, but nevertheless there is quite a lot to do, including some notably long descents (read 'The slopes').

Highlights among the reds include run 11 from Rotkoglhütte into Rettenbachtal – long and quite testing – and run 7 below that, down to the village.

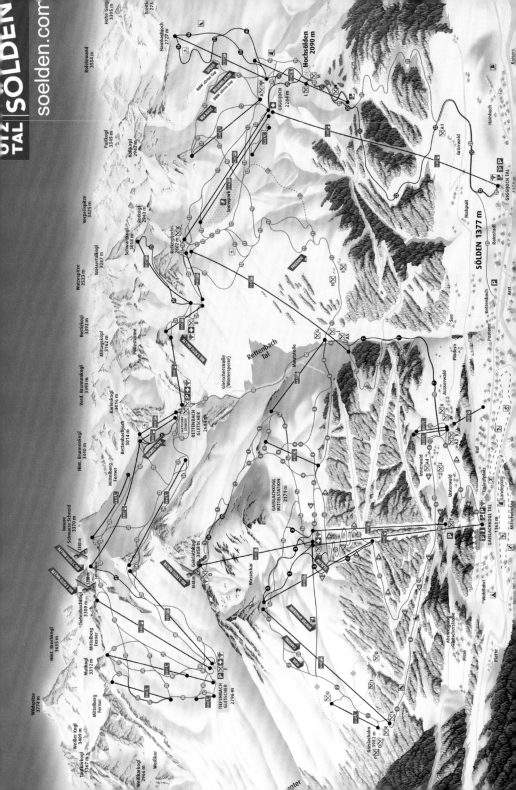

Run 1, from the top of Gaislachkogl, gives great views and is a proper red at the start but then softens, and may leave you wondering whether the construction of the gondola was worthwhile. Experts might take a different view (read the next section). You ski past the Gratl double chair – an opportunity for some relaxed laps on runs 4 and 5, nice open reds.

Most of the blacks are relatively easy – more on this below. The several blacks on Gaislachkogl numbered 3 really could be classified red.

For experts

Although some of the black pistes may not justify the classification, those on Giggijoch are worth a try even if they are not notably steep; and there are steeper sections, for example at the top of the more direct of the two blacks numbered 14, on the extreme right of the map.

Run 25 from Schwarzkogl is a good black, though not seriously steep. Run 31 at the bottom of the Rettenbach glacier is a genuine black, and designated as a mogul run.

Despite these attractions, you may spend more time on the long, leg-testing red runs.

There is a lot of off-piste to be explored. At Giggijoch, for example, the Rosskirpl chair to Hainbachjoch accesses some good slopes, and there are huge areas of terrain lower down, into Rettenbachtal. The Schwarzkogl chair also serves off-piste alternatives to its one piste.

From Gaislachkogl there are demanding routes in various directions – into Rettenbachtal, down the Wasserkar bowl towards the gondola mid-station and off the back of the mountain – and lower down large areas are reachable by traversing from the pistes.

Some of these routes are serious stuff. Several schools offer off-piste guidance.

Fancy stuff

The Area 47 Snowpark is a sizeable affair at Giggijoch, with beginner and medium areas plus a jib area. There's a dedicated website at www.snowpark-soelden.com. Next to the park is the 700m funslope.

Sölden – the resort

Sölden is essentially traditional in style but with some modern development along the main through-road in the shape of glitzy shops and bars. This hectic strip linking the two lift stations is separated by the river from a much more relaxed suburb to the east, where many of the smaller guest houses are located.

The resort is famous for its vibrant nightlife, but it is not in the Ischgl league; there are still bars with semi-naked girls on display, but the tacky advertising is less pronounced than it once was.

Convenience

It's essentially a linear place, with the two access gondolas close to either end, almost a mile apart. Most of the development is in the northern half of the town, within ten minutes' walk of the Giggijoch gondola. The ski-bus runs every 10 minutes. So all in all, it's adequately convenient for most visitors.

Lodgings

Ski Total has a good chalet hotel above the town, reachable (just) on skis, but most of the lodgings are in middle-market hotels, guest houses and apartments. There are over 30 hotels, mostly 4-star

but with a good choice of cheaper places.

The Central Spa is the one 5-star hotel, by the river and away from the main drag, a bearable walk to the Giggijoch gondola. Two distinctively cool 4-stars, both with rooftop pools, are the Bergland, in the centre, near the funicular to Innerwald, and the recently built Berge, over the river but well placed for the Giggijoch lift.

Bars and restaurants

Drive into Sölden after the lifts have closed and you'll get an idea of what goes on here – the umbrella bar in front of the hotel Liebe Sonne will be spilling happy beer drinkers into the street. Over the road, Fire and Ice has glass walls to keep its customers contained.

The après starts well before this in various huts on the hill, pivotal places being Bubi's Schihütte on Gaislachkogl and Eugen's Obstlerhütte below Hochsölden, on the run down from Giggijoch. If you're descending from Rettenbachtal and manage to get past the cluster of places at the treeline, Philipp's Eisbar at Innerwald may draw you in.

Later on there are countless places to go, ranging from quiet drinks at Die Alm through live music venues to places with striptease and table dancing.

Most of the eating out options are in hotels and traditional in style, but of course there are several pizzerias.

Off the slopes

The Freizeit Arena is an excellent leisure centre with tennis, bowling and a fitness centre as well as an adventure pool with whitewater channel, slides etc. The big Aqua Dome at Längenfeld (12km down the valley) has no less than 12 different pools. Neither of these places is cheap, but some hotels are in partner schemes.

There is a floodlit 5km toboggan run down the road from Gaislachalm, on the extreme left of the piste map, but bizarrely

it doesn't open until 10.45pm. It's not far up the valley to Pill, and the Hochgurgl toboggan run.

There is an ice rink, which offers not only skating and Bavarian curling but the kit you need to stage your own hockey match.

For families

Of course, it's possible to have a satisfactory family holiday here if you pick your location with care, but the busy, towny resort isn't a natural family spot. There are kindergartens at Giggijoch and Innerwald (ie at the nursery slopes just above the town).

The Hochsölden option

Hochsölden is a neatly traditional ski-in, ski-out mini-resort (no more than 300m end to end) set below Giggijoch, reachable from there by skiing down a red run or by road from Sölden. The Rotkogl double chair lift runs up beside the 'village' – so it's a good spot for getting on the snow early.

There are five 4-star hotels, and a few smaller b&b places and apartments – and that's about it. Be sure to take your e-reader.

Innerwald and the village nursery slopes – the view on arrival on piste 8 from Gaislachalm; mid-March 2012

Obergurgl

Obergurgl / Hochgurgl

There is nowhere quite like Obergurgl, combining as it does a traditional-style village with skiing more or less to your door at the kind of altitude (and snow) you associate more with soulless, purpose-built French ski stations. Add in a lack of road traffic, crowd-free slopes and jolly après-ski, and you have a formula that brings many visitors back year-on-year to the same room in the same hotel, quite a few of them from Britain.

For sceptics, the village is a bit lacking in focus and diversions, and the hoteliers a bit too pleased with themselves. More objectively, the ski area is too small. The new shared lift pass deal with Sölden helps in this respect, and keen skiers will want to make full use of it.

The mountains in brief

Size One of the smallest areas in these pages – but the regulars don't care
Slopes Intermediate gradients, practically all above the trees
Snow Relax: at these altitudes, they've got you covered
System, Lift Nearly all fast lifts, well able to meet demand – excellent
Sustenance Some good places, though the best gets busy
For beginners Excellent slopes, but be ready to pay for a full lift pass
For true blue skiers You'll be able to get around the whole area – great!
For the confident Plan on a couple of outings down to Sölden
For experts Plenty to do off-piste, and you won't face much competition
Fancy stuff A good-looking park, and funslopes above both villages

Obergurgl – the resort in brief

Convenience You'll do a bit of walking, but not a lot
Lodgings Book early, and don't expect any bargains
Bars and restaurants Legendary tea-time action, then ... not a lot
Off the slopes Skating in Obergurgl, sledging in Hochgurgl
For families One of the best – just pray the weather doesn't sock in

Pass notes	Key facts		Key ratings	
For 2017/18, at least, passes for 3+ days are also valid in Sölden, 20min away by bus (covered by the pass). Beginner day passes are no longer available: beginners need a full pass from day one – madness. A pedestrian lift pass is available.	Altitude	1930m	Size	*
	Range	1795–3080m	Snow	*****
	Slopes (claim)	110km	Fast lifts	*****
	Where to stay, ideally		Mountain rest's	****
	At the far southern end of the village, close to the Hohe Mut gondola and Rosskar chair-lift.		Beginner	*****
			True blue	*****
			Confident	***
			Expert	***
	More info www.obergurgl.com		Convenience	****
			Families	****
			Village charm	****

The mountains in detail

The slopes of Obergurgl and Hochgurgl are separate, and in the dim past were linked only by bus services. These days a long (3.6km, 8mins) gondola links them – though only until the ridiculously early hour of 4pm.

Obergurgl's slopes fall into two sectors separated by the deep Gaisbergtal. The higher Festkogl is reached by a gondola from the northern end of the village, while from the southern end there is a fast chair towards Festkogl and a gondola towards the second sector, Hohe Mut. A blue run crosses from the Festkogl sector to the lower Hohe Mut slopes.

Hochgurgl's slopes spread across a gentle mountainside. A gondola from the village followed by a fast chair take you up over a gentle central bowl to the area high-point of Wurmkogl (3080m), where there are fabulous views south-east towards the Dolomites.

There is more challenging skiing to either side of this central bowl. To skier's left are two drags starting some way down into the forest, while to skier's right the Grosse Karbahn serves a couple of red-gradient blacks, and a tedious traverse brings you to the Kirchenkar gondola, which is due to get a second stage in 2018, opening up a new high red run.

Size

The resort claims 110km of pistes, which would make this a middle-ranking area on a par with St Anton, for example – a clear exaggeration. Christoph Schrahe (read the book's introduction) puts the area at about 60km, which is what it feels like.

It is, in other words, one of the smallest areas in these pages.

Note that Obergurgl and Sölden now have a proper pass sharing deal, meaning that you can spend as many days as you like skiing the other resort, 20min away by regular shuttle-bus.

Slopes

There is a good range of intermediate skiing, typically a bit easier than the piste classifications suggest.

Practically all the skiing is on open slopes above the treeline, with typical descents in the range 500–900m vertical. But a single red run drops down the wooded mountainside below Hochgurgl to a gondola base station near Pill, offering a total vertical from Wurmkogl of almost 1300m. And the lower slopes below Hohe Mut are lightly wooded.

There are ski routes in both Obergurgl sectors, but curiously none at Hochgurgl. The status of these routes is not explained on the piste map. The tourist office says they are operated just like pistes – groomed and patrolled; weird.

A long-standing complaint is that a number of pistes have serious drops to one side that are not marked – take great care in a white-out.

Once a week you can join a guided group to ride the Festkogl gondola at 7.30am and get first tracks skiing over to Hohe Mut for a high-altitude breakfast. It's not cheap.

Snow

A key attraction: at these altitudes, you can be pretty confident of good snow throughout a long season. The resort claims to have snowmaking on 99% of its pistes; strange that they haven't bothered to kit out that final few metres.

System, Lift

The lifts are now impressively slick in general. With the construction of the Kirchenkar gondola in 2015, the only slow relics now are the two Vorderer Wormkogl drags on skier's left at Hochgurgl and the slow quad Bruggenboden chair on the lower Hohe Mut slopes. The lack of queues here is one of the resort's great draws.

Sustenance

There are about 10 huts, located in most of the obvious spots, ranging in style from the cosily traditional to cutting edge glass-and-steel.

The pick is Hohe Mut Alm, combining excellent food with a choice of a lovely woody interior or fab views from a big terrace; gets packed, though. Lower down in this sector, Nederhütte deserves a mention for efficient service as well as for its famous après party.

At Hochgurgl, Top Mountain Star at Wurmkogl is a cool modern place with even better views and a varied menu. For a complete contrast, head for the simple but very satisfactory Kirchenkarhütte – limited menu but hearty meals.

Top Mountain Crosspoint is an extraordinary place, presumably aimed at the summer tourism market (it is on the road – closed in winter – that goes up to the Timmelsjoch pass on the Italian border). As well as an exceptionally attractive modern restaurant doing a wide range of good food, it has an impressive motorcycle museum (not free).

More on the slopes

For beginners

First, the bad news. For 2017/18, at least, there will be no cheap beginner lift passes sold here; beginners must now buy a full lift pass. This is a minor disgrace, making your first week on skis more expensive than it need be.

From every other point of view, this is an excellent place to start, with good nursery slopes conveniently to hand at village level, served by the Wiesenlift and Mahdstuhllift. And there are good longer slopes to progress to: the run down the first stage of the Hohe Mut gondola, and the other slope reached by that same first stage, running down beside the Bruggenboden slow chair – an ideal area for building confidence.

For true blue skiers

This is a great resort for the near-beginner or cautious intermediate. Not only are there good mid-mountain blue slopes in the Festkogl sector above Obergurgl and all across the mountainside above Hochgurgl, but many of the reds are not appreciably steeper. You can expect to get around the whole area, either sticking to blues or giving the occasional red a go. You'll find more to do at Hochgurgl than Obergurgl, but the link is pretty quick so it doesn't matter where you choose to stay.

For confident intermediates

It's difficult to be so enthusiastic about the place for a more confident skier. There are rewarding runs; the problem is that

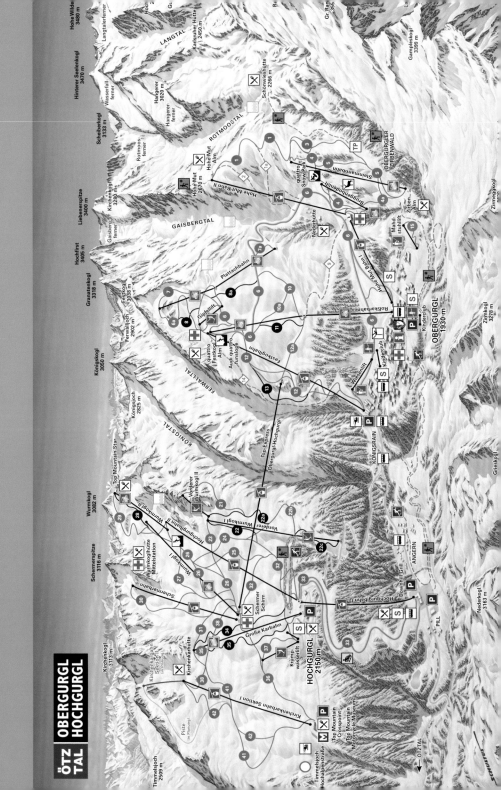

there aren't many of them. Be prepared to make day trips to Sölden.

Above Obergurgl, two of the most interesting runs are red 12 down the Festkoglbahn and red 1 from Hohe Mut. The ski route variants on these pistes can be quite challenging. The lower reds in the Hohe Mut sector, served by the Steinmann chair, are nicely wooded but could be blue.

At Hochgurgl, the Schermerbahn serves a good red down most of its length. Below it, the two runs beside the Grosse Karbahn marked black are really of enjoyable red gradient. The runs from the Vorderer Wurmkogl drags are good red stuff, too.

Run 33 through the woods from Hochgurgl to Pill is not long (350m vertical) but excellent – a lovely winding genuine red.

For experts

As the previous section suggests, the pistes offer precious few challenges – the black runs could be classified red, except for the occasional steeper pitch – run 28 at the very top of Wurmkogl, for example.

The several ski routes are well worth exploring. Unlike most Austrian resorts these days, Obergurgl doesn't seem to groom its ski routes, so if you are keen on bumps …

There is lots of off-piste to be explored within the lift network, especially from the lifts on the northern side (skier's right) of Hochgurgl – that is the Grosse Karbahn, Kirchenkarbahn and Schermerbahn – and it doesn't get skied out immediately. And from the top heights of Wurmkogl and Hohe Mut there are more ambitious routes to be explored, into the side-valleys that break up this mountainside.

There are transceiver checkpoints at those high-points, and on Festkogl. And there is an Ortovox transceiver training park near the Hohe Mut mid-station.

Of course, you really should have guidance for practically all of this. The main ski school now runs an Alpin Center, devoted to guiding off-piste and touring.

Fancy stuff

There's a good-looking terrain park served by the Bruggenboden chair at the bottom of Hohe Mut – over 20 obstacles in 2017. There are funslopes at mid-mountain on Festkogl and on the upper slopes of Hochgurgl. Check out the resort website for more information.

Obergurgl, the hotels at the Festkogel gondola out of shot on the left; the rounded peak is Hohe Mut

Obergurgl – the resort

Obergurgl has attractions – it is traditional in style, quiet and almost traffic-free, and on a fine day its high setting is splendid. As a place to spend time, though, it is hardly compelling. Essentially, it consists of nothing but hotels, guest houses and apartments. You venture outside in the evening basically to hurry to the cellar bar of some other hotel, not to wander about enjoying the ambience.

It's a small place, but quite long, and a village of parts – driving in, you come to one group of hotels at the village entrance, around the Festkogl gondola, then a second below the road on the right, then a third on the left, up on a low hill above the road, and finally a cluster around the little square that passes for a village centre.

Convenience

Few lodgings are actually ski-in and even fewer are ski-out, but it's a small village (about 1km end to end) with its major lift stations helpfully positioned at each end, so you don't have far to walk – unless, that is, you have foolishly picked a hotel that happens to be remote from your ski school's standard meeting place. There are ski-buses to deal with that, but matching your hotel and your school makes more sense.

Lodgings

There are 25 hotels – nearly all 4-star, many with pools – plus a similar number of guest houses and many more apartment buildings. Demand for rooms exceeds supply, which seems to lead to a degree of complacency – and does mean you need to book early. The 4-star Bergwelt is excellent in all respects except location – up the steep little hill between the lift bases.

Sister companies Ski Total and Esprit Ski (family specialists) now have a range of catered chalets here.

Bars and restaurants

The main lift base area is quite lively at close of play. Après festivities start slightly higher up at the famous Nederhütte, close to the Hohe Mut mid-station, where lunch slides seamlessly into music (often live) and dancing on the tables. David's Hütte, further down the hill, can be lively too. Further fun is to be had at the two competing umbrella bars at the lift base, attached to the adjacent hotels, and other bars nearby.

There is a reasonable range of restaurants in hotels designed for non-residents, plus a few independent ones – including a notably good pizzeria, the Belmonte.

Several hotels have cellar bars offering music in various forms later on. The Josl Keller seems to lead the field.

Off the slopes

There are short langlauf loops just below the village, and what looks an excellent walking route from the same area up to the Schönwieshütte on the southern fringes of the ski area.

The dinky little ice rink offers the Bavarian form of curling as well as skating; open from mid-afternoon through the evening. The hotel Edelweiss, amazingly, offers indoor riding lessons on its lovely Haflinger horses.

For serious tobogganing, as opposed to messing about on the snow, you'll need to head for Hochgurgl (or for Pill, at the bottom of the run – free bus in the evening).

Your other options off the slopes are pretty much down to what your hotel has to offer, or the spas that a couple of other hotels make accessible for a fee. There's a leisure centre down in Sölden (not cheap), and thermal spa enthusiasts can take a bus a further 12km down the valley to the seriously impressive Aqua Dome in Längenfeld.

Shopping? The resort website has an exciting online shopfinder – it brings up two mini-markets, a hairdresser and a post office. Oh, and multiple branches of three sport/fashion shops.

For families

From most points of view, Obergurgl makes an excellent place for young children, with easy access to snow and few hazards. There are two dedicated areas for infant beginners, more or less at opposite ends of the village, both with indoor kindergartens.

Some hotels run their own kindergartens, but the catered chalets of specialist family tour operator Esprit Ski are likely to be the obvious choice for most British families. At the time of writing, in 2017, one of them has the crucial feature of a residents' bar.

If the resort has a flaw for families, it is that it's a cold and bleak place in bad weather. But children are tough.

The Hochgurgl option

If you're going to stay in a high, bleak spot, there is something to be said for staying in the highest, bleakest part of it. At 2150m, Hochgurgl is 220m higher than Obergurgl.

Hochgurgl is a tiny place, no more than 400m end to end, centred on the two main lift stations. Even so, you may have to plod a few yards from the door to ski.

There are half a dozen hotels, a mix of 3-star, 4-star and one 5-star, the cleverly named Top Hotel Hochgurgl. Most have pools. The hotels have bars and restaurants, of course, but the only establishment with much of an independent reputation is Toni's Almhütte, a cosy wood-beamed chalet attached to the Olymp. It does food, and may have live music.

Off the slopes the highlight is a toboggan run down through the forest to Pill on the valley floor, at the base of the Hochgurglbahn gondola. Open in the daytime, and in the evenings once or twice a week (when the lift is free to ski pass holders). There is a short floodlit langlauf loop.

Hochgurgl: a few hotels beneath broad, open snowfields, and a single red run plunging into the woods below

Saalbach

Saalbach / Hinterglemm / Vorderglemm / Fieberbrunn / Leogang

Saalbach is the headline act in the 'ski circus' that includes Hinterglemm, 3km up the valley, smaller Leogang over the hill and (since 2015) Fieberbrunn, a couple of valleys away. That last link made this area clearly Austria's biggest. The Arlberg then seized the crown – but for how long?

Size apart, the area has many attractive features – not least, its top-notch lift system. But it has a snow problem: not only are the slopes rather low but about half of them are also excessively sunny.

Saalbach is appealingly traditional in style and car-free in the centre, and has become known for vibrant après-ski and nightlife. Hinterglemm is more ordinary, but in other ways has clear attractions.

The mountains in brief

Size Second biggest in Austria, with the worthwhile Fieberbrunn addition
Slopes Generally gentle, partly wooded, some worthwhile steeps
Snow Snowmaking keeps runs open, but sun and altitude affect conditions
System, Lift Hugely impressive system: virtually all fast chairs and gondolas
Sustenance Plenty of good spots with table service – a highlight
For beginners Pretty good nursery slopes, and excellent longer runs
For true blue skiers Few better places in Austria, despite some no-go areas
For the confident Huge amounts of genuine reds – and worthwhile blues
For experts Easy groomed blacks but some challenging routes and off-piste
Fancy stuff A rarity: a big park at village level – though it's at Hinterglemm

Saalbach – the resort in brief

Convenience Plenty of lodgings within walking distance of the main lifts
Lodgings The usual Austrian formula, with plenty of choice
Bars and restaurants One of the liveliest, from mid-afternoon until late
Off the slopes Good walks and sledging; skating and tubing at Hinterglemm
For families Satisfactory if you pick your lodgings with care

Pass notes	Key facts		Key ratings	
For a small extra cost, the Super Ski card covers everything from Hintertux to Schladming, including nearby Zell am See-Kaprun. There is a free drag-lift on the small nursery slope in central Saalbach, and points cards are available for use on all other lifts.	Altitude	1000m	Size	★★★★
	Range	800–2096m	Snow	★★
	Slopes	270km	Fast lifts	★★★★★
			Mountain rest's	★★★★
	Where to stay, ideally		Beginner	★★★★
	In or close to the heart of Saalbach, between the access lifts.		True blue	★★★★
			Confident	★★★★★
	Websites		Expert	★★★
	saalbach.com		Convenience	★★★★
	saalfelden-leogang.com		Families	★★★★
	kitzbueheler-alpen.com		Village charm	★★★★
	bergbahnen-fieberbrunn.at			

The mountains in detail

The curving Glemmtal runs roughly east-west, with Hinterglemm about 3km further up-valley than Saalbach. At each village, and at an anonymous valley station west of Hinterglemm, major lifts go up the north- and south-facing slopes; and at the opposite extremity, east of Saalbach, at Vorderglemm, is a fourth station with a lift up the sunny slopes only.

The south-facing slopes have a series of high-points linked by a network of runs split at Saalbach by a valley that caters only for walkers and tobogganers. The north-facing slopes have far fewer lifts and runs, on three well-defined peaks – Schattberg Ost and West, and Zwölferkogel.

All of this forms a circuit that you can ski in either direction (or, if you prefer, taking a route forming a figure of 8). Skiing anti-clockwise, you can cover the whole valley, crossing at the extreme easterly and westerly points; but skiing clockwise you must cross the valley at Saalbach, missing out Vorderglemm, where there is no clockwise lift.

The links to the other resorts go northwards from high-points on the sunny side of the valley. From Wildenkarkogel, above Vorderglemm, a long chain of lifts and runs goes off to two points near Leogang, in the next valley. And from Reiterkogel, above both Saalbach and Hinterglemm, a newly created red run goes to the southern tip of the Fieberbrunn slopes.

The Fieberbrunn network is a complex affair, but essentially consists of a chain of lifts from the Saalbach link on open slopes below the peak of Henne, and woodland runs close to the village, below the low peak of Lärchfilzkogel.

Size

Saalbach's stated slopes total of 270km is verified by the independent consultant Christoph Schrahe, so it's reliable. Briefly Austria's biggest area, it now comes second only to the Arlberg. But read on.

From the Seekar lift in the south-west corner of the area, behind Zwölferkogel, it's over 13km to Fieberbrunn, and a huge 17km to Leogang. So exploring the area can give a real sensation of travel.

At the eastern end of the sunny slopes, a blue piste goes away from the lifts to the village of Viehhofen, 4.5km down the valley from Vorderglemm and 8km from Saalbach. Here, a short new gondola is planned for construction in 2018 to complete the link (started in 2016) with Zell am See's Schmitten area. You could argue that the two ski areas could then be treated as one, which might put Saalbach ahead of the Arlberg again. But to ski Saalbach from Zell you'll need a bus to the lift at Vorderglemm – so by the unwritten rules of ski resort marketing they may be denied union.

Slopes

Most of the skiing is easy-intermediate stuff, with some tougher runs on the north-facing slopes of the main valley and on the slopes of Fieberbrunn.

You're likely to spend a lot of time on the runs above mid-mountain, which offer verticals of about 400m. But runs to the valley stations are in the order of 800m–1000m, including the run to Leogang, probably the longest, which is about 6km long.

The main sunny slopes have patches of forest dotted about, but much of the skiing feels quite open; the runs on the Magic 6er chair are relatively sheltered. The steeper slopes on the shady side of the valley are more heavily wooded. Most of the slopes you're likely to spend time on at Fieberbrunn are more or less treeless.

There are a few short ski routes in the main valley, but more numerous and lengthy ones in the Fieberbrunn sector. The piste map gives no explanation; assume that they are not patrolled.

The key gondola to get you back from Fieberbrunn closes at 3.30. Better news is that from mid-January several major lifts are open from 8am.

Snow

The combination of low altitude and a huge area of excessively sunny slopes is a drawback for anyone planning a trip after midwinter. Snowmaking covers about 90% of the pistes, and these days is so effective that you can count on being able to ski the whole area. The worry, later in the season, is more about the quality of the surface – slush in the afternoons, icy concrete next morning.

Fieberbrunn has the reputation of being a 'snow-pocket', and the numbers bear this out – it gets about as much snow as St Anton and Obergurgl, and much more than nearby Kitzbühel.

System, Lift

Over recent years, this area has set the pace for investment in modern lifts. For all practical purposes, the system now consists entirely of fast lifts – gondolas and detachable chair-lifts. If you want to experience the tranquility of a km-long T-bar ride, you have to head out to the Seekar drag, behind Zwölferkogel.

Lift queues are rare. But, of course, the other side of the coin can't be escaped: in high season, notably during Austrian school holidays, many of the runs get unpleasantly crowded. It's worth bearing in mind that runs forming part of the main circuit will be busier than others.

Sustenance

The whole area – the few steep, shady black pistes excepted – is dotted with attractive rustic huts, many doing table service. They are all marked and named on the piste map.

Pick of the restaurants is the huge brick-built AsitzBräu, at the top of the Leogang gondolas, rebuilt in 2010 and incorporating lots of brewing relics in its woody interior. It's spacious and relaxed, with small individual tables as an alternative to the usual communal affairs. The menu is very traditional, but much wider than the norm. The Alte Schmiede, across the piste and in the same stable, is another very attractive spot.

Wieseralm, on the sunny slopes directly above Hinterglemm, is a characterful woody place with a fine terrace, good food and cheerful service. It's an outpost of the excellent hotel Wiesergut in Hinterglemm.

In the central 'circus' area, most of the runs are on the gentle, lightly wooded sunny side of the valley

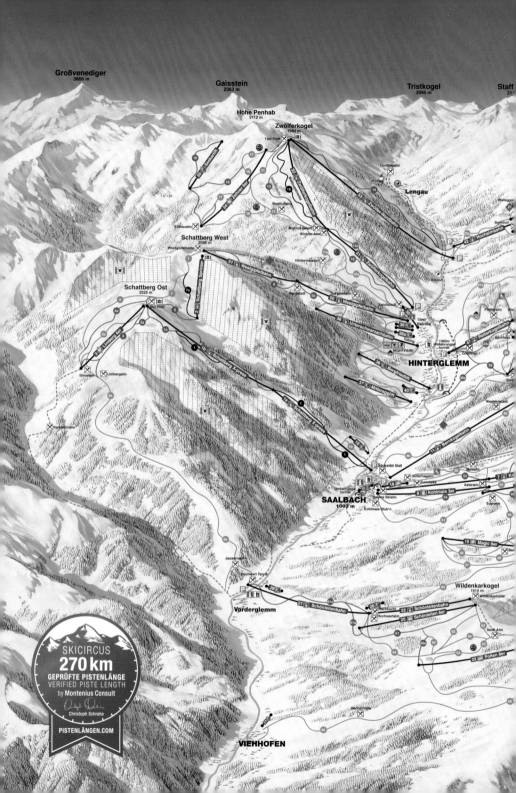

More on the slopes

For beginners

Right in the heart of Saalbach, detached from the main slopes, is a nursery slope with the 110m Kreuzkapelle drag-lift. And at the foot of the main pistes is a much bigger slope served by the 400m Turm six-seat chair-lift. These aren't the gentlest of slopes, but they're pretty good. The bigger slope does get a lot of through-traffic. The Kreuzkapelle drag is free, and points cards are available for all other lifts.

There are excellent long blue runs to progress to, reached by the adjacent Kohlmais gondola.

For true blue skiers

Given good snow, there are few better areas than this for an intermediate skier wanting to build confidence.

It's not without problems. The circular tour presents difficulties: the twin peaks of Schattberg, on the steep, shady side of Saalbach. The runs on the front are genuine reds and a soft black, and you should be very wary of the lovely blue run round the back to Vorderglemm – it gets steep and tricky over the last quarter of its length, with the difficulty often compounded by crowds and by snow that can be slushy or rock-hard.

But elsewhere, you have a network of plentiful, amiable blue pistes to play on, spread right across the sunny side of the valley.

Which is not to say all the blues are super-easy. Look first for runs that take roundabout routes or go across the mountainside, and avoid those that go down beside the lifts, which can be as steep as nearby reds. From the Panorama chair, for example, keep to skier's right on blue 52, which curls away from the lifts. One blue down the line of a lift that is genuinely easy is that by the Bernkogel chair-lift; it steepens lower down, but not by much.

Don't overlook the pistes over the hill towards Leogang, which often have better snow than Saalbach's sunny runs. The Steinberg gondola, on skier's right, has a lovely winding blue down its length, cut through the forest. In good snow don't be afraid to embark on the long run away from the lifts to Viehhofen, with a bus back to the lift system at Vorderglemm.

For confident intermediates

It's a paradise for the keen, confident intermediate, with long, genuine red runs to valley level in practically every sector – those on the shady side of the valley from Schattberg and Zwölferkogel are particularly rewarding – and some worthwhile higher slopes where you might enjoy doing laps. Many of the blues are entertaining, too – this is not a resort where the blues are motorways.

The Fieberbrunn link runs (on both the Saalbach and the Fieberbrunn sides of the intervening valley) are excellent, long, testing reds. You may hear nasty rumours that the shady run from Reiterkogel towards Fieberbrunn is of black steepness. Well, no: it has one pitch halfway down that is certainly at the tough end of the red spectrum, followed by a shelf that is pretty awkward when bumped up and crowded. But the run is properly classified red. The rest of Fieberbrunn is worth exploring, too.

Whether you'll enjoy the black pistes or the ski routes depends, crucially, on the snow conditions. The blacks are not seriously steep, but tricky when icy.

For experts

The black runs on the shady side of the valley are not seriously steep but definitely black; the Nordabfahrt on Zwölferkogel is probably the steepest – it certainly is in average terms over its length. These pistes get groomed, so for moguls you must look elsewhere.

A good start is to look to the ski routes under Fieberbrunn's Hochhörndlerspitze; these are good long runs, dropping over 900m to the lift.

There is plenty of scope for getting off-piste on the sunny side of the valley, particularly from Reichendlkopf and from Spieleckkogel at the western end. And the linking lift from Fieberbrunn has opened up steep options on the shady back side of Reichendlkopf and Hochalmspitze, to the link lift base.

There are also off-piste routes from the same lifts as the ski routes mentioned above, going around the back of Hochhörndlerspitze. And there are more routes further into the Fieberbrunn terrain.

For an extreme challenge you could hike for 40 minutes from Fieberbrunn's Hochhörndl chair-lift to ski the 70° north-east face of the 2118m Wildseeloder.

This is the regular Austrian venue for the Freeride World Tour, which reaches its famous climax in Verbier. Good luck.

Fancy stuff

Saalbach itself doesn't have a terrain park nearby, but up the valley at Hinterglemm is one of the best-located big parks in the Alps, next to the nursery slopes: beginner, medium and pro lines, served by a gondola and floodlit every evening – hence its name, Nightpark. There's another sizeable park at altitude between Saalbach and Leogang – the Nitro park, at the Asitzmulden lift, with a bag jump.

Two 'freeride parks' have been created, combining deep snow with obstacles 'integrated into the terrain'. There's one 800m long at Lärchfilzkogel, two lifts up from Fieberbrunn (so a bit of a schlep from Saalbach), and a much shorter one at the Asitzmulden lift.

There's a 'funcross' on the Hochalm top chair-lift, and a 'learn to ride' park on the Bernkogel top chair. And Fieberbrunn has an Easy-Park at mid-mountain.

Saalbach – the resort

While HInterglemm has expanded, Saalbach has retained its village character, with a pleasant, traditional pedestrian core. It's a distinctly lively resort, with boisterous après bars at the base; it's not unusual to find skiers weaving their way home in ski boots in the late evening.

Convenience

The core of Saalbach is quite compact – the three main lift bases form a triangle, about 300m across. But the village spreads along the valley, and across the hillside at the foot of the Kohlmais lifts, and you can find yourself staying 1km from a lift. Ski-buses run along the valley.

Lodgings

There is the usual Austrian range. In Hinterglemm there is a glitzy 5-star place, but the valley's hotels are otherwise equally split into 4-star and 3-star ratings. If planning to stay in the centre, check that your room is not exposed to disco noise or revellers-in-the-street noise.

Central Saalbach is quite compact; the Schattberg gondola (in the shade) is 300m from these Kohlmais slopes.

As its name suggests, the Art and Ski-In Hotel Hinterhag is a bit special – lovingly built of ancient timbers, and in a good position on the slopes above the village. The 3-star hotel Astrid is also well placed on the piste, with good food.

Bars and restaurants

Après-ski action is highly developed. One standard way for party animals to wrap up their day is to arrive at Berger Alm by the Magic 6er chair (wrongly labelled Hochalm on the piste map) as happy hour starts at 3.30; then to progress down piste 66 to Hinterhag Alm, just above the village, for a two-storey party driven by live music; and then to descend the final 70m vertical to Bauer's Schi-Alm, which will already be rammed. There are alternatives, though. Later on there are lots of lively places, including the table-dancing dives common to Austrian resorts of this ilk. The resort website lists over 20 places under the heading of nightlife, though this does include Hinterglemm.

This is very much a half-board resort, with few restaurants outside hotels. Some of the après places and mountain restaurants also function as restaurants in the evening. We've enjoyed dinner at the hotel Astrid's Kohlmais Stub'n. Another good spot is down the valley at Vorderglemm – the hotel Tiroler Buam.

Off the slopes

If you take Hinterglemm into account, there is quite a bit to do. Get hold of the excellent Winter Sports Alternatives leaflet (downloadable). A 3km toboggan run (open day and evening) goes from Spielberghaus to the village, with uplift by snowcat (or you can walk). There's a lift-served run at Hinterglemm, too.

There's a bit of cross-country skiing in the valley, and rather more walking, including strenuous routes up both sides to mountain restaurants.

For families

Saalbach does have at least one ski school snow garden, but really for families Saalbach's villagey character counts for less than Hinterglemm's more spacious nursery slopes and off-slope activities. It also has a couple of attractive hotels surrounded by snow. Head up the valley.

Alternatives to Saalbach

As well as being the most charming village, Saalbach is arguably the best base for skiing the whole area; but Hinterglemm runs it close, and has good off-slope diversions. Leogang is much less well placed, out on its limb. Fieberbrunn is rather plain, and even more distant from the main circuit; it really makes sense only as a base for skiing ... Fieberbrunn.

Hinterglemm 1040m

Although the valley road was long since shifted from central Hinterglemm into a bypass tunnel, the village retains the linear layout of its formative years, which makes it less immediately appealing than Saalbach. But it is pleasant enough, and its facilities may count for more for some visitors, especially for families.

There are excellent nursery slopes and kids' facilities next to the village (and another beginner lift at mid-mountain on the sunny side). The Unterschwarzach gondola serves a good longer blue run that is floodlit six nights a week, as well as the impressive Nightpark.

Convenience It's a rather spread-out place, roughly a mile long, with its main lift bases about 750m apart. But there are several short lifts on the shady side of the valley that help you get to the main lifts.

Lodgings Plenty of choice, including the valley's only 5-star hotel, the Alpine Palace. Among the most interesting places is the Wiesergut 'design' hotel – a harmonious modern development of an ancient house, west of the centre.

Bars and restaurants Goaßstall, on the Reiterkogel slopes a short climb above the gondola station, is an Austrian classic, now well into its third decade of doing lunch until 3pm, then a monster drinking party, then dinner, then another monster party. Some specialists rate it the best après venue in the Alps. There are of course alternative spots in Hinterglemm.

Off the slopes Most of the valley's diversions are concentrated here.

The Reiterkogel lift accesses a 3.5km toboggan run (twisty, with braking said to be required); open day and evenings; lift passes are valid. There's a 120m tubing hill on the nursery slopes; evenings only, lift passes valid, tubes free. The sports centre has an ice rink offering skating and curling, open daytime and evenings; tennis courts, ditto.

Families A sound bet, with good kids' facilities on the nursery slopes, and the off-slope stuff listed above.

Vorderglemm 940m

There's not much in Vorderglemm apart from a handful of roadside hotels and guest houses (the Tiroler Buam has a good restaurant) but it does have a ski school – and free short drag-lifts, both at village level and up at the mid-station of the gondola into Saalbach's sunny slopes.

Fieberbrunn 820m

Driving through Fieberbrunn on the road from Saalfelden to St Johann, you might not realise it's a ski resort. The village spreads for a couple of miles along the road; the centre is bypassed, but it's no charmer. The lift base is a mile away, and a couple of the better hotels are located there, so it seems the obvious base.

From that base, gondolas diverge to go over wooded lower slopes, one serving red runs, the other blue runs around the mid-mountain lift junction of Streuböden; higher up, the two sectors are linked, and there is a further link to the higher Hochhörndl sector, at the foot of which is the gondola link to Saalbach. To get to Reiterkogel takes roughly five lifts and two pistes. There are beginner lifts at the main lift base and at Streuböden.

Along the Pillersee Tal there is plenty of walking and cross-country skiing. Up at Streuböden there's a 1.2km sled-on-rails coaster ride.

Leogang 800m

Leogang is the community at the north-east corner of this area, but the runs and lifts are a mile or more from the village itself. The original Asitz gondola base is at Hütten, where there is a cluster of lodgings, and the newer Steinbergbahn starts from the isolated hotel Krallerhof, now the obvious place to stay (though there are also simpler places in a little suburb 200m up the nursery slope). There are toboggan runs from the mid-station of the Asitz gondola, day and evening. And there's a zip-wire.

The excellent, testing Zwölferkogel puts the walks to the head of the valley in the shade in midwinter

Salzburger Sportwelt

Flachau-Wagrain-Alpendorf / Zauchensee-Flachauwinkl-Kleinarl

Two extensive multi-valley areas, not widely offered in the UK

Salzburger Sportwelt is a lift pass, not a ski area, but at its heart are two
sizeable multi-valley areas covered by this chapter. One uses the catchy
name Snow Space Flachau-Wagrain-St Johann-Alpendorf (even though
St Johann isn't part of it). We've called this Sportwelt North. The other is
a two-part affair; one part, between Kleinarl and Flachauwinkl is called
Shuttleberg; the second part goes by the name of its central resort,
Zauchensee. We've christened the pair Sportwelt South.

The north area is highly developed, with thriving resorts at each end
and the busy little town of Wagrain at its heart. The south one is less
commercialised, with a much more limited choice of lodgings.

There are plans to link the two lift systems, creating a ✳✳✳✳ area –
possibly in 2019. For now, buses link Wagrain and Kleinarl four times an
hour. Buses will also get you to other small areas covered by the pass.

This is an area of gentle wooded slopes, mainly of interest to
intermediate skiers and beginners, although there is some off-piste
potential to amuse experts when the conditions are right. This whole area
is covered by the Ski Amadé regional lift pass; the associated website,
skiamade.com, has an excellent 3D interactive piste map.

A minor attraction of the Sportwelt is its ease of access from Salzburg
airport, which is only 80km away from Flachau, practically all of that on the
motorway. Book a late flight home, and you can ski until close of play.

Spacious, gentle slopes towards the top of Flachau's Griessenkareck, in the Sportwelt North area

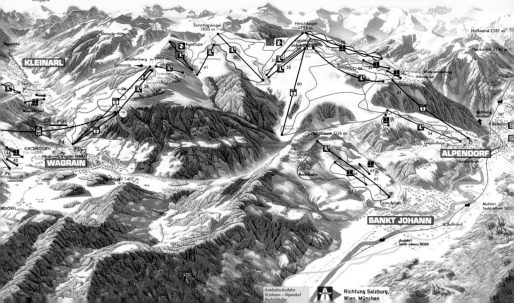

Sportwelt North – Wagrain

Wagrain / Flachau / Alpendorf

This, the bigger and much more commercial of the two main Sportwelt lift networks, straddles two broad mountains of mainly intermediate difficulty and links three quite different resort villages.

At the eastern end, Flachau has grown to become quite a big resort, spreading spaciously across a wide, flat valley. At the western end, Alpendorf is just a compact collection of skiers' hotels, detached from its parent town, St Johann im Pongau. But the ideal base for exploration of the whole area is the central valley, which is occupied by Wagrain – a towny, busy little village squeezed into the narrow valley bottom. High above it, the G-Link cable car links the two mountains.

The mountains in brief

Size A bit limited on its own, but North and South add up to a decent area

Slopes Generally red-gradient, wooded slopes; some good long descents

Snow Comprehensive, effective snowmaking, but altitude has its effects

System, Lift Virtually all fast lifts, with multiple access lifts in each resort

Sustenance Huge numbers of cosy places on the main home slopes

For beginners Good nursery slopes, but then things get a bit awkward

For true blue skiers Far from ideal; if you have the choice, go for Alpendorf

For the confident Good: lots of genuine red-run skiing; but snow non-ideal

For experts Not a great deal to amuse you, on- or off-piste

Fancy stuff A worthwhile funslope on Grafenberg, and a decent park

Wagrain – the resort in brief

Convenience There are conveniently placed lodgings, but not many

Lodgings Unusually, more choice at 3-star than 4-star level

Bars and restaurants Not a lot of choice, but just about enough

Off the slopes Reasonable facilities, though no proper toboggan run

For families Some good facilities – make sure your base is close by

Pass notes	Key facts		Key ratings	
The standard weekly pass is the Ski Amadé one, also covering Hochkönig, Schladming and the Gastein valley. Beginners can buy points cards, apparently valid for all the lifts.	Altitude	860m	Size	**
	Range	800–1980m	Snow	***
	Slopes (claimed)	120km	Fast lifts	****
	Websites		Mountain rest's	****
	wagrain-kleinarl.at		Beginner	*
	bergbahnen-wagrain.at		True blue	*
	flachau.com (resort)		Confident	****
Where to stay, ideally	flachau.at (lift company)		Expert	**
A walk from one of Wagrain's two main lifts	alpendorf.com		Convenience	**
	skiamade.com		Families	***
			Village charm	****

The mountains in detail

The area's two mountains have in common modest altitudes and wooded slopes mainly of red-run gradient – but are in other ways rather different.

The slopes between Flachau and Wagrain are arranged radially about the shoulder of Griessenkareck: single red runs go north to the isolated Rote 8er chair-lift base and west to Wagrain (or rather to the suburb of Kirchboden, above and outside the centre); and a web of runs go north-east to Flachau, where there are three quite widely spaced lift bases. Two of these and the Rote 8er have huge car parks.

At mid-mountain above Wagrain, a big cable car links Griessenkareck to Grafenberg. From here, runs go north-east to Wagrain and are served by two gondolas starting 600m from the town centre; going west, runs and lifts in a couple of little bowls below Sonntagskogel link with Gernkogel above Alpendorf, where a fast chair and a gondola provide access.

Size

The Sportwelt North area claims 120km of pistes. Christoph Schrahe puts the total a bit lower than that, and the lift company has declined to explain exactly how they arrive at their higher figure. Having skied the area, we rate it **✳✳** for extent. Add in Sportwelt South, though, and the combined areas merit a **✳✳✳✳** rating.

The area measures 15km across, from Alpendorf to Flachau, and there is a real sensation of travel across the valleys.

Slopes

The mountains are essentially wooded from top to bottom, although the pistes are mainly wide, and there are more open areas on the upper slopes.

The terrain is mostly of red gradient, with few black slopes and blue slopes confined to certain areas.

There are lots of long runs to the valleys – it's not difficult to put together descents of 900m or 1000m vertical to all the lift bases. Even if snow conditions

The bowl beneath Sonntagskogel, at the top of Alpendorf – the most interestingly varied sector; note the park

at the bottom lead you to truncate these runs, there are plenty of lift stations allowing descents of 500m–700m. The biggest descent, from the Top Liner chair-lift on Griessenkareck to Wagrain, is over 1050m vertical.

There are half a dozen short ski routes, unexplained on the piste map. They don't amount to much, so they don't pose much of a hazard if unpatrolled, as they presumably are.

This area seems very keen on slope closure shortly after the lifts close; but the home run to Alpendorf is open to 7pm.

Snow

The altitudes here are modest – most of the top heights are under 1900m and many under 1800m – and it is not a notably snowy corner of the Alps; but snowmaking covers all the pistes and is used very effectively. So piste skiers need only worry about snow quality, not quantity.

System, Lift

Gondolas and six-seat chair-lifts abound, particularly at the lower levels, and there are multiple lifts out of each resort. The main queuing threat arises on good weekends, when the giant car parks fill with day visitors. There is one slow quad chair, Sonntagskogel 2, which is inescapable when skiing from Wagrain towards Alpendorf; and the black runs on the back of Hirschkogel, above Alpendorf, are served by a T-bar. But all in all, it's an excellent system.

Sustenance

Restaurants litter the main slopes above the three resorts; if you set about it, you could take in as many as a dozen in a single descent to Flachau – although you'll pass far fewer in a descent under the Roter 8er or Flying Mozart gondolas. They are all marked and named on the piste map distributed locally (but not on ours, sadly).

The huts are mainly traditional and cosy in style, with table service. A less rustic exception is the woody but stylish Lisa Alm, at mid-mountain on the Starjet, above Flachau, doing interesting food. Halfway down the run from Griessenkareck to Wagrain, Auhofalm is another place with a bit of contemporary flair about it.

More on the slopes

For beginners

There are good nursery slopes near the Kirchboden lift base (on the Flachau side of the Wagrain valley), including a 330m button lift. But beyond the beginner slopes things get a bit awkward (read the next section).

There are no free lifts or special beginner lift passes, but you can buy points cards, valid on all lifts.

For true blue skiers

The run classification is fairly reliable, and you would be correct to interpret the red-dominated piste map to mean that this is not a great area for early intermediates lacking confidence.

From Wagrain, the two obvious options are to bus out to the Rote 8er gondola to ski the winding blue run down the bottom stage, or to ride the local gondola to Grafenberg. The runs here down the Hachau chair-lift are lovely, but short. Sadly, run 40c down the longer Sonntagskogel 1 chair is borderline blue/red in gradient, and if you want to work your way further across the mountain, you have to come back on red run 41 (or descend to Alpendorf, which is a long way from Wagrain).

The blue runs further west above Alpendorf are genuine blues, although far from being motorways.

To sum up: if you prefer easy blues but can handle stiff ones, you'll be fine here. If you really are freaked by anything approaching red gradient, you'd be much better off elsewhere.

For confident intermediates

This is a great area for the keen piste basher, provided you get good snow or (later in the season) you time your skiing to avoid afternoon slush. Many of the blue runs are well worth skiing, in addition to the serious quantity of good red skiing.

The long descents to the valleys are very rewarding – the blue to Alpendorf as well as the reds to all the Griessenkareck lift bases and run 36 on Grafenberg, curling away from the lifts to the Wagrain lift base. Run 60 to the Buchau gondola is a nicely varied red with a vertical approaching 750m – not bad for a single lift. The blacks served by the Stegbach

GRIESSENKARECK
WAGRAIN
BERGBAHNEN
GRAFENBERG
Grießenkareck 1991 m
Ennskraxn 2436 m
Sonntagskogel 1850 m
Hirschkogel 1755 m
1980 m
1880 m
TOP LINER
KLEINARL
Grafenberg 1702 m
G-LINK
WAGRAIN
G-LINK Wagrain
FLYING MOZART
GRAFENBERG
WAGRAIN
FLACHAU
ALPENDORF
ST. JOHANN
Kirchboden
Markt
Hahnbaum 1200 m
starjet 1
starjet 3
achterjet
spacejet 1
HERMANN MAIER
RODELBAHN LUCKY FLITZER
ROTE 8ER WAGRAIN
ANSCHLUSS TAUERNLOIPE
LOIPE
WINTERWANDERWEG
RICHTUNG WAGRAIN
Moos
Schweighof
Salzburg,
Wien, München
Salzburg
163

drag, on the back of Hirschkogel, don't really merit black classification (one of them used to be classed red).

For experts

Black pistes are dotted about the upper slopes, particularly in the Sonntagskogel sector. Some, as noted above, could be red, but 40b on the Sonntagskogel 1 chair-lift is appreciably steeper, as is 50a from Sonntagskogel 2. The Alpendorf website bigs up a very short run 52 as the steepest, but it's not on the map and we never came across it.

There is a limited amount of off-piste terrain between the pistes on the higher, more open slopes, but you'll soon exhaust these shots. And this is far from being a classic area for more serious routes outside the lift system, largely because of the dense forest. But in both halves of the area there are some more open slopes from the high-points, leading down to the adjacent valleys.

Fancy stuff

There's a 600m funslope on the Sonntagskogel, with waves, steep turns, tunnels, jumps, boxes and a giant snail. The proper park, called Betterpark, is on Hirschkogel above Alpendorf. It's a fair-sized affair (about 800m long, overall) with some big kickers. Keen freestylers should stay over there.

Wagrain – the resort

Wagrain is a towny little village that doesn't seem to care much for ski-resort-hood: it has kept the pistes and lifts at arm's length, and has relatively few lodging options. It makes quite a refreshing change.

Convenience

Wagrain is not a big place, but it's not designed for the convenience of skiers. As so often, everything depends on where exactly you stay. The heart of the village is a little triangular space close to the junction of the Flachau–St Johann road and the road south to Kleinarl (in the Sportwelt South ski area). The lifts for Grafenberg and Alpendorf are 600m up this road. The lift for Griessenkareck and Flachau is even further from the

Wagrain's lift bases are widely separated, so the two mountains are linked by cable car on the lower slopes

centre, in the slightly elevated suburb of Kirchboden. You can stay close to either lift base or, for more village atmosphere, right in the centre. Ski-buses run frequently between the lift bases, and between the Grafenberg lift and the centre; about two per hour run to the Rote 8er gondola base.

Lodgings

There are many more apartments and rooms to rent than hotels and guest houses, and 4-star hotels are clearly outnumbered by 3-stars. Best in town is actually just out of town opposite the Grafenberg lift base – the Sporthotel Wagrain, the only 4-star S (Superior) place. There is a cluster of hotels near the Kirchboden lift base and nursery slopes – mainly 3-star, but including the 4-star Alpina. Read 'For families' for another option. The Almmonte bar/restaurant at the lift base is planning to shake things up in 2018 with a new boutique/design hotel.

Bars and restaurants

Après-ski kicks off in mid-mountain restaurants on both sectors – Auhofalm on Griessenkareck may have table-dancers, while things seem more muted at Krapfenalm and Sonnalm on Grafenberg. There are of course bars at the lift bases – Kuhstall at the Flying Mozart gets pretty boisterous, as does Kühbergalm at the Grafenberg base.

Almmonte is another option at the Flying Mozart, but it seems more popular as a restaurant. There are several restaurants in the village centre, the best of which are in hotels – the Grafenwirt is arguably the best. But the best restaurant in these parts is the Aichhorn, a few miles up the valley in Kleinarl.

Off the slopes

There's an artificial ice rink at Kirchboden, open afternoon and evening, and a curling rink in the village open two evenings a week. Cross-country trails go out towards Flachau and up the valley to Kleinarl (and well beyond). Wasserwelt is a good aquatic centre with indoor and outdoor pools and a spa. For serious tobogganing (as opposed to mucking about on the nursery slopes) it seems you need to head up the valley to Kleinarl.

For families

At the mid-station of the Rote 8er gondola (3km from central Wagrain, and reachable by road) is the excellent Wagraini's Winterwelt – an extensive kids' practice area with two magic carpets and two rope-tows. There's a tubing slope, too. If this appeals, you might consider staying at the 4-star hotel Edelweiss, nearby. But there are also kids' areas nearer the village, at the main lift bases. The hotel Alpina at Kirchboden is also very family oriented.

Alternatives to Wagrain

Wagrain is the natural base for skiing this area. But Alpendorf also has merit – its local slopes are the most varied and interesting in the area – and Flachau is a more conventional holiday resort than the others.

Flachau 890m

Flachau has grown in a way that seems unplanned. It has no obvious centre; around the Starjet chair-lift base it begins to feel like a village, but the place then spreads along the Flachauer Strasse for miles. And then, separated from all this by flat fields is the suburb of Hundsdörfl, at the Achterjet gondola base. It's all pleasant enough, built in chalet style.

There are good beginner slopes near the Starjet and Spacejet access lifts. But there's a bit of a problem with progression beyond the nursery slopes.
Convenience It's a widely spread resort

– 2.5km from end to end. You can stay close to the Achterjet or Starjet, but most people rely on the frequent ski-buses shuttling between the two lift bases, and circling the village from the Starjet. Buses also run to Flachauwinkl, in the centre of the Sportwelt South area – frequently in the morning, less so in the afternoon.
Lodgings There is the usual Austrian range of lodgings, with 4-star hotels slightly outnumbering the 3-stars. Given that the village centre doesn't amount to much, you may as well stay close to one of the main lifts. The well-run Montanara is right opposite the Achterjet.

Bars and restaurants On the lower slopes Zur Brennhütt'n and Munzen under the Achterjet get some business at close of play, while Lisa Alm across at the Starjet throbs. There are big, lively bars at all the lift bases – Hofstadl at the Starjet base, Dampfkessel at the Spacejet and Herzerlalm at the Achterjet. All these places do food, and there are quite a few other options for dinner. The hotel Montanara's à la carte restaurant, Gaumenlust, gets two toques from the Gault-Millau guide.

Off the slopes Next to the Achterjet base is a sled-on-rails coaster, the Lucky Flitzer. There's proper tobogganing, day and evening, from the Brennhütt'n and Munzen restaurants – 2km floodlit run, walk up or ride the Spacejet chair (day only) or take a taxi. Across the valley there is a longer run from the gasthof Sattelbauer. That's also the target of one of the more strenuous walks available. There are lots of cross-country trails – you can string together some long trips. On the outskirts of Altenmarkt, 4km away, is Therme Amadé, a big spa with countless pools; it's not cheap for adults.

Families Flachau has some appeal for families. The Sport am Jet school has an excellent snow-sure kids' practice area with various lifts at the top of the Achterjet gondola, and although English-speaking guests aren't numerous the school does make an effort on the language front.

Alpendorf 800m

Alpendorf is a curious place, bearing no resemblance to a village. It consists of about ten 4-star hotels (most of them 4-star S, actually), apartment buildings and car parks arranged either side of a street rising gently from the main gondola station to the secondary six-seat chair-lift. Further up are scattered suburbs, with simpler guest houses.

The hotel Oberforsthof earns a toque from the Gault-Millau guide, which offers one way of picking a place to stay.

The two lifts go up to different points on the hill. In each case there are beginner slopes at mid-mountain; it seems a full lift pass is required.

There's a 4km cross-country trail at resort level, a 3km one at the top of the gondola and a longer easy one on the valley floor, by the river. There are cleared paths up into the ski area. Sadly, facilities and diversions for families (including a toboggan run and a big ice rink) seem to be concentrated on St Johann's 'home' mountain of Hahnbaum, miles away.

Flachau spreads widely at the foot of wooded Griessenkareck, with three widely separated access lifts

Sportwelt South – Zauchensee

Zauchensee / Flachauwinkl / Kleinarl

The southern Sportwelt area is an unconventional three-valley system: it consists of two very distinct halves, with nothing resembling a resort in the central valley where they (almost) meet, at Flachauwinkl.

At present, the obvious base for most skiers is the very small ski station of Zauchensee, at the heart of the bigger, eastern sector. But Kleinarl, a pleasant, spacious village at the western extremity of the smaller sector, will have a stronger case when its slopes are linked to Wagrain in Sportwelt North, perhaps as soon as 2019/20.

The slopes are more varied than those of the North area, with more to offer the expert and the true blue skier.

The mountains in brief

Size On the small side, but the North area is close, and reachable by bus
Slopes Intermediate gradients, some open, some wooded; some long runs
Snow Generally effective snowmaking, but afternoon-sun slopes vulnerable
System, Lift Only a couple of slow lifts, and fewer weekend crowds here
Sustenance A good sprinkling of cosy, traditional places
For beginners Pretty close to ideal – gentle, convenient slopes
For true blue skiers Lots of good slopes, with few traps for the unwary
For the confident A bit limited – expect to spend some time up North
For experts More to do here than in the North area, including nice glades
Fancy stuff A serious park and a very serious pipe on Shuttleberg

Zauchensee – the resort in brief

Convenience It's a tiny place, with nothing more than a short walk away
Lodgings Several attractive 4-star hotels – and that's about it
Bars and restaurants There's an umbrella bar, and a nightclub (good luck)
Off the slopes There's a toboggan run, and then it's all down to your hotel
For families If only they kept the cars out – then it would be perfect

Pass notes	Key facts		Key ratings	
The standard weekly pass is the Ski Amadé one, also covering Hochkönig, Schladming and the Gastein valley. There are no free lifts or special passes for beginners but you can buy points cards, apparently valid for all the lifts.	Altitude	1350m	Size	**
	Range	1000–2175m	Snow	***
	Size (see text)	110km	Fast lifts	****
	Where to stay, ideally		Mountain rest's	***
	In Zauchensee – it doesn't matter where.		Beginner	*****
			True blue	****
	Websites		Confident	***
	altenmarkt-zauchensee.at		Expert	***
	zauchensee.at (lift co)		Convenience	*****
	wagrain-kleinarl.at		Families	*****
	shuttleberg.com		Village charm	***

The mountains in detail

Although Sportwelt South looks like a three-valley network, it's better to think of it as two mountains – there are two very separate lift companies, and two piste maps.

In the eastern valley, Zauchensee has a couple of runs on the afternoon-sun side, and a short easy run on the back of that hill, in the 'fourth valley'. Its main slopes – and the major concentration of lifts and runs in the whole South area – are on the morning-sun side, in two separate sectors. Each is served by a choice of bottom-to-top gondola or multiple chair-lifts. Gamskogel offers the greater vertical, and a World Cup downhill course that makes an excellent long red run for the rest of us. Rosskopf, appreciably lower, is the link to the central valley; over the ridge, red and blue runs descend to Flachauwinkl.

The westerly mountain, Shuttleberg (its fast chair-lifts are all called Something Shuttle), makes a clear pitch for the family market, but actually has quite a wide appeal. From Kleinarl in the western valley, two Shuttles take you up to the ridge. On the morning-sun side, above Flachauwinkl, there is a more complex web of runs and lifts.

Size

The slopes of the Shuttleberg sector have been certified by Christoph Schrahe (read the book's introduction) as amounting to 40km. The Zauchensee sector claims 70km; we don't doubt it is bigger than Shuttleberg, but we're not convinced it's that much bigger. So the Sportwelt South areas taken together rate ✱✱ for size; add the North area, and you get ✱✱✱✱.

In overall dimensions this area is a tad smaller than Sportwelt North – about 13km from end to end.

Slopes

This is intermediate terrain – some of it basically red-gradient, with blues taking winding routes, some more naturally suited to blue runs. The lower slopes are generally wooded, in some parts less densely than Sportwelt North, and higher up there is quite a lot of open terrain and glades – the latter quite unusual in the Alps. So there is more scope for off-piste exploration here.

There are good long runs of around 900m vertical to Flachauwinkl and Kleinarl, clocking up 5–6km; Zauchensee, being a bit higher, doesn't offer quite such long runs.

On both mountains there are freeride trails or ski routes, without explanation except that the Shuttleberg map reveals in German that they are not prepared.

Snow

The altitudes here are a bit higher than usual for the region – Zauchensee in particular is way higher than any other resort in the Sportwelt – which helps with snowmaking as well as snowfall. The snowmaking is almost comprehensive, and is well used. So no particular worries on the snow front.

System, Lift

By definition, Shuttleberg is equipped entirely with Shuttles – fast, detachable chair-lifts. Zauchensee is less thoroughly equipped – the Unterberg chair-lifts in parallel with the Rosskopf gondola are slow, and there are a couple of drags, one of them serving the 'fourth valley' slope.

At the time of writing in 2017, a new six-seat chair-lift is being built from a point low in the Shuttleberg Kleinarl slopes more or less to the top. This should ease the main bottleneck in the system – the upper chair above Kleinarl, which has to handle people arriving from the valley and people skiing the upper slopes.

Sustenance

The Gamskogel sector has only one restaurant, at mid-mountain, but there are plenty elsewhere; both maps name them.

Burgstallhütte, on the lower slopes above Flachauwinkl, gets very good reports and has a wider than usual menu.

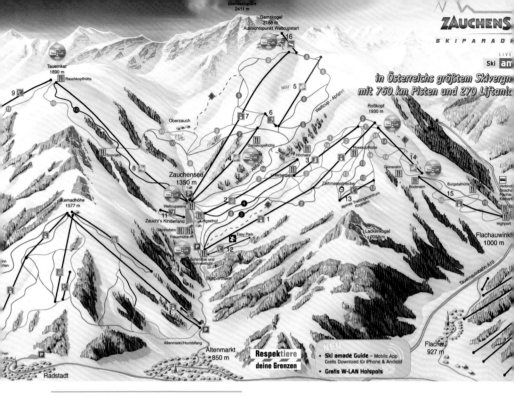

More on the slopes

For beginners

As you should be able to discern from the one of the photos overleaf, Zauchensee has an ideal nursery slope right next to the village – extensive, gentle, free of through-traffic, sunny. At an altitude of 1350m, you can expect good snow. And there are good blue runs to progress to.

There are no free lifts or special beginner lift passes, but you can buy points cards, valid on all lifts.

The only flaw is that this is about the least entertaining resort in the Alps for a non-skier. So if you decide after a miserable day that skiing is not for you, you're in for some serious Kindle-reading.

For true blue skiers

The piste map looks enticing: blue runs top to bottom on all five mountainsides. One or two runs are uncomfortably challenging: run 9 on Gamskogel is a bit tricky in places – a borderline blue/red, really. But most are genuine blues. In particular, the two major morning-sun areas have lovely long, broad runs top to

bottom, plus various other options on the upper slopes. The runs on Tauenkar, on the east side of Zauchensee, are genuine blues; run 11 on the back is lovely but has a steepish start – keep to starboard.

The lower slopes of the afternoon-sun mountainsides down to Flachauwinkl and Kleinarl aren't so delightful. Blue 15 from Rosskopf to Flachauwinkl is a cat-track, so not very appealing at the best of times – and as spring approaches it may run out of snow. There is a gondola alternative, in case you are determined to get to Shuttleberg. The lower half of the Family Run to Kleinarl – new for 2017, they say – is better: a proper piste for much of its length although it does eventually fade into a narrow cat-track.

For confident intermediates

There is a quite a bit of good red-run skiing here. The highlight is probably the World Cup downhill race course (6/5/5a) from Gamskogel to the village. Ride the tiny funicular to the very top if you fancy skiing the precipitous start, and add a few metres to the 750m vertical of the excellent red run.

The reds on both flanks of Rosskopf are well worthwhile, and the blacks here and on Tauernkar are not seriously steep.

Over on Shuttleberg there is good skiing on the upper part of the sunny side and the shady side – but for the final descent to Kleinarl your choice is the blue 'family run' or a testing black.

So there's good, interesting skiing, but there's not a great deal of it. In the course of a week you'll probably want to hop on the frequent bus to Wagrain and the Sportwelt North area.

For experts

Unless you hit ice, there are few serious challenges on-piste. At Zauchensee black 10 runs the full length of the chair-lift on Tauernkar, but it barely deserves the classification – it is basically a red-gradient mountain. There are a couple of short, sharp blacks just above the village on the lower slopes of Rosskopf. At Kleinarl the black k2 to the village looks like the real thing; on our recent visit we didn't have time to try it.

The main interest is likely to lie in the ski routes. These are not classified for difficulty. They were unskiable when we visited, but the ones from Gamskogel looked to be of black gradient, particularly run 3 on skier's right of the pistes. On Shuttleberg the two highest ski routes are gentler, but form part of The Stash which offers some lovely glade skiing (read 'Fancy stuff' and check out the photo below). There is quite a bit of off-piste terrain outside the ski routes. And from Gamskogel there is a descent on the back of the hill coming round to the resort, but it looks a bit messy.

Fancy stuff

Shuttleberg makes quite a fuss about its Absolut Park, with wild-west entry gates at the top and a cool Chill House at the bottom (with climbing wall and indoor skateboard ramp). It's a pretty serious affair, about 1km long, with several sections aimed at different groups, and over 100 obstacles in all. It includes a 'funpipe' with 4m walls. Down the hill a bit is the real beast, the 7m Superpipe.

Then on a separate hill there's The Stash, a sort of freeride/freestyle hybrid, as in Avoriaz and various other resorts around the world. And for kids there is the 'Lil Stash' nearby.

There's more info on all this at absolutpark.com.

A welcome sight in the Alps – glades; the top of Shuttleberg, The Stash on the left, seen from Absolut Park

Snowmaking delivered the goods at tiny Zauchensee in late March 2017; note the excellent beginner area

Zauchensee – the resort

Zauchensee is a tiny resort near the head of the valley south of Altenmarkt, just above the eponymous lake; it has been purpose-built, in traditional style, for skiers and summer visitors. In scale and character it resembles elevated satellite resorts like Hochsölden – but it is in the valley bottom.

Convenience

Zauchensee is about as convenient for skiing as a valley-bottom village could be but does require some walking. The village is less than 300m end-to-end, with lifts departing from two points, and the main lift station a further 150m away.

Lodgings

There are a couple of small apartment houses but basically the resort consists of half a dozen 4-star and one or two 3-star hotels. Location is scarcely crucial, but the hotel Salzburgerhof probably enjoys the best position, between the two lifts at the foot of the morning-sun slopes – and it gets very good reports from visitors.

Bars and restaurants

As you might expect, this is not a great après resort. Next to the sister hotels Zentral and Zauchenseehof is an umbrella bar that's popular at close of play, and the latter hotel has a nightclub in the basement, the Almbar.

Off the slopes

In a place this size you can't expect a wide range of diversions. But there's a 3km floodlit toboggan run from Sonnalm to the shore of the lake; walk up and reward yourself with a beer, or get a toboggan taxi. There's a cross-country trail down the valley to Altenmarkt – and lots of trails beyond that.

For families

Zauchensee is not traffic-free, but in all other respects the place could have been designed for families, with the nursery slopes perfectly positioned a short walk from all the hotels. Stay in a hotel with a suitable pool and other amusements, and you're sorted.

Alternatives to Zauchensee

In a three-valley ski area you might reasonably expect a choice of three resorts. In this case, it's more like two resorts and a pair of lift stations – Flachauwinkl amounts to little more than that, but offers speedy transfers from Salzburg as well as a central position in the system. Kleinarl is a proper village in what feels like a remote valley setting, although it is only 6km up the valley from Wagrain.

Kleinarl 1000m

Kleinarl is a pleasant, spacious, linear village running south from its lift station for over 1km. It has a decent range of accommodation, with a handful of 4-star hotels; most are a bit of a walk from the lift, but the Zirbenhof is right next to it.

There is some après life in the huts on the lower slopes, but more in the places at the base – notably the Schirmstüberl. The Aichhorn is a highly regarded restaurant awarded two toques by the Gault-Millau guide.

There's a floodlit 2.5km toboggan run from the Ennskraxn hut. For enthusiasts, across the valley you can hike for two hours to the Kleinarlerhütte for a 7km descent. There are cross-country trails and walks up and down the valley.

Flachauwinkl 1020m

Flachauwinkl consists mainly of two lift stations separated by 600m and the A10 motorway, and linked by a shuttle-bus – and some sizeable car parks.

At the bottom of Shuttleberg are a good beginner slope and a kids' area with magic carpet, and just across the piste the welcoming and woody Walchauhof guest house. A little umbrella bar completes the micro-resort. From the Winklalm restaurant there's a 3.5km toboggan run, served during the day by the first chair-lift out of the valley; it's floodlit one night a week, with 'rodeltaxi' access.

Across the valley next to the lift station for Zauchensee the lift company runs a modest 26-room hotel, the Sporthotel Flachauwinkl.

Kleinarl spreads quite a way along the valley from the chair-lift base on the left; can you spot the walkers?

Schladming

Schladming / Haus im Ennstal / Pichl / Gleiming

Schladming is a bit further east than British skiers are accustomed to travelling, and not very well known internationally except to followers of ski-racing (it hosted the World Championships in 2013). It's unusual in some ways: it's a sizeable valley town, definitely not a village, and its skiing ranges across four adjacent (and linked) wooded mountain ridges.

A regular criticism is that the four hills are a bit samey, and they are, but they offer a decent amount of good skiing and a sense of travel. The 'Dachstein' that gets added to the name (eg in the web address) is the rocky peak to the north; just short of 3000m, it has a small glacier area on the back, and off-piste routes on the front.

The mountains in brief

Size Mid-sized, but with some extra areas nearby and on the lift pass

Slopes Mostly wooded, red-gradient mountains, with roundabout blues

Snow Good snowmaking, but the resorts are low, so quality can suffer

System, Lift A good system marred by some curiously poor links

Sustenance Huge numbers of good spots with table service – a highlight

For beginners Good slopes, but inconvenient for many; you need a lift pass

For true blue skiers Some excellent terrain, but only in certain sectors

For the confident Good runs on all four hills; but they are all rather similar

For experts Quite a bit to do, when you add it up (and include Dachstein)

Fancy stuff Parks large and small, and multiple funslopes to play on

Schladming – the resort in brief

Convenience The walks are mostly bearable, and ski-in ski-out is possible

Lodgings Lots of 3-star lodgings, and an adequate choice of 4-star

Bars and restaurants The biggest après bar in the Alps, good restaurants

Off the slopes Plenty to do, although the toboggan run is some way out

For families Rohrmoos beckons – it comes close to being an ideal location

Pass notes	Key facts		Key ratings	
The standard weekly pass is the Ski Amadé one, also covering the Sportwelt, Hochkönig and Gastein valley. There are low-season, short-break ski school deals, but in general beginners must buy a full lift pass from the start.	**Altitude**	745m	Size	***
	Range	745–2015m	Snow	***
	Slopes	123km	Fast lifts	****
			Mountain rest's	****
	Where to stay, ideally		Beginner	***
	Near the Planai gondola, or up at Rohrmoos.		True blue	***
			Confident	****
	Websites		Expert	***
	schladming-dachstein.at		Convenience	***
	planai.at		Families	****
	reiteralm.at		Village charm	***
	hauser-kaibling.at			
	derdachstein.at			

The mountains in detail

Schladming's row of four similar mountains, neatly arranged in a north-facing row, is unusual to say the least. The resort makes a half-hearted attempt to capitalise on this asset with various forms of branding along the lines of '4 Berge Ski'. There's even a website at 4berge.at (but it's only in German, which really is half-hearted).

The easternmost hill is Hauser Kaibling, its name derived from the small village of Haus im Ennstal at its base where a toy cable car and a proper gondola access the mountain. Above the main wooded slopes, lifts and runs link to what is definitely the main mountain, Planai.

Planai's main gondola and massive base facilities (built for the aforementioned World Championships) are only a short walk from the pedestrian square at the heart of the town. On the western fringes is a second lift base; here, the Planai West gondola offers another way into Planai, and a slow chair goes up towards the next hill, Hochwurzen, over the gentle snowfields of the spacious suburb of Rohrmoos.

Hochwurzen is linked to the westernmost mountain in the Schladming chain, Reiteralm, at Pichl; although the mountain's lifts are generally slick, the long access lift is notoriously ancient and slow – the mountain is mostly accessed by the fast lift at Gleiming.

Further west, and not linked, is a more limited but peaceful fifth mountain, Fageralm. We've never found time to visit another outlier, Galsterbergalm, well to the east of the main area.

Size

Here's a rare thing: a resort that publicises a piste extent figure that's less than the figure measured by Christoph Schrahe. The difference (which isn't great) may be down to the few short ski routes, given that Schladming claims 123km of pistes, which would exclude ski routes. Anyway: it's a decent area, coming towards the top end of our ✱✱✱ category.

Slopes

These are essentially wooded mountains – there is the odd patch of pasture here and there, but really it's only at the very top that there are open slopes.

The mountains are generally of red gradient – there are some direct blacks, but the blues almost without exception take indirect routes across the hillside. The main exception is the upper part of Kaibling, which is relatively gentle.

Many visitors arrive at the view, with some justification, that the skiing lacks variety: on each of the four hills, the recipe is much the same.

Depending on the snow (read 'Snow') there are some long, rewarding descents to be done, in the order of 1100m vertical and about 5km in length. The network is an impressive 16km across.

The piste map shows one short ski route on Kaibling and three on Planai. They are unexplained. A 3km red run at the top of Hochwurzen is floodlit most evenings; you need a special lift pass (or take your touring gear).

A distinctive feature of the area is that roads up into the slopes are kept clear, and buses run to several mid-mountain lift stations, where there is some parking.

This area is covered by the Ski Amadé regional lift pass. There's an excellent 3D interactive piste map (normally a contradiction in terms) at skiamade.com.

Snow

Like most resorts in this part of the world, Schladming has an altitude problem – in fact, at 745m it is possibly the lowest resort in these pages. This means the snow quality on the lower slopes is always going to be unreliable. But the snowmaking is comprehensive and well used, and practically all the skiing is north-facing, so things could be worse.

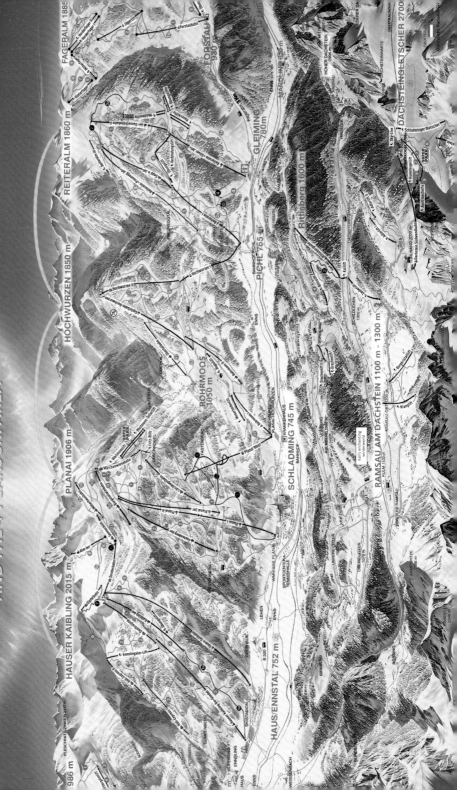

System, Lift

Although the lift system as a whole is pretty slick, all the westward lift links between sectors are poor. Planai and Hochwurzen, in the same ownership, are linked by a 40-year-old double chair-lift – but happily there are plans to replace it with a gondola, maybe by 2020. The link from Hochwurzen to Reiteralm involves an even more ancient double chair that is also over a mile long. Both of these slow chairs can build queues in high season. The high-altitude link between Kaibling and Planai is less of a problem – it employs a quad, with higher capacity.

Each of the hills has powerful lifts from other valley stations, so customers arriving by car or bus are better catered for, and all the key lifts on the upper mountains are fast. Arrange to keep your movements between sectors to the minimum and you will have few problems. But one might be the Planai gondola out of Schladming, now over 30 years old, and no longer up to the job. So it's good to hear that this is also to be replaced – again, possibly by 2020.

Sustenance

Amazingly, the general four-mountain map does not even mark restaurants. But there are maps for each hill that do.

There are countless huts – over 50, for sure – with table service at the great majority (100% of those on Hauser Kaibling, they say). With one or two lift-station exceptions, the style is resolutely traditional, and the general standard is high; you can hardly go wrong. To get you started, here are top tips for each hill.

On Planai, Onkel Willy's Hütte is a traditional favourite – good atmosphere and service, satisfying but limited food (go downstairs to find some space). Schafalm is excellent, too. On Kaibling, Schoarlhütte is a cosy little place, crammed with Alps-bilia; beef stew a speciality. Krummholzhütte at the top of the gondolas is a fine old refuge. Near the top of Hochwurzen, Hochwurzenalm is a cute little hut with good food. Low down on Reiteralm, Schnepf'n Alm is exceptional – the restaurant of a little 4-star 'hotel village', with a wide-ranging menu. On Fageralm, Zefferer Hütte is tiny and cosy, perfectly in tune with this low-key mountain.

More on the slopes

For beginners

Schladming doesn't have village-level nursery slopes – given its altitude, quite sensible. The most convenient slopes are about 300m higher at Rohrmoos, on the lower slopes of Hochwurzen, reachable by bus. These are excellent slopes, wide and gentle. The Reiteralm ski school meets at mid-mountain, where there are extensive, gentle beginner slopes reached by gondola from Gleiming. Kaibling has a beginner slope at mid-mountain, but it's a bit steep to our eyes.

If you start skiing at Rohrmoos, you will naturally graduate to the longer blue runs down the nearby six-seat chair – essentially an extension of the nursery slopes. But progression from there isn't straightforward unless you have guidance, as explained below.

In general you have to buy a full lift pass from the start, even to ski Rohrmoos – not a good arrangement.

For true blue skiers

Planai, Hochwurzen and Reiteralm are challenging for nervous intermediates – you can get around the mountains only by picking the easier reds to link together the blue bits. This isn't easy to do reliably, unless you are following a good instructor.

Kaibling is excellent, with good runs on both left and right of the upper slopes, and (right at the back of the area, well away from other lifts) down the Alm six-seat chair-lift. All these have fast lifts.

Unlinked Fageralm is also worth a look. The lack of crowds is an advantage, but that's not all: the upper mountain is a lovely area of gentle slopes, whether blue or red. You have to ski red run 2 to get home, but it borders on blue gradient.

For confident intermediates

On Kaibling there is basically a single top-to-bottom red, indistinguishable from the parallel blue around mid-mountain.

Planai has much more to offer. There are four good red runs down the upper mountain, funnelling into one red piste to the main lift base and blacks to that point and the Hochwurzen link. You'll want to ski Schladming's pride and joy – the 1050m-vertical World Cup downhill course, more or less down the line of the gondola, to the town. The last third of the course is black – correctly so, although not steep by black standards – but you can bail out just before the final drop.

At the top of Planai there are short but worthwhile runs (about 330m vertical) on the north-east flank of the mountain, good for laps – both lifts are eight-seaters.

Hochwurzen and Reiteralm essentially offer more of the same. Reiteralm has more runs, with roughly speaking three descents to the main lift bases, plus one into the Preuneggtal.

For experts

The black pistes don't add up to much, but some do present some short, sharp challenges. Black Rose, at the top of Reiteralm, is very steep near the start – 41° they say. At only 100m vertical it's one of the longer ones in Reiteralm's vaunted Black Quartet of runs. The other three are regular blacks; but very short.

The lower slopes of Planai, including the end of the downhill course, are justifiably black, and can be icy too. Both of the ski routes on the open north-east-facing slopes at the top of Planai are of black steepness, with very steep starts.

The black on the lower part of Kaibling really has only one pitch that might merit

the classification. The short black at the very top is easy. The same lift accesses a popular ski route which is a bit more challenging but very short (200m vertical).

Most of the mountains have open areas at the top where there is off-piste terrain outside the pistes; the valley linking Kaibling and Planai is a favourite area. From the top of Kaibling you can head east for a longer descent into the Gumpental. If you're prepared to do some hiking, that will open up other routes – for example from Krahbergzinken behind Planai, from Gasselhöhe behind Reiteralm and from Rossfeld behind Hochwurzen.

And then there is the Dachstein, a short bus or taxi ride away. Routes on the south face are accessed by a ladder and tunnel from the glacier.

Fancy stuff

Planai's Superpark by the Weitmoos drag-lifts has four lines to suit everyone from beginner to pro. Reiteralm has a beginner park, X-Point, at mid-mountain, with jumps, turns and waves.

There are funslopes at Rohrmoos on Hochwurzen and at Kaiblingalm on Kaibling. And at the time of writing, in 2017, a new Crosspark funslope is being shaped on the upper slopes of Reiteralm.

The hills are wooded more or less from top to bottom; this is the main valley station for Hauser Kaibling

Schladming – the resort

Schladming is a substantial valley town, its original prosperity based on mining. Much of the town doesn't really feel part of the ski holiday business, but the part that definitely is – a spacious, traffic-free square only a short walk from the huge, slick main Planai lift base development – is very pleasant. Rohrmoos is a key component of the resort – a rustic suburb at the foot of Hochwurzen, right on the best nursery slopes.

Convenience

It's quite a big town, several km across, but it's not difficult to find lodgings within walking distance of either the main Planai lift base or the Planai West/Hochwurzen lifts. On the elevated shelf of Rohrmoos, where the most convenient nursery slopes are located, there are ski-in ski-out places. Ski-buses run on various lines, the two main ones shuttling between the two Planai lift bases and linking all the valley lift stations.

Lodgings

There is the usual Austrian range of accommodation but, unusually, 3-star hotels outnumber 4-stars by some way.

Right at the lift base you have a choice between two conspicuously modern places – the 3-star adults-only TUI Blue Pulse and the 4-star Planai. In contrast, a walk away on the main pedestrian square is the ancient 4-star Posthotel.

There are hotels and guest houses dotted all over the gentle slopes of Rohrmoos. The 3-star Pariente is perfectly placed for the nursery slope; nearby is the 4-star Shütterhof, with spa.

Bars and restaurants

Several mountain restaurants are lively in the afternoon – Almrausch near the top of Planai ('have fun and be safe – pistes close at 19.30') is probably the most boisterous; live music or 'go-go girls' some days. On Hochwurzen, Seiterhütte is on the floodlit piste, and both hut and piste are open until 11pm. It doesn't bear thinking about.

At the Planai main lift base, Hohenhaus Tenne (sister of the one in Hintertux) is an extraordinary, giant place, claimed to be the biggest après bar in the Alps. It gets rammed; people love it or hate it. There are alternatives – notably the Platzhirsch-Alm over the road, with noisy front bar and quiet back bar.

Hohenhaus Tenne re-opens after a mid-evening pause, and is equally popular then. CultClub is the main alternative.

The town has an unusually good range of restaurants. Best in town are probably Julius, Die Tischlerei and Johann in the central Posthotel. In a slightly different league, Maria's Mexican is deservedly popular for its ambience and food, if you like that kind of thing.

Off the slopes

There's plenty to do. Get hold of the very useful booklet (downloadable) on off-slope activities, called Winter Glint.

Just to the east of the town centre is a large activity centre with leisure pool, 25m lanes and kids' pools, plus spa and fitness rooms.

There's a serious 7km toboggan run on the upper part of Hochwurzen, day and evening, accessed by the summit gondola. Although it's not shown on the map, there is a 4km run on Reiteralm from Hochalm down to Almdorf – walk up or take a skidoo taxi. There are skating rinks in central Schladming and in Haus, and several places for curling.

Walks include paths up into the ski slopes, with a special lift pass available for walkers. There's cross-country skiing in various spots, including the Untertal between Planai and Hochwurzen, and nearby Ramsau, with limitless trails (including ones up on the Dachstein).

For families

There are impressive kids' practice areas on all the mountains – at the top and bottom of Kaibling (the latter rather shady in midwinter), at mid-mountain on Planai, at Rohrmoos on Hochwurzen and at mid-mountain on Reiteralm. Fageralm also has good kids' facilities.

The obvious strategy is to base yourself in a hotel at Rohrmoos and use the facilities there, which are near-ideal for kids and adult novices alike.

Alternatives to Schladming

Schladming is the obvious place to stay, but the alternatives are all viable if you want a quiet time. Haus is at the foot of its own mountain, Hauser Kaibling. Pichl is at the lift base where Hochwurzen meets Reiteralm. And nearby Gleiming is the major lift base for Reiteralm.

Haus im Ennstal 750m

Haus, 6km east of Schladming, is a proper little village, and a pleasantly relaxed place to stay. Although the skiers who fill its sizeable car parks are in the majority, it does have some accommodation. Neither the really minute, 60-year-old cable car out of the village nor the gondola 1km to the east has much in the way of handy lodgings, but in the village centre there is a handful of 3-star and 4-star hotels, the pick being the 4-star Herrschaftstaverne. There's a small artificial ice rink.

Pichl 765m

Pichl, 5km west of Schladming, is the main lift base for Hochwurzen, and also the base of the famously inadequate double-chair link to Reiteralm. Its hotels and guest houses are dotted around the surrounding fields.

Directly across the valley in a fine elevated position, 400m from the lifts, is the extraordinary 4-star hotel Pichlmayrgut – a multi-building complex with excellent facilities (pools, squash, tennis). For skiing purposes, though, you may prefer a place on the slopes, such as the 4-star Raunerhof, in a ski-in ski-out position 200m above the valley. Or the Almwelt, another 200m higher, the 4-star 'hotel village' mentioned in the 'Sustenance' section, with its accommodation in neat wooden chalets. From either hotel you can ski to Gleiming, for fast access to Reiteralm, or to Pichl for the Hochwurzen lift.

Gleiming 780m

Gleiming, a further 1km west from Pichl, consists of a scattering of hotels and guest houses around the main lift base for Reiteralm. You can ski to this lift from the two on-piste hotels mentioned above. Close to the lift station is the 3-star hotel Gleimingerhof.

Schladming is a big town at the foot of Planai; on the right is Rohrmoos, leading to Hochwurzen (out of shot)

Serfaus

Serfaus / Fiss / Ladis

These three resorts market their shared area as Serfaus-Fiss-Ladis; but we reckon they'd be well advised to follow the lead of Saalbach-Hinterglemm-Leogang-Fieberbrunn – pick one two-syllable village name, and stick to it.

It's an area that merits serious attention for its size, altitudes and facilities. It makes a big pitch for the family market, aided by the fact that Serfaus is car-free, by the exemplary kids' areas (at mid-mountain above Serfaus and just outside Fiss), and by the resorts' impressive sunshine record. The pitch seems to work – but it's slightly surprising to find that the slopes in general suit keen, confident skiers, with plenty of challenges, and aren't nearly so good for inexperienced skiers.

The mountains in brief

Size A mid-sized area, though not as big as the tourist office wishes it was

Slopes Mostly open slopes, very few of them gentle

Snow Snowfall record isn't great, but altitude helps, up to a point

System, Lift Impressive, with slow lifts only in places that don't matter

Sustenance Table service isn't standard here – but some good spots

For beginners Excellent slopes, but in Serfaus you need a full lift pass

For true blue skiers There is good blue skiing to do, but not a lot of it

For the confident Excellent: extensive, varied slopes with a sense of travel

For experts Quite a lot to amuse, but most of it requires good snow

Fancy stuff Various forms of terrain park all over the place

Serfaus – the resort in brief

Convenience Thanks to the tube, walks are not excessive

Lodgings Plenty of choice, especially for families

Bars and restaurants A bit of après activity, and some choice of restaurants

Off the slopes Quite a lot to do, but more evening tobogganing needed

For families A veritable winter wonderland

Pass notes	Key facts		Key ratings	
This is one of the few areas in the book with no shared or regional pass deals available.	Altitude	1430m	Size	✳✳✳
	Range	1200–2820m	Snow	✳✳✳
	Slopes (see text)	162km	Fast lifts	✳✳✳✳✳
Beginners in Serfaus must go up to mid-mountain, and need a full lift pass from day one. In Fiss or Ladis you can get a day pass for the extensive beginner area between the villages, including the Ladis-Fiss gondola.	**Where to stay, ideally**		Mountain rest's	✳✳✳
	Close to the lift stations in Serfaus – or, for families, close to Murmlipark.		Beginner	✳✳✳✳
			True blue	✳✳✳
	Websites		Confident	✳✳✳✳✳
	serfaus-fiss-ladis.at		Expert	✳✳✳
	feelfree-sfl.at		Convenience	✳✳✳
	murmli-berta.at		Families	✳✳✳✳✳
			Village charm	✳✳✳✳

The mountains in detail

This is an unusual area. Above Serfaus is a broad bowl reaching a long way towards the peaks that separate this area from Ischgl's Paznauntal; two gondolas go up into the slopes on the left of the bowl, where there are lifts to three points on a high ridge. Beyond that, runs and lifts stretch a further 5km in a more or less linear fashion via the peak of Pezid and the col of Arrezjoch to Masnerkopf, high-point of the area at 2820m.

A third gondola from Serfaus goes to the right, to the ridge separating the Serfaus sector from the slopes of Fiss. Here there is another bowl, accessed again by three gondolas from the village, with the rightmost going up to another ridge, with further skiing on the shady back side of the ridge. A fourth gondola from Fiss goes to a low hill where the nursery slopes are set, with a long, gentle run on the far side down to Ladis.

Size

This is a fair-sized area, at the top end of our ✳✳✳ size rating. The 162km we quote is the resort's figure; Christoph Schrahe puts it a bit lower. The resort now wants to claim more: '214km when skied, 162km when measured,' says the piste map. Read the introduction to the book to understand what's going on here.

The extraordinary shape of the area, with the chain of lifts extending west of Serfaus to Masnerkopf, results in an overall length of 15km.

Slopes

Practically all the skiing is on open slopes, with just a few short runs to village level in the trees (both Serfaus and Fiss have a run tellingly named Waldabfahrt – Forest Piste). The mountains are mainly quite challenging, with easy runs in quite limited areas.

We congratulate the lift company on the comprehensive altitude information they have put on their piste map – the best we've ever seen in this respect. It reveals that, although there are

The lower slopes have some wooded runs, but once away from the villages you are in open, treeless terrain

1000m-vertical runs to the villages, the runs in the more remote sectors are much shorter – 300m–500m in the western part of the Serfaus sector, in particular.

The Frommesabfahrt, looping down to Fiss on the right of the area, is the longest run, widely touted to be 10km; but even if you start from Zwölferkopf and link several pistes together the whole amounts to more like 7km.

There are ten ski routes on the map, without explanation. They are about equally divided into 'intermediate' and 'difficult' categories.

Once a week there is a 'first tracks' opportunity, with breakfast included, but the deal is wildly expensive (€68 in 2017).

Snow

The area's impressive sunshine record points to a less than impressive snow record, but the villages and the slopes are relatively high – you spend most of your time skiing above 1800m – which helps keep natural snow in good nick. It also aids snowmaking, which covers 80% of the pistes; but the map doesn't distinguish the lucky ones.

System, Lift

The system couldn't be called state of the art, but is excellent in practice, with gondolas and fast chairs in all the key places. There's a 1km T-bar in the middle of the Fiss slopes, and two shorter slow quads that are easily avoided. If everyone sets off for Masnerkopf, you can expect to find queues for the Pezid gondola now that two fast chair-lifts feed into that sector, but if you do, you can always head back to the Serfaus bowl for a bit.

Sustenance

There are over 20 restaurants marked on the piste map, not counting a few slightly away from the pistes. The map describes 14 that are owned by the lift company, and of these only about half offer table service. Some of the self-service places are quite impressive, including the glass-walled BergDiamant at Schönjoch.

The rustic Schalber Alm does a good range of excellent food, efficiently served – not surprising, given that it is run by the 5-star hotel Schalber. The larger but still traditional Zirbenhütte at the far side of Fiss has a very good menu and takes table reservations (a rarity in Austria).

More on the slopes

For beginners

Up at Komperdell there are vast, gentle slopes served by everything from moving carpets to fast chair-lifts. At about 2000m you can expect good snow, too. The only snag is that you need a full lift pass. If you resent this, as well you might, you could look at staying in Fiss or Ladis.

There are some good blue runs to progress to – probably enough to satisfy a first-week skier.

For true blue skiers

You might think resorts that make such a strong pitch for family business would have largely amiable blue cruising pistes, but you would be wrong – the mountains are mainly of red gradient. There is blue skiing to be done, but not a lot of it.

It is centred on the extensive area of blue skiing at Komperdell, and happily includes a genuine blue descent to the village. Higher up, on the Plansegg chair, is Zanboden, genuinely blue except perhaps at the start – but, bizarrely, you can avoid this by starting on the red Seables. The Lazid gondola goes to the top of the wide, sunny Lawens blue, which would be ideal except that it is advertised as a carving piste, which can mean confident skiers travelling at high speed. You'll need to ride the gondola back down to Komperdell.

There is a bit more blue skiing to be done over at Fiss, but bear in mind that the Sattel-Süd-Serfaus run back to Serfaus isn't the easiest of blues. The Möseralm red down to Fiss is fairly easy, and from there you have one or two other options, including the long, flatteringly easy blue run from the Fiss nursery slopes down to Ladis.

For confident intermediates

This is a good area for the keen intermediate, offering multiple different mountainsides all with worthwhile red skiing.

All the lifts above and beyond Komperdell are worth spending time on, with some easy blacks to tempt you as well as rewarding reds. Don't overlook the lovely winding Wald run through the forest on Alpkopf – the perfect place to be in a storm. And above Fiss both the

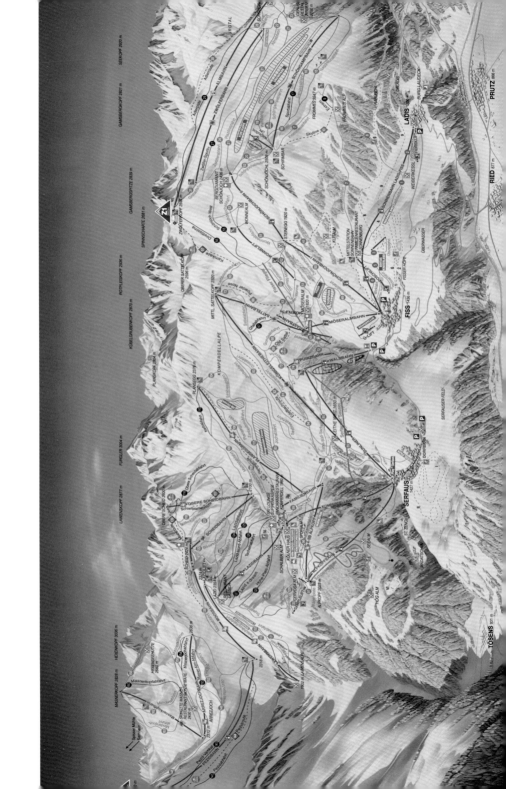

front sunny side and the back shady side of the Schönjoch ridge have satisfying runs. The long Frommes run, looping away from the lifts, is pleasantly scenic but mostly of blue gradient.

Don't expect too much of the long excursion to Masnerkopf. The red runs on Masnerkopf itself are OK although not very challenging (unlike the black), but the skiing on the way there doesn't amount to much and the blue run back from Arrezjoch is pretty tedious.

The red-graded ski routes are worth exploring when the snow is good. The Plansegg and Edelbach routes are about the easiest. Note also the remarks in the next section on the black runs.

For experts

There are quite a few black runs spread across the piste map. Many hardly deserve the classification – Kerb, Obere Scheid and Pezid, for example. Hohe-Pleis may be a real black, but only just – and it was smooth and soft when we skied it in 2017. Others are quite tough, especially when the snow is hard – Masnerkopf, particularly, and Direttissima and Schönjoch West on Zwölferkopf.

The ski routes add up to quite a lot of skiing, and some are challenging.

Kamikaze offers more sustained steepness than the Direttissima piste next to it. Schleifplatten, under the Obere Scheid chair, is serious stuff – said to reach 38°.

There is also a great deal of unmarked off-piste terrain accessible within the lift system. For an excursion slightly away from it, from Zwölferkopf you can branch right off the Kamikaze ski route to descend a broad valley leading to the Urgtal and so back to the lifts.

The ski schools lead regular touring groups over to Samnaun and to See in the Paznauntal, with avalanche kit, touring skis and return taxis included in the deal.

Of course, most of the above requires good natural snow, so the relatively poor snowfall record is of some concern on what are quite rocky mountains. On the other hand, the off-piste doesn't get skied out quickly here.

Fancy stuff

In both sectors there are multiple terrain parks – from several aimed at beginners through to the advanced Snowpark (with air bag) on the north-facing slopes of Schönjoch at Fiss. Next to that is a long funslope. There's more information at the resort's special website feelfree-sfl.at.

Serfaus is a long village, stretching almost a mile from the lift base at this end to the car parks at the far end

Serfaus – the resort

Anyone familiar with Saas-Fee in Switzerland would find Serfaus quite familiar. Cars are parked at the entrance to the village (after you've dumped your bags, so not quite the Swiss model) and the lifts are at the opposite end. In between is a charming, traditional, traffic-free village – the only resort of its kind in Austria, as far as we know. The difference is that here, under the main street, is a tube train – opened in 1985 and now being doubled in carrying capacity for 2019.

Convenience

It's a long, thin village, with the lifts at the western end about 1.4km from the car parks at the entrance. But the two points are linked by the underground hover-train, with two intermediate stops along the way. So no one has to walk very far – about 300m at the most. There are large-scale kit lockers at the lift base, too, so no need to walk in ski boots.

Lodgings

There's a wide choice of hotels, guest houses and apartments. Hotels (many of which, naturally, stress their family orientation) are mostly 4-star, with a good number of 3-stars and two 5-stars. The 4-star Gabriela occupies pole position, just a few yards above the lift base; but the 4-star Superior hotel Bär will appeal more to families – it's in the centre of the village, next to the Murmlipark snow garden (read 'For families') and has its own fab kids' play facilities. (It also has a serious wine cellar, so there are compensations.)

Bars and restaurants

The emphasis Serfaus places on family holidays naturally means that après-ski action here is relatively muted by Austria's boisterous standards. But it is certainly not absent – there is an umbrella bar at Komperdell that gets some afternoon business, and at the lift base the long-established Patschi bar reportedly gets pretty lively. There are other après places too – the Posthotel in the main street has an umbrella bar – and of course there are some late-night spots.

There's a reasonable range of restaurants, many within hotels but some not. In the latter group, s'Hannes stands out – traditionally based dishes with a modern twist.

Off the slopes

There's quite a bit to do. A 4km toboggan run from Komperdell is open in daytime but floodlit in the evening only once a week. And on Alpkopf there's a 1.5km sled-on-rails coaster, open daytime only. The Serfauser Sauser is a kind of zip-wire but with bends; no, we haven't tried it. An 'icetaxi' runs to Ladis for an hour's curling in the evenings, with a glass of glühwein thrown in. Two hotels admit the public to their swimming pools.

There are cross-country trails next to the village and up at Komperdell, and more at Fiss, including a long one contouring around the mountain to Schöngampalm. Countless cleared paths are provided, going around the mountains and up into the ski slopes. An excellent leaflet (downloadable) details all the trails and paths.

There's a weekly musical extravaganza up at Komperdell.

For families

A car-free village at an altitude where you can expect snow to lie in the streets is a good start for a family resort. And the kids' facilities are very impressive, both here and in Fiss.

In the centre of the village is Murmlipark, with a carousel and two moving carpets, and all the usual trimmings. But up at mid-mountain is the KinderSchneealm, which is about five times the size. There's even a printed piste map covering this and the Fiss equivalent. At the lift base there is a big indoor play centre, with all kinds of activities. At Komperdell there's a mini-snowmobile circuit.

Although British visitors are few, there are many Dutch, so the instructors and other staff are quite accustomed to speaking English.

Alternatives to Serfaus

Serfaus makes the best base for keen skiers wanting to make the most of the skiing – it's as close to the centre of the area as you can get, and it's the most appealing village. Little Ladis, on the other hand, is as far from the centre of things as you can get, and really makes sense as a base only for novices. Fiss has more hotels than Serfaus, including some that might sway your choice, and shares excellent beginner slopes with Ladis.

Fiss 1435m

Fiss is a pleasantly traditional village spread widely across a sloping site, with its main ski lifts at the top. (There's a second lift base below the village, for the convenience of car-borne skiers.) It is more diffuse than Serfaus, without much central focus. The beginner slopes are just above the village, and from there you have a lovely, long, gentle run down to Ladis to progress to.

Convenience It's quite a sprawling village, and lodgings are up to 800m from the lift base. The better hotels run shuttles to the lifts, of course. There are kit lockers at the lift base for everyone staying in the village – a very impressive facility.

Lodgings The range is much like Serfaus. The 4-star hotel Chesa Monte in the village centre, 600m from the lift base, is excellent, with notably good half-board food. It runs a shuttle to the lifts.

Bars and restaurants Hexenalm is a woody chalet at the gondola base that gets busy but far from boisterous at teatime.

Off the slopes There's a 3.5km toboggan run down the first stage of the Schönjoch gondola, and floodlit tobogganing once a week from Möseralm. The Fisser Flieger is a kind of zip-wire taking four at a time, and the Skyswing is a fairground swing-ride. As in Serfaus, there is a weekly musical show at mid-mountain.

Families The kids' facilities are about as good as such things get – countless moving carpets, tubing, a funslope, dedicated restaurants, an Indian village ... all just above the village, accessible by a gondola from the lift base that goes on to link with Ladis.

Ladis 1200m

Ladis is smaller than the other villages, but not as small as it looks from the blue run down from Fiss – it stretches away for about 1km. A medieval castle stands over the village, and nearby is a small lake which you hope to find frozen for skating and curling purposes. There is a cluster of 4-star hotels around the base of the gondola up to Fiss.

Ladis stretches away from its lift base (out of shot on the left) to its ancient castle, and beyond

Ski Juwel – Alpbach

Alpbach / Inneralpbach / Auffach / Niederau

Ski Juwel is a classic example of the logic of ski resort links. In 2012 little Alpbach and littler Auffach in the next-door Wildschönau area both doubled their appeal to keen skiers (and justified higher lift pass prices) by building one connecting lift and laying out an (almost) connecting piste.

Both areas are old British favourites (the Wildschönau, strangely, on account of tiny Niederau). Each offered the popular Tirolean formula of amiable wooded mountains, cosy traditional villages and jolly, beer-fuelled après-ski, but you had to accept extremely limited slopes. Together, they make a more attractive proposition for those who like some variety from day to day. But let's be clear: they still don't add up to a big area.

The mountains in brief

Size Even now, one of the smallest areas to get a chapter in these pages

Slopes Red-gradient mountains, with open top slopes dropping into forest

Snow Shady orientation, many runs on the upper slopes, 85% snowmaking

System, Lift Generally good, though the higher chair-lifts are slow

Sustenance Some pleasant spots, but the huts are hardly a highlight

For beginners Adequate nursery slopes; but think about progression

For true blue skiers Disappointing: limited unless you experiment with reds

For the confident Lots to do, within the limits of a small area

For experts Hope for good snow, to tackle off-piste routes to the valleys

Fancy stuff Decent parks on both mountains – and half-pipes on both

Alpbach – the resort in brief

Convenience If commuting by bus isn't your thing, look at Inneralpbach

Lodgings Not many hotels to choose from – but some very good ones

Bars and restaurants Just because it's small, that doesn't mean it's dead

Off the slopes Disappointing: no convenient tobogganing or skating?

For families Depends on your point of view; we're not convinced

Pass notes

At a small extra cost you can buy an AllStar/Super Ski card covering Mayrhofen to the west and SkiWelt to the east, and 20 other ski areas. Beginners can buy points cards which can be used not only on beginner lifts but also on the gondolas used to reach the higher beginner slopes.

Key facts

Altitude	1000m
Range	875–2025m
Slopes (see text)	109km

Where to stay, ideally
For quintessential Alpine charm, central Alpbach.
For daily convenience, Inneralpbach.

Websites
skijuwel.com
alpbachtal.at
wildschoenau.com

Key ratings

Size	*
Snow	***
Fast lifts	****
Mountain rest's	***
Beginner	***
True blue	**
Confident	****
Expert	**
Convenience	**
Families	***
Village charm	****

The mountains in detail

Alpbach's Wiedersberger Horn has skiing on two flanks – on the north-facing slopes served by the Wiedersbergerhornbahn gondola, starting beside the road up to the resort, and on the east-facing slopes served by the Pöglbahn gondola starting at Inneralpbach, a separate village. On the open upper slopes reached by these gondolas are several chair-lifts and two drags, with high-points at Gmahkopf (1900m) and Horn Alm (2025m).

Inneralpbach is now the hub of the Ski Juwel slopes, because it is also the start of the linking gondola to Schatzberg (1903m) at the top of the Auffach slopes, also reached by a gondola from Auffach (upgraded to an eight-seater in 2017). Again, there are chairs and drags on the open upper slopes above Auffach.

Niederau's slopes are not connected to the main area. The area is very small, and relatively low – a chair-lift goes to Lanerköpfl (1621m) and a gondola to Markbachjoch (1500m), with runs to the village from both, and there are a couple of drags on the latter.

Size

The lift company publicises both realistic and inflated figures for piste km, but they are based on the 'greater' Ski Juwel lift pass area, not just the linked Alpbach-Auffach area. The realistic figure for the whole Juwel area is 109km (145km 'active skiing'), but the Schrahe report (read the intro to the book) puts the linked area at only 59km. That's small.

Snow

The altitudes here are not great, but there are many lower Austrian resorts than these. There are plenty of lifts above mid-mountain, including the upper stages of the two longest gondolas, so it's easy to spend most of your time above 1300m. Most of the slopes face north-east or north, which helps a lot. Snowmaking is said to cover 85% of the pistes.

Slopes

These are classic Tirolean mountains: wooded low down, open towards the top, generally red gradient – Alpbach has clearly struggled to form blue pistes on the Wiedersberger Horn (which we abbreviate to Wi Horn), and Auffach, disgracefully, hasn't bothered except in a small area at mid-mountain.

There are three good long runs to the valley lift stations (with verticals in the 900m–1000m region), but not from Schatzberg to Inneralpbach, where there is no piste down the lower stage of the gondola. But most of the skiing is on the upper slopes, with much smaller verticals. The two longest chair-lifts on the Wi Horn are only about 400m vertical, while the two six-packs at the top of Schatzberg are even shorter.

There are several ski routes, which are not explained on the piste map. One is within the lift network on the Wi Horn, the others offering alternative descents to the valley from both Wi Horn and Schatzberg.

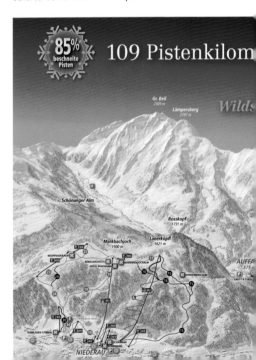

System, Lift

Most of the key lifts are fast and of adequate capacity. The Schatzbergbahn out of Auffach is being upgraded to an eight-seat gondola as we write in 2017. The Wiedersbergerhornbahn (Wi-bahn) dates from the late 80s and has modest capacity for a six-seater. But with three gondolas out of the valley the Alpbachtal seems adequately equipped.

The one conspicuous weakness in the system is on the highest slopes of the Wi Horn, where there are two 500m-long slow chairs and one that is 1.1km long – the Hornbahn at the very top.

Sustenance

Restaurants are marked and named on the piste map. They are adequate in number, but quite a few are self-service despite their traditional appearance.

The very atmospheric Böglalm on the Wi Horn just above Inneralpbach is famous for its roast chicken (book in advance). Higher up, try Dauerstoa Alm – or the splendid glass-walled Hornalm, newly built in 2016 to replace the incinerated Wiedersbergerhornhütte. At the top of Schatzberg, Gipfö Hit ticks most of the key boxes – friendly, efficient service of well done traditional fodder in a welcoming, woody space.

More on the slopes

For beginners

In the village there is a sunny nursery slope with a 300m button lift; it's not the gentlest of slopes, and the shorter one at Inneralpbach is gentler. There are also short slopes up at Gmahkopf, the gentlest of which is on the 200m Hornboden drag.

There are easy longer blue runs to progress to on the Wi Horn; but in case you make quick progress you should take account of the next section.

For true blue skiers

At first sight, the area around Gmahkopf on the upper slopes of the Wi Horn appears to offer quite a bit of blue-run skiing, but the reality is seriously disappointing. Blue 62, served by the drag on the back of the hill, is sweet but very short. And the longer runs shown on the piste map are not very satisfactory.

As you might guess from the map, blue 52 is made up of linking tracks across the mountainside – not fun at all. Blue 46, served by the upper stage of the gondola and the Gmahbahn six-seat chair-lift, looks promising, but is actually a mixture of bumpy open slopes and cat-tracks that are quite challenging in places.

SKI JUWEL – ALPBACH

143

The red skiing is not particularly steep, but mostly it does represent quite a step up in difficulty. The runs over on the upper slopes of Schatzberg are a tad easier, so if you have exhausted the Wi Horn blues, you might consider heading up the linking gondola – try runs 5 and 6 first.

The runs to valley level are proper reds, so you'll be descending by gondola until confident to tackle them.

For confident intermediates

Practically all of the red runs are worth exploring, and the black runs are not difficult – most could be classified red. So there is plenty to do, within the constraints of an undeniably small area.

The open upper-slope areas on both mountains have nicely varied runs, but they are short – those on Schtazberg particularly so.

The runs down the gondolas are the highlight – well worth doing for fun, not just to get home. Both the red and black options down the Wi-bahn gondola are excellent – you may find the black in better shape because of less traffic. Red 47 to Inneralpbach is a cracker – a sequence of good, steep red slopes down the fall line, linked by traverses; the last of the steeper pitches is the steepest and may have poor snow at times, but has a blue variation.

Run 13 down the upper stage of the linking Schatzberg gondola is an excellent proper red, with a lovely view of the

Alpbachtal – and because the gondola follows a dog-leg route it doesn't get as much sun as you might expect on this south-west-facing mountainside.

For experts

Most of the black pistes are borderline black/red in gradient, so on-piste the main satisfaction lies in the long red runs to the valley. But there is quite a bit of off-piste terrain between the pistes to play on.

Given good snow to valley level, there are more serious off-piste opportunities than you might expect. From Wi Horn you can go in three directions – to skier's left of the lift network to the Wi-bahn base station, to skier's right of the network to Inneralpbach or off the back of the hill into the Zillertal, with return by taxi. From Schatzberg you can descend to Auffach on skier's right of the lifts, or towards Alpbach down the top section of the linking gondola, or all the way to Inneralpbach on skier's left of the gondola. With a bit of hiking, other options are opened up.

Fancy stuff

There are decent parks on both mountains – Snowpark below Gmahkopf on Wi Horn and Snowboard Park, with novice and pro lines, on the fringes of upper Schatzberg. Amazingly, both parks have a half-pipe (no indication of depth). Just across the hill from the Snowpark is a funslope.

Alpbach – the resort

Alpbach is one of the pin-up villages of Austrian skiing – a cluster of heavily wood-built chalets on a gentle slope around its church, dissolving rapidly into open fields. It has a local lift and slope, but for most people the day starts and ends with a ski-bus to and from lift bases a mile or two away.

Convenience

Your daily routine revolves around a ski-bus shuttling frequently between the village centre and the Wi-bahn gondola. Apparently there is no service to Inneralpbach, location of the ski kindergartens and the gondola to Schatzberg, which seems a bit poor. It's a small village, but big enough for some services to go beyond the centre to an outlying 4-star hotel (the Alphof). There are ski depots at the lift bases.

Lodgings

The choice of lodgings in this very small village is naturally a bit limited – there are countless private chalets and rooms to rent, but only a handful of 3-star and 4-star hotels, and a slightly greater number of guest houses.

The 4-star S (Superior) hotels Alpbacherhof and Böglerhof are both lovely places to stay, the latter occupying pole position in the village next to the village slope and the ski-bus stop.

Bars and restaurants

Après activity here seems to start at the lift bases. Joe's Salett'l is a popular umbrella bar at the base of the Pöglbahn in Inneralpbach, and there's another umbrella across the piste. At the other gondola base, the Liftstüberl provides an alternative to standing at the bus stop. Helpfully, all are clearly marked on the piste map.

In downtown Alpbach, the Postalm and the gasthof Jakober are long-established favourites; both operate as restaurants as well as lively bars; you might find live music in either. The Postalm is the late-night spot.

Off the slopes

There are several tobogganing options, though none is super-convenient. If you're feeling energetic, you can walk up to the head of the valley south-east of Inneralpbach for a 5km run from Faulbaumgartenalm. Or, closer to home, get a taxi from Bischoferalm near Alpbach up to Bischoferjoch for a floodlit 4km run from there. But the big one is the 6.5km run from Reither Kogel above Reith, down the valley, accessed by gondola.

At the top of the Wi-bahn gondola is a new sled-on-rails coaster, the Lauser Sauser. To find an ice rink or public swimming pool, you would have to travel down to the Inn valley.

There are excellent cleared walking paths across the sunny mountainsides around Alpbach, and quite long cross-country trails up the valleys that branch south-west and south-east from Inneralpbach.

For families

A small, friendly village with a sunny nursery slope at its heart ought to be just right for young families. That nursery slope is a good place for kids to have fun in the snow, but seems to be not part of the local ski school set-up. So off we go on the bus ...

Two of the ski schools operate kids' snow gardens at Inneralpbach, with the usual carousel, moving carpets and play objects. One of these schools, at least, operates a taxi shuttle from Alpbach. A third school has its kids' practice area up at the top of the Wi-bahn gondola.

Obviously, having the snow gardens at the foot or the top of the main mountain aids the transition to proper skiing. From other points of view it seems regrettable.

The upper slopes of Wi Horn are mostly tree-free; the central Gmah chair-lift now starts lower down the hill

Alternatives to Alpbach

The obvious alternative is Inneralpbach, ideally positioned for spending time on both mountains with minimum exertion. Auffach may not have quite the charm of Alpbach, but it is more of a village than Inneralpbach and is equally convenient for skiing, or at least for skiing Schatzberg. Niederau is detached, at the foot of its own tiny, low ski area.

Inneralpbach 1050m

Inneralpbach is pleasant enough, but doesn't really feel like a village. Although there are plenty of chalets and rooms to rent, there are only two hotels – the 4-star Wiedersbergerhorn and the 4-star S Galtenberg Family and Wellness hotel, both near the base of the Galtenberg drag-lift. Not much happens here in the evening after the umbrella bar phase.

Auffach 875m

Auffach is a quite long, narrow valley-bottom village, with something like a centre just north of the lift station.
Convenience You can stay near the lift or rely on the frequent ski-bus service.
Lodgings As over the hill, a limited but adequate choice. The 4-star Auffacherhof hotel is only yards from the lift base.
Bars and restaurants Après drinking starts at the umbrella bar at the gondola mid-station, and continues at the base. The village is a bit lifeless later on.
Off the slopes From the mid-station there is a 5km toboggan run to the village; not lit, but twice a week you can do it in the evening using toboggans with lights.
Families The kids' practice area is on lovely gentle slopes at mid-mountain.

Niederau 830m

Niederau is a rather diffuse little village at the foot of its own small mountain, 8km by road from Auffach. A keen skier can cover the whole mountain in a couple of hours. It's not without challenge, though. There's a row of good nursery slopes next to the village, and further gentle slopes at the top of the mountain. The choice of lodgings is adequate, some of them conveniently located, and there's some life in the bars at close of play.

A cute view of Inneralpbach, though it's not one you're likely to see unless you make a special effort

SkiWelt – Brixen im Thale

Brixen / Westendorf / Söll / Ellmau and several others

The SkiWelt Wilder Kaiser-Brixental is one of Austria's big linked ski areas, now ranking third behind Saalbach and the Arlberg. Back in the day (when it was called Grossraum), Söll was the area's chief representative in the UK market, but these days the best base for the whole SkiWelt is Brixen.

Brixen is the point where the core area of the SkiWelt – low, rounded, partly wooded hills, with populated valleys on all sides – meets the separate slopes of Westendorf. From here you have a choice of three directions each morning: towards prominent Hohe Salve, then Söll or Hopfgarten; towards Scheffau and Ellmau; or towards the Westendorf slopes (and from there perhaps the almost-linked Kitzbühel area).

The mountains in brief

Size It's big, challenging Saalbach for second place in the Austrian rankings

Slopes Generally gentle, partly wooded, long in the right conditions

Snow At these altitudes, don't bank on good conditions low down

System, Lift Generally impressive, but with more than a few slow lifts still

Sustenance Plenty of good spots with table service – a highlight

For beginners Pretty good, if you don't mind starting at mid-mountain

For true blue skiers Lots to do, including long descents when snow is good

For the confident Long, rewarding descents, but lots of short easy runs too

For experts Some good ski routes (given good snow) and short blacks

Fancy stuff An impressive park within reach at Westendorf

Brixen – the resort in brief

Convenience OK if you pick your spot, but most people need the ski-bus

Lodgings Limited but adequate choice of 4-star hotels and gasthofs

Bars and restaurants It's quiet, but it's not entirely dead, at teatime anyway

Off the slopes It's a small place – don't expect too much

For families Make the right arrangements, and all will be well

Pass notes

For a small premium, the AllStarCard covers a huge range of resorts including two large areas nearby – Kitzbühel and the Saalbach area reachable via Fieberbrunn. It also covers the Kitzbühel train. Beginners can buy points cards, and a special lift pass deal is said to be available via the ski schools.

Key facts

Altitude	800m
Range	620–1867m
Slopes (see text)	272km

Where to stay, ideally
Within walking distance of the two Brixen gondolas.

Websites
skiwelt.at
kitzbueheler-alpen.com
wilderkaiser.info

Key ratings

Size	★★★★
Snow	★★
Fast lifts	★★★★
Mountain rest's	★★★★
Beginner	★★★★
True blue	★★★★
Confident	★★★★
Expert	★★
Convenience	★★
Families	★★★
Village charm	★★★

The mountains in detail

The main SkiWelt area can be divided into two major sectors. Hochbrixen, at the top of the eponymous gondola from Brixen, is where they meet. To the west are the slopes around the dominant high-point of Hohe Salve (with runs to Hopfgarten, Söll and the isolated lift station of Schwendt). To the east is the core area of the SkiWelt – the slopes on the multiple minor peaks of Zinsberg, Eiberg, Brandstadl (with runs to Blaiken near Scheffau) and Hartkaiser (with runs to Ellmau). There is then a third sector on Astberg, above Ellmau; this is very low and very small, and really of interest only to those based in Ellmau.

Then, in the opposite direction from Brixen are the slopes of Westendorf, which spread around a horseshoe arrangement of peaks from Choralpe via Nachtsöllberg and Fleiding (the SkiWelt high-point at about 1865m) to the shoulder of Gampenkogel. From here a run descends to the valley bus link with Kitzbühel's Pengelstein gondola.

Size

The 272km in our facts panel is arrived at by adding up the published lengths of runs in the linked SkiWelt area, omitting a few outlying bits and pieces. Checks on one or two runs suggest that it's probably about right, although some runs in the list are not on the current map – and last time Christoph Schrahe checked the area he found the total overstated by about 10% (read the intro to the book). So we reckon Saalbach is currently ahead of the SkiWelt by a few km. Anyway: it's big.

Note that with an AllStar/Super Ski pass you can ski Kitzbühel as well – it's only a two-minute bus ride from the far end of the Westendorf slopes.

Slopes

First, a discovery. To our amazement we now realise that the area has been fibbing about its top height, claiming 1957m (the peak of Westendorf's Gampenkogel) when in fact the lift on that hill goes nowhere near the top. The high-point of the SkiWelt is actually the shoulder of Fleiding, about 90m lower. Tsk, tsk.

Although these are low and essentially wooded mountains, large areas at altitude and on the sunny southern slopes to the valley are open, presumably because they make good summer grazing. So in bad weather the trees aren't always as much help as you might hope. Much of the area is of gentle gradient, but there are lots of steeper parts, notably around the high-point of the core area, Hohe

Salve, and at Westendorf.

The SkiWelt rightly makes a bit of a fuss about its valley runs. Depending on how you count them, there are about a dozen in the core area and two or three at Westendorf. The biggest descent, from Hohe Salve to Hopfgarten, clocks up 1200m vertical, while Hartkaiser to Ellmau is more like 700m. Hohe Salve to Söll is said to be over 7km in length.

On the other hand, the core area from Hochbrixen to Hartkaiser is made up of countless short runs; many lifts have verticals in the order of 250–400m.

Some of the valley descents are ski routes, unexplained on the map and not classified for difficulty.

This is a complex area, and the aforementioned map is a complete nightmare – a classic example of a map designed for marketing purposes, not as an aid for skiers. Views differ on the signposting: once you get the hang of it, even consultant editor Watts can get from A to B without too much difficulty, but we've heard from others who can't get the hang of it.

Snow

Our standard warning about the low resorts in this part of the world applies: these days, snowmaking may be good enough to keep runs to the valley reliably open (here it covers 80% of the slopes); but with lift bases below 900m you can't expect great snow conditions on the lower slopes, especially later in the season. Be prepared for ice and/or slush, and count yourself lucky if you find packed powder.

This area can get big snowfalls when weather comes in from the north-west, but that's not the way it is, usually.

In this area, concerns over altitude are compounded by some concerns over orientation: the runs towards Brixen get full sun, and can get seriously slushy at the bottom.

System, Lift

Overall it's an impressive lift system, but there are still quite a few slow lifts dotted around – about ten T-bars over 500m long, a dozen slow quads, half a dozen triples and doubles. Helpfully, the piste map legend attempts to distinguish fast quads from slow, but uses the same symbol for both.

Sustenance

There are dozens of attractive, traditional huts all over the area – although there is a curious desert south of Hartkaiser, and you might get dehydrated on run 30 to Schwendt. They are all marked and named on the map, along with an indication that Wi-Fi is or is not available. A better idea would be to indicate instead whether table service is available.

Editorial favourites are Stöcklalm, at the bottom of the Hochsöll slopes; Rübezahl Alm above Ellmau – a lovely old hut with multiple small rooms; KaiserLounge, also above Ellmau but quite different – woody but cool, with an innovative menu; Tanzbodenalm above Scheffau – modern but woody; and Brechhornhaus, at the far end of the Westendorf slopes. But there are many others worth trying.

More on the slopes

For beginners

The nursery slopes are up at sunny Hochbrixen (about 1300m), reached by gondola. There are two rope-tows and two button lifts, on gentle slopes. So, all good. There are lots of longer easy runs to progress to, but you'll want someone with you to decipher the hideously confusing piste map.

We're told that the ski schools offer special lift pass deals, so that you don't have to buy a full-price pass on day one.

We're sorry to report that neither of the Brixen ski schools has bothered to

Steep, rounded Hohe Salve, seen here from Westendorf's Choralpe, is the most prominent feature of the area

90 CABLE CARS
284 KM OF SKI RUNS
77 REFRESHMENT STOPS

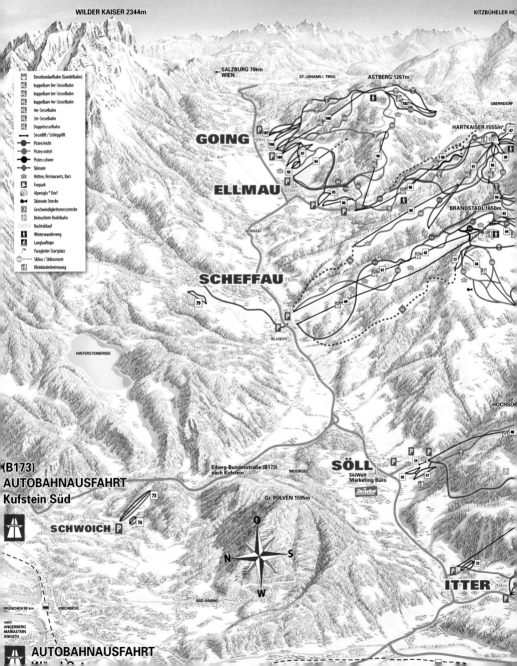

www.skiwelt.at

welt
BRIXENTAL

REAL BIG

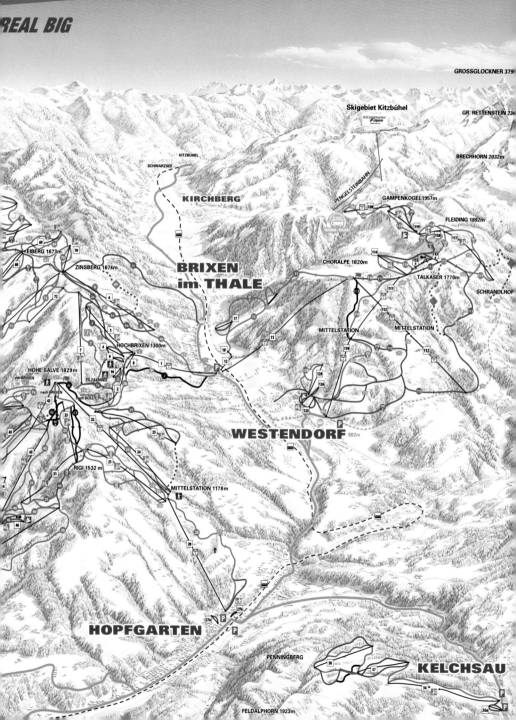

GROSSGLOCKNER 379

Skigebiet Kitzbühel

GR. RETTENSTEIN 23

KITZBÜHEL

BRECHHORN 2032m

SCHWARZSEE

KIRCHBERG

GAMPENKOGEL 1957m

FLEIDING 1892m

EIBERG 1673m

BRIXEN im THALE

CHORALPE 1820m

ZINSBERG 1674m

TALKASER 1770m

SCHRANDLHOF

HOCHBRIXEN 1300m

MITTELSTATION

MITTELSTATION

HOHE SALVE 1829m

FILZALMSEE
von BRIXEN

nach BRIXEN
nach SÖLL

WESTENDORF 802m

RIGI 1532 m

MITTELSTATION 1178m

HOPFGARTEN 620m

PENNINGBERG

KELCHSAU

FELDALPHORN 1923m

create an English-language version of its website, which doesn't bode well. They claim to offer classes in English, of course, but you might want to make it clear that you won't settle for less.

For true blue skiers

From Zinsberg, the minor peak above Hochbrixen, there are blue runs in three directions – back to Hochbrixen, on towards lifts for the next peaks (Eiberg and Brandstadl), or down to Brixen. The valley run is a genuine blue, with just one slightly steeper section midway, but bear in mind that excessively sunny, low runs like this can be challenging because of the snow conditions.

We believe you can ski all the way to Scheffau or Ellmau and back, entirely on blue runs. But we haven't actually tried it, and the map is so poor it's impossible to be sure.

Many of the red runs in the core area are actually of blue gradient; but not all – and the problem is identifying the soft options. Don't be tempted to set off from Hochbrixen in the direction of Hohe Salve; it will end in tears.

There is some good skiing to do at Westendorf, notably the long and interesting run 111. To get home, take 110a

from one of the gondola mid-stations, or ride gondola 11 all the way down.

For confident intermediates

If you like to be flattered rather than persistently challenged, this is a great area – lots to do, and a great sense of travel. The valley runs (read 'Slopes') are the highlight when conditions are good. In warm weather it's worth skiing the run to Brixen at just the right time to get it at its best, and then riding the gondola down at the end of the day to avoid it at its worst. The north-facing valley runs are of course much less temperamental.

The Westendorf slopes are generally more challenging than those in the core area, and well worth exploring – including the runs at the far end, on Fleiding, which look a bit trivial on the map but aren't. Don't miss the excellent testing red run from Choralpe down to Brixen, with a genuine black stretch in the middle.

An outing to Kitzbühel may seem unnecessary, given the extent of the SkiWelt, but if you haven't skied that area, it's worth a visit. The run down to the short bus link was once red, then blue, now red once again. For most of its length it is a good blue, with a red pitch near the end.

The ornate interior of Brixen's church is worth a look, if you like that kind of thing; note the lack of traffic

For experts

There aren't many black runs on the map, but in our experience they are all genuine – those on several flanks of Hohe Salve, in particular. The very sunny run 1 from Hochbrixen looks good, but we've never found it open. Run 112 Alpe Seite at the top of Westendorf's Choralpe is said to be the steepest around, at 39°/80%. We're a bit sceptical about the extreme figures, but it is seriously steep.

We've never encountered snow conditions here to tempt us to try the ski routes to the valley, but route 63 to Scheffau is said to be pretty testing, especially at the top.

This isn't a great area for off-piste, but there are short pitches to be found between the pistes on the open upper slopes, and a few descents to the valleys, notably to Hopfgarten and Brixen, including lift lines, of course. There are routes from the Westendorf lifts into the Brixenbachtal, leading back towards Brixen.

Fancy stuff

There's no fancy stuff immediately above Brixen, but you can quite easily get to the parks above some of the other villages (read the entries at the end of this chapter). The main park in the SkiWelt area is at the far end of the Westendorf slopes – the 650m-long Boarders Playground, with easy, medium and pro lines.

Brixen – the resort

Brixen's merits as a base for the SkiWelt were boosted a decade ago when the SkiWelt gondola to Choralpe was built, giving access to the slopes of Westendorf, and, at much the same time, the valley through-traffic was banished to a bypass. With its grand ornate church, the place now makes a quietly attractive resort.

Convenience

It's a long, thin village, spreading for over 2km along its meandering main street, with the main concentration of shops and lodgings 1km east of the lift base, around the railway station – an area the maps prefer to call Lauterbach. The ski-bus runs about twice an hour between the eastern extremity of the village, where the blue home run arrives, and the lift base.

There are now 300 heated kit lockers at the lift base station.

Lodgings

Most of the lodgings are in apartments, small b&b houses and private rooms, with just a handful of 4-star hotels and another handful of places in the 'inn' category. One of these is the spick-and-span Gasthof Hoferwirt, 200m from the lifts. The 4-star hotel Hubertus is the nearest hotel, 300m away. You can stay in your very own igloo up at Alpeniglu (read 'Off the slopes').

Bars and restaurants

It's a quiet village by Austrian standards, but not entirely without life. Skiing Westendorf, Kandleralm on the home run 11 is a good spot for a last drink on the hill, but if you delay too long, the rope-tow and carpet lift to get you up to the lift base in Brixen will be closed. At the lift base, the PapalaPub and Brixner Stadl compete. The latter is open until 2am, and there are one or two other options in the village.

Off the slopes

Alpeniglu is a 'theme park with a difference' up at Hochbrixen – a 'village' of 18 igloos incorporating an ice art exhibition, bar and restaurant.

There are extensive cross-country trails in the Brixental, including a 2km trail up at Hochbrixen. Information on walks is curiously badly organised, but there are quite a few options in fact, including one from Hochbrixen to the village. Another goes up the side valley south of Brixen to Brixenbachalm, where there is a 5km toboggan run. There is a curling rink.

If swimming is your thing, you have a choice between staying at the hotel Alpenhof or Sporthotel Brixen (both a bus ride from the lifts) or making excursions to the aquatic centres at St Johann or Kitzbühel.

For families

The Brixen ski school has a splendid large kids' practice area up at Hochbrixen, next to the Alpeniglu, with multiple moving carpets – sunny but pretty snow-sure.

The quiet village seems appealing to families, but note the limited range of off-slope activities (picking one of the hotels with a pool would be a good plan, for a start).

Alternatives to Brixen

There are half a dozen other villages at or near the SkiWelt's lift bases. Brixen's position in the SkiWelt is unrivalled, and that's a key consideration; but some of the other resorts have other attractions. Most offer a wider range of lodgings, and more going on in the evening. Those on the shady side of the mountains offer a better chance of enjoyable skiing to the base in warm weather. There's better tobogganing and night skiing at Söll, vast valley-level nursery slopes at Ellmau.

Westendorf 800m

Westendorf is a pretty, rustic village set on a slightly elevated shelf. There are good nursery slopes right next to the village, along with a beginners'/kids' Mini Playground. The gondola station, 500m from the centre, can be reached by using the beginner lifts, or riding the ski-bus. There are also buses to Brixen, for quick access to the main SkiWelt area.

There are about ten hotels and gasthofs in the village, more 3-star than 4-star. Amazingly, none is anywhere near the lift base, though there are simple places on the slopes above. Which leaves the central 4-star Schermer and Jakobwirt as the obvious recommendations – both with pools.

There is apparently an ice rink in the middle of the village, although it's never caught the editorial eye. A toboggan run a mighty 7.5km in length is advertised from Talkaser, high on the slopes (reached by the gondola), via Fleidlingalm to Schrandlhof, with a free shuttle back to Westendorf. If you don't have the luxury

Ellmau has big, gentle nursery slopes next to the village, and grand views of the craggy Wilder Kaiser

of a hotel pool, for swimming it's off to the excellent facilities in Wörgl or Kitzbühel.

Sonnalm near the mid-station of the gondola makes a pleasant stop on the way home. The village is quite lively for a small place, with numerous bars doing good business at teatime and later.

Hopfgarten 620m

Hopfgarten is a little market town with old houses tightly huddled around its grand, twin-towered church. The gondola towards Hohe Salve goes up from one end of the village (well away from the industrial development at the other end), where there is also a nursery slope with a 100m moving carpet. The home run is an excellent red, but it gets the full afternoon sun so can suffer in warm weather.

There are half a dozen hotels, split equally 3-star and 4-star. Sportresort Hohe Salve is a 4-star right at the lift base, and Familotel Hopfgarten is just across the nursery slope. Both have pools.

There's a 2km toboggan run, floodlit, from Sunnseit Hütte to the village. At Salvenaland 2km south of the village there is skating and curling on a small lake.

Söll 700m

Söll is a pleasant but sprawling village which seems to be mostly suburb without much in the way of urb: the compact centre doesn't have much to offer. The gondola to Hochsöll – the smallest of mid-mountain satellite resorts, with a scattered handful of small guest houses – goes from a station 900m from the village centre, and some of the aforementioned suburbs are 700m further away, so life revolves around ski-buses. The nursery slope is also at the lift base.

Hochsöll is a key feature of the resort. There are various short lifts and runs here, and the resort's snowparks – the Crazy Kangaroo terrain park on the Rinner chair with easy and intermediate lines, and the Skiparcours Hans im Glück kids' fun park.

There is an excellent big area of floodlit skiing here, and the runs to the valley are lit too – it adds up to Austria's biggest area, they say. And two floodlit toboggan runs go from Hochsöll to the valley, easy and not so easy. Back in the day, Söll had a good little leisure centre, but it folded long ago, and now you have to travel down to Wörgl or along to Ellmau

to find a public swimming pool.

Söll has more hotel accommodation than any of the other SkiWelt bases – about 20 hotels and gasthofs, equally split 3-star and 4-star. The sister 4-star hotels Hexenalm and Hexenblick are at the lift base, on the nursery slope.

Söll isn't quite the après hotspot it was 30 years ago, but there are still some lively spots at the lift base and later on in the village.

Scheffau 745m

Scheffau is a much expanded little village about 1km away from the big Blaiken lift base, where two gondolas go up the Brandstadl, about in the middle of the core SkiWelt skiing. There's a gentle piste down to Blaiken, with buses to bring you back. Or you can bus both ways and leave your kit at Blaiken. There are modest hotels and guest houses in the heart of the village, and bigger, smarter places below and above it.

Ellmau 800m

Ellmau is a pleasantly traditional village clustered around its elegant church, with nursery slopes on two sides where lifts go up to little Astberg or to Hartkaiser for access to the core of the SkiWelt. To get to the Hartkaiser lift you must ride a nursery lift or take a ski-bus.
Up the mountain on the Tanzbodenbahn is Ellmau's snowpark, Kaiserpark, with easy and expert lines.

There is a floodlit toboggan run from Astberg. The Kaiserbad leisure centre has tennis, climbing walls and saunas as well as multiple pools.

There are a dozen hotels, more 4-star than 3-star. On the slopes above the lift base is an exceptional place – the 5-star S (Superior) hotel Kaiserhof.

There is some life in the village in the evening. A key après spot is the Ellmauer Alm, at the foot of Astberg.

Going 800m

Going is only a mile down the road from Ellmau, and they more or less share a broad area of nursery slopes from which a chair-lift goes up to the small, low ski area of Astberg. It's a quiet, pretty village, but it is in the worst possible position for skiing the SkiWelt as a whole. East of the village is a famously wonderful 5-star hotel, the Stanglwirt.

Stubaier Gletscher – Neustift

Neustift

The Stubaier Gletscher, at the head of the long Stubai valley, south-west of Innsbruck, may offer the world's best glacier skiing; or that accolade may belong to the Hintertux glacier, covered in the Ziller valley chapter at the end of the book. It doesn't matter – they're both great little ski areas blessed with excellent snow. The main lifts here go up from 2300m.

Hintertux is a tiny village, but at the valley station of this glacier there is only an isolated hotel; for resort diversions and atmosphere, you must look down the valley. There are hamlets with hotels and guest houses, but the first sizeable place is Neustift, 16km away. It's a pleasant village, with the bonus of its own wooded ski slopes for bad-weather days.

The mountains in brief

Size Small by normal standards, but this is as big as glacier areas go
Slopes Mainly treeless; large gentle areas but also plenty of challenges
Snow Mostly not glacial, in fact, but the altitudes ensure good snow
System, Lift As usual on glaciers, there are drags; but the main lifts are fast
Sustenance Few options, but some good and distinctive spots among them
For beginners There are many better places to start
For true blue skiers You can get around most of the area – enjoy the snow!
For the confident You need to be happy on the unprepared ski routes
For experts You'll soon exhaust the ski routes, and be tempted off-piste
Fancy stuff An impressive park, tucked away at the back of the area

Neustift – the resort in brief

Convenience It's a bus ride of almost half an hour to the glacier lifts
Lodgings A strikingly wide choice of hotels and guest houses
Bars and restaurants The après scene is muted; some good restaurants
Off the slopes A good public pool, and a choice of epic toboggan runs
For families You can take Tom and Dot up to the glacier if you must ...

Pass notes	Key facts		Key ratings	
For a small extra charge, the Stubaier Super Ski pass covers all the areas in the valley – and the swimming pools in Neustift and Telfes. The glacier offers no special pass deals for beginners, but there are very cheap passes for the valley-level beginner lift at Krössbach.	Altitude	1000m	Size	*
	Range	1695–3210m	Snow	*****
	Slopes	64km	Fast lifts	***
			Mountain rest's	****
	Where to stay, ideally		Beginner	**
	If skiing is everything, at the lift base. Otherwise, in central Neustift.		True blue	***
			Confident	***
	Websites		Expert	***
	stubaier-gletscher.com stubai.at		Convenience	**
			Families	***
			Village charm	****

The mountains in detail

At the head of the Stubai valley, gondolas go up to the glacier from two stations about 500m apart. The first gondola you reach is the major one (a three-cable lift with 32-person cabins) that goes via the Fernau middle station to Eisgrat; the second, minor gondola goes to the lower but focal point of Gamsgarten (shown in the photo over the page). The main slopes are above those points, but there are also very worthwhile slopes on the left of the map, above Fernau. There are ski routes to the valley from Gamsgarten and Fernau.

Size

This is one of the areas that responded positively to the work of Christoph Schrahe (read the intro to the book). It now publicises a modest 64km of runs (wrongly described as the 'fall line' figure) along with an inflated 'effective route' figure of 108km. So it rates only ✳ – but it claims to be Austria's biggest glacier ski area, and it possibly is.

Slopes

Although the area does offer summer skiing, it's on a much reduced area – roughly speaking, only the slopes above Eisgrat are on the glacier. But the whole area above Fernau is treeless, and most of it has typically gentle glacial gradients, though there are much steeper sections.

One third of the runs here are ski routes. They are neither prepared

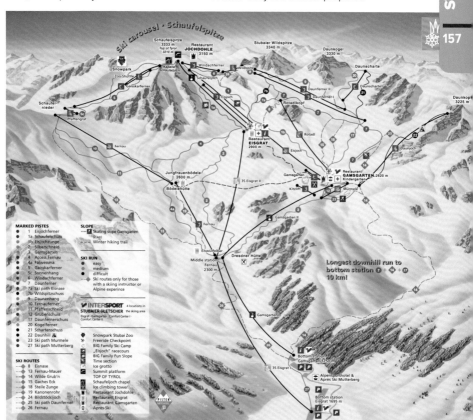

MARKED PISTES
- 1 Eisjochferner
- 1a Schaufelschuss
- 1b Eisjochzunge
- 2 Silberschneid
- 3 Gamsgarten
- 4 Access Fernau
- 4a Falavesina
- 5 Gaisskarferner
- 5c Sonnenhang
- 6 Windachferner
- 7 Daunferner
- 7a Ski path Eisrinse
- 7b Wildspitzschuss
- 9 Daunenhang
- 10 Fernauferner
- 11 Pfaffenschneid
- 12 Grubenschuss
- 17 Daunfernerschuss
- 20 Kogelferner
- 21 Schartenschuss
- 22 Daunhill ⚠
- 23 Ski path Murmele
- 27 Ski path Mutterberg

SKI ROUTES
- 8 Eisrinse
- 13 Fernau-Mauer
- 14 Wilde Grub'n
- 15 Gaches Eck
- 18 Steile Zunge
- 19 Kanonenrohr
- 24 Bildstöckljoch
- 25 Ski path Daunferner
- 26 Fernau

SLOPE
- Skating slope Gamsgarten (2 km)
- Winter hiking trail

SKI RUN
- ● easy
- ● medium
- ● difficult
- Ski routes only for those with a skiing instructor or Alpine experience

INTERSPORT 4 locations in
STUBAIER GLETSCHER the skiing area
Eisgrat · Gamsgarten · Comfort Center I ·
Comfort Center II

- Snowpark Stubai Zoo
- Freeride Checkpoint
- BIG Family Ski Camp „Eisjoch" racecourse
- BIG Family Fun Slope
- Time section
- Ice grotto
- Summit platform
- TOP OF TYROL
- Schaufeljoch chapel
- Ice climbing tower
- Restaurant Jochdohle
- Restaurant Eisgrat
- Restaurant Gamsgarten
- Après-Ski

Longest downhill run to bottom station ❶ · ⑮ · ㉗ 10 km!

nor patrolled. Adding to the standard confusion in Austria, the piste map here also says: 'only for those with a skiing instructor or Alpine experience'. Over to you – do you qualify?

The lift company also publicises 13 off-piste routes which are marked and described on a separate map (downloadable) and can be followed using a special smartphone app. These are not avalanche-safe – they are not declared open or closed.

Leading skiers to go off-piste with only an app for guidance sounds like a big mistake. But wait! 'The freeride runs should be undertaken exclusively with state certified ... guides,' says the small print. So why the map, and the app? The lift company is pretending to facilitate freeriding, while covering its back.

The core area above Fernau offers a worthwhile vertical of just over 900m, while a full top-to-bottom descent amounts to over 1500m vertical and a length of 10km – impressive statistics.

Snow

For a conventional winter holiday, you should have no worries about snow. The area's winter season runs from mid-October to early May.

System, Lift

The access lifts are impressively powerful, and all the long chair-lifts are fast. On the higher glacial slopes there are drag-lifts, as usual on such slopes. The main flaw is that the left-hand lift above Fernau, nowhere near the glacier, is a T-bar 900m long. The Eisjoch six-seat chair-lift from Gamsgarten, stretching 2.7km to the top of the area, is naturally popular, so can build queues.

Sustenance

There aren't many restaurants, but enough for a small area, and there are some special spots.

Dresdner Hütte, at the bottom of the main slopes near Fernau, is a big stone-built refuge for climbers and walkers, managed by the same family for 100 years, with lovely panelled rooms. At the main mid-stations, as well as big, efficient self-service options there are two excellent table-service restaurants – Zur Goldenen Gams at Gamsgarten and the more ambitious Schaufelspitz at Eisgrat. At the top of the slopes, and said to be the highest eatery in the Tirol, the self-service Jochdohle would appeal mightily to one of two of our skiing chums: it specialises in giant schnitzels.

The mid-mountain facilities at Gamsgarten are big-scale – including an impressive children's nursery area

More on the slopes

For beginners

There are beginner lifts at Gamsgarten, but there is no sign of an economic way to use them – you need a full pass – and you face the hassle getting to and riding the access lifts for precious little benefit.

For true blue skiers

In traditional glacier-area style, most of the upper slopes are thoroughly gentle. In both the main sector above the two big mid-stations and in the Fernau sector on the left of the map, there is great easy cruising. There's blue skiing at the very top, on the back of the peak, as well.

There are some negatives to take into account. There is no very easy piste from Eisgrat down to Gamsgarten (though the red is an easy one, and you can get there by two roundabout routes involving lifts). And, more importantly, there is no easy run to the valley station – the two ski routes are genuine red routes.

For confident intermediates

The key thing to note is that a great deal of the red that dominates the map is in the form of ski routes. If you can hack them, the routes are very rewarding; but they mostly have pitches approaching black gradient, which you can expect to be heavily mogulled. And, of course, after a snowfall they'll be blanketed in deep powder. They're also unpatrolled, so not to be skied alone.

The most demanding route is on the left of the map, run 13 Fernau-Mauer, which after a long cruise plunges down a proper black pitch. The routes to the valley are excellent.

The higher red pistes are mainly indistinguishable from the adjacent blue runs. Run 11 Pfaffenschneid, for example, is of red steepness only at the very end. The two runs that go lower, to Fernau, are proper reds, and very enjoyable. But they don't add up to a lot of skiing.

For experts

The pistes don't offer much in the way of challenge – the short blacks on the high slopes touch black gradient only briefly, and the longer run 22 Daunhill mainly cuts across the steep slope at the top.

The ski routes can be entertaining, but they don't add up to a lot, so you'll naturally be drawn to the off-piste routes described under 'Slopes'. And you'll then have to decide whether to follow the injunction to ski only with a guide. Some of these off-piste routes are difficult to resist – taking a steeper way down from the Daunjoch chair that serves the Daunhill piste, for example.

Fancy stuff

The impressive Zoo Park is on the sunny back side of Schaufelspitze, with easy, medium and pro lines, served by a drag-lift. It opens with a well-established hardware test weekend in late October. There's a 1km family funslope on the Eisjoch drag-lift.

Neustift – the resort

Neustift is an attractive village on the gently sloping sunny side of the Stubaital. Among its attractions are a good leisure centre, and a small area of low, wooded skiing in the Elfer area. This has a red run of 800m vertical served by a gondola from the edge of the village, and a couple of short drags at the top, one of them adding a further 250m vertical – a good option for bad-weather days. The bigger Schlick 2000 area is 6km away.

Convenience

The village overall is about 1.2km long, and the Elfer gondola is at one end, about 400m from the centre. Ski-bus services run the length of the Stubai valley, with several per hour to the glacier and the Elfer lift at peak times. To reach the glacier lifts takes about 25 minutes.

Lodgings

There is a surprising amount of accommodation spread along the valley, of all kinds. The Jagdhof is a Relais & Châteaux 5-star just outside the village – remote from the Elfer lift, where there is a cluster of big 4-star hotels; choose between two with the Superior classification – the Sporthotel Neustift and the Alpeiner. For a more modest place in the heart of the village you won't beat the welcoming Hoferwirt.

Bars and restaurants

You may well have started your post-skiing indulgence up on the glacier, of course – the glass-walled Schneekristall bar at Gamsgarten aims to attract après business with live music. There are, of course, bars in Neustift (eg the Dorf), but this is not a resort that attracts a big-drinking crowd.

The Hoferwirt has a good mid-market restaurant, and naturally the luxy Jagdhof has a top-notch one, the Hubertus Stube, with two toques from the Gault-Millau guide. There are plenty of more modest places – the funky Herr Klaus does good steaks and burgers.

Off the slopes

There's a leisure centre with bowling, a smart pool, 70m slide, sauna, steam, massage etc; entry is covered by the valley lift pass, which is an excellent deal. On the Elfer there are two toboggan runs, both claimed to be 8km long, open daytime and three evenings a week.

There are walking routes up on the ski slopes and in the next-door Pinnistal.

For families

The glacier lift company goes out of its way to appeal to families, and there are excellent kids' facilities at Gamsgarten. We're not sure we see the point of dragging kids up to 2600m, though. A better plan might be to use the gentle village slopes at Krössbach, 5km up the valley from Neustift, where very cheap passes are available.

Neustift isn't quite within sight of the Stubaier glacier, but it is the nearest resort village, 16km from the lifts

Zell am See-Kaprun

Zell am See / Schüttdorf / Kaprun

As a glance at the piste map and the photo following it will show, Zell is a most unusual ski resort, set on a promontory on a fair-sized lake. As you might guess, it enjoys good business in the summer, and as a result has grown into a sizeable town, with a definite urban feel.

Zell's mountain, Schmitten, is unusual too: horseshoe-shaped, with steep runs down into the central valley. It is a small area, but in 2018 should complete a link with Saalbach in the next valley – an imperfect link, involving a short bus ride, but good enough to make outings viable.

Zell markets itself with Kaprun, 6km away, which has the key asset of the fair-sized Kitzsteinhorn glacier area.

The mountains in brief

Size One of the smallest areas in the book – but the Saalbach link is coming
Slopes Packs in a wide variety, from open cruises to forest steeps
Snow Altitude and orientation countered by comprehensive snowmaking
System, Lift Generally impressive, though with some problem areas
Sustenance Plenty of good spots with table service
For beginners Adequate slopes, but they're not handy for central Zell
For true blue skiers If you really do ski only blue runs, you could go mad
For the confident Lots to do, within the constraints of the area's small size
For experts One or two proper black pistes, but not much off-piste
Fancy stuff A modest terrain park, but an impressively long funslope

Zell am See – the resort in brief

Convenience Bearable walks in general, and some slope-side lodgings
Lodgings The usual Austrian range, with lots of 4-star hotels
Bars and restaurants Lively bars; a better range of restaurants than usual
Off the slopes Unimpressive tobogganing; great aquatic centre at Kaprun
For families OK if you stay out at Schüttdorf (or Kaprun)

Pass notes	Key facts		Key ratings	
Passes for 2+ days are also valid for Kitzsteinhorn/ Kaprun. For a small extra cost, the Super Ski card covers everything from Hintertux to Schladming, including nearby Saalbach and its linked resorts. Beginners can pay for valley lifts by the ride or buy special day passes for valley lifts.	Altitude	760m	Size	*
	Range (Zell)	760–2000m	Snow	**
	Slopes (see text)	77km	Fast lifts	****
	Where to stay, ideally		Mountain rest's	****
	In Zell, within walking distance of the CityXpress gondola.		Beginner	***
			True blue	**
	Websites		Confident	****
	zellamsee-kaprun.com schmitten.at kitzsteinhorn.at		Expert	***
			Convenience	***
			Families	***
			Village charm	****

The mountains in detail

You can access the southern ridge of the Schmitten horseshoe by riding a gondola from the fringes of Zell; or you can take a bus a mile or two into the heart of the horseshoe, where another gondola and a cable car go up to the area high-point of Schmittenhöhe. There are runs along the southern arm back to Zell and to Schüttdorf (where there is another gondola, upgraded in 2017) and, from the arm, steeply down into the central valley.

From that valley another cable car goes up to an area of sunny runs on the northern arm of the horseshoe. There are runs outside the horseshoe, too, including an isolated long run into the next-door Saalbach valley.

Size

Zell claims 77km of runs, ski routes included. This seems a bit high for an area you can ski, more or less, in a morning – and the lift company admits it does apply a multiplier to its run lengths to arrive at its published figure (read the book's introduction for more on this).

But 2018 should see the completion of the short lower stage of the gondola up from Viehhofen in the Saalbach valley. Saalbach has a piste to Viehhofen, but no lift from there – so accessing Saalbach from Zell will involve a short bus ride to the lift at Vorderglemm. Mileage-hungry skiers will find it well worthwhile. But will Saalbach-Zell dare to present itself as a single area? We guess not.

Keen skiers will also want to make day trips to Kaprun's Kitzsteinhorn. The buses are frequent at key times, but the trip takes a tedious 35 minutes.

Slopes

Although most of the skiing is below the treeline, many runs are very broad and open-feeling. At the top, on the back of the hill, the runs are largely open but with some lightly wooded slopes – glades, you might call them. The mountain offers a good range of gradient.

Many of the runs are quite short, but a fair few offer satisfying verticals, at least when snow low down is good. The southern ridge offers a descent of over 1100m vertical from the top of the Areit gondola, and the TrassXpress gondola serving the Trass black run into the central valley offers a vertical of around 950m. The red run to Viehhofen currently offers about 800m vertical, to which another 200m or so will be added when the link is completed.

There are several short ski routes, unexplained on the map.

Snow

Our standard warning about the low resorts in this part of the world applies: these days, snowmaking may be good enough to keep runs to the valley reliably open but, with lift bases under 800m, you can't expect great snow conditions on the lower slopes, especially later in the season. Be prepared for ice and/or slush, and count yourself lucky if you find packed powder.

In this case, the orientation isn't ideal, either: the runs along the southern ridge face south-east, and a lot of the skiing on the northern ridge faces south. But there is quite a bit of skiing above 1400m.

Of course, if conditions are poor, you have the backup of skiing on the Kitzsteinhorn, but you won't be alone.

There's floodlit skiing three evenings per week from the Ebenberg chair-lift on the lower slopes, overlooking the town.

System, Lift

The system is pretty slick, with gondolas or fast chairs in all the key positions. The first stage of the Schüttdorf gondola was upgraded in 2017, increasing its capacity by 50%. There are some short slow lifts on the northern ridge, and on the back of the hill, but they don't have much impact on your enjoyment of the area.

Six of the cabins on the lift back from Saalbach have built-in jukebox systems controlled by smartphone apps; sounds like an absolute nightmare.

Sustenance

There are almost 20 restaurants, which is a good number for a small area, and all but one do table service. (About half do self-service as well, we note without much interest.) They are named as well as marked on the piste map.

The pick is Hochzelleralm on the northern ridge – good food and friendly service in a cosily beamed hut; head upstairs for more space. AreitAlm at the top of the first stage of the gondola from Schüttdorf has been rebuilt in fine style as AreitLounge. Pinzgauer Hütte is a bit special – in a lovely secluded position about 600m away from the pistes; skidoo tows back to the piste are available.

More on the slopes

For beginners

There are various beginner slopes, but none is close to downtown Zell. Between Schüttdorf and the base station of the Areit gondola are the gentlest slopes, served by the Schmidolins moving carpet and the 80m Bambilift rope-tow. At the major lift base in the Schmittental are the 100m Schmidolin rope-tow and the 330m Fallegg drag. Day or part-day passes are available for these lifts.

There are also beginner lifts higher up. At the top of the gondola from the town is the 100m Enzian rope-tow. At the top of the Areit gondola from Schüttdorf is a kids' moving carpet with tunnel.

All in all, these are not great options if you choose to stay amid the bright lights of the resort, and you might want to consider staying in Schüttdorf or in the Schmittental for more direct access.

For true blue skiers

There are short gentle blue slopes on the back of Schmittenhöhe, and slightly longer ones at mid-mountain on the southern ridge of the horseshoe. The blue linking those two areas, on the upper part of the ridge, is a bit more testing in places, but properly classified blue. From mid-mountain there is a winding blue run to the valley, but we thought it tricky – too narrow, too busy, too bumpy for comfort.

So for a blue-run skier there is skiing to be done, but not a great deal of it.

The lakeside setting is fab, and they say the lake does freeze over, at times; note the black runs on the right

When the lift link with Saalbach is completed, blue-run skiers will be able to explore that area, perhaps with more confident friends, by riding the linking gondola down to Viehhofen.

For confident intermediates

For confident and competent intermediates, this is a much better mountain. The blue along the southern ridge is not so easy as to be pointless, and the red runs are genuine reds.

Run 4 to Schüttdorf is a long, varied red, rewarding in good snow – very testing when its quite sunny orientation is having an effect. The sunny runs below Sonnkogel are well worth spending time on, and on the back of the ridge the shady black run down to the Ketting chair-lift is nothing to be afraid of. But perhaps the highlight of the skiing on the northern ridge is the new red run (actually a revived old ski route) to Viehhofen – shady, long and of proper red gradient.

If you're tempted by the blacks dropping into the Schmittental from the southern ridge, take snow conditions into account. Read the next section.

Outings to Kaprun's Kitzsteinhorn are well worthwhile in good weather, even if the snow on the Schmitten is OK.

For experts

Zell makes quite a fuss about its two major black pistes, and they are indeed excellent runs, though not particularly steep. Run 13 is great fun, following a quite tight, shady, winding course through the woods, but it's only just black in gradient, and less than 500m vertical. Run 14 Trass is more of a test: longer (almost 800m), more prone to ice, broader but steeper – they say 35°/70%, but that must be over a very short pitch in its central section.

The other blacks dotted around the map are short and generally easy. There's more challenge to be found in the numerous short ski routes, mostly on the northern ridge of the horseshoe.

Off-piste terrain is pretty much limited to the small open and glade areas on the back of Schmittenhöhe and on the top part of the northern ridge. There's much more at Kitzsteinhorn.

Fancy stuff

Zell's fancy stuff is on the sunny slopes below Sonnkogel – a modest terrain park with beginner and intermediate sections, and a funslope that is anything but modest – Zell claims it is the longest such slope in the world, at 1.3km.

Zell – the resort

Zell is an important town as well as a winter and summer resort – it has shops obviously serving locals as well as visitors, and a prosperous urban ambience. The major through-road is buried in a tunnel, and the heart of the town is traffic-free, but there is still quite a bit of local traffic through the town. It's all very different from your typical Austrian ski-resort village.

Convenience

The CityXPress gondola is close to the centre, and there are hotels nearby. Most are in or around the central pedestrian zone, typically 300m from the lift.

Lodgings

There is the usual range; 4-star hotels outnumber 3-stars. There are two 4-star hotels in ski-in ski-out locations on the home slopes: the Alpin is above the gondola base, the Berner nearer the chair. In the Schmittental, the 4-star AlpineResort is next to the nursery slope.

Bars and restaurants

Right at the top of the hill, the big terrace of the Berghotel's SchnapsHans bar gets very lively in the afternoon, as does the first hut on the way down to Zell, Breiteckalm. There are several places to go in the town, from the tiny sports bar O'Flannigans and the rather smoother Ginhouse to the more animated Pinzgauer Diele and Villa Crazy Daisy, both open until 4am.

Crazy Daisy does decent food, and there is an unusually wide choice of other good restaurants at all budget levels, up to the swanky Stube of the hotel Salzburgerhof. Good mid-market options include the central hotel zum Hirschen.

Off the slopes

300m from the centre is a leisure centre with spa, 25m pool, kids' pool and tube-slide, bowling and big ice rink. (Tauern Spa at Kaprun is much more fun, though.) Tobogganing is limited to a floodlit run of about 1km down the Schmittental from the Köhlergraben guest house. There are lots of marked footpaths, some at altitude, and very extensive cross-country trails.

The Kitzsteinhorn is an extensive glacier area, with something for everybody – experts included

For families

A towny resort like this isn't a natural fit for a family holiday. Of course there are kids' practice areas, and by the Glockner chair-lift at mid-mountain there is a kids' funslope, with obstacles, waves and tunnels. Schüttdorf makes the best base.

The Schüttdorf option

Schüttdorf is now bigger than Zell, but it isn't a conventional holiday resort – it has only a handful of hotels, all 4-star. The Latini is by the nursery slopes, 300m from the Areit lift.

Kaprun / Kitzsteinhorn

Kaprun is a pleasant, sizeable resort a 35-minute bus ride from Zell, with the tiny Maiskogel area on the edge of the village, peaking at 1730m, and an extensive glacier ski area beneath the splendid peak of Kitzsteinhorn.

Kitzsteinhorn

It's an area of two halves, roughly, divided by the big, multipurpose Alpincenter complex – a larger upper area of intermediate pistes and a lower area of stiffer slopes, mostly ski routes.

Size Doing the sums with the claimed size figures for all the local ski areas, we arrive at a claimed extent of about 40km – small. There is an impressive plan to bridge the 4km gap between the Kitzsteinhorn and the smaller Maiskogel with a three-cable gondola in 2019.

Slopes Only the highest part of the ski area is actually on the glacier, but much of it is on rock shaped by the glacier, so it is treeless, and largely gentle. But there are also some steeper ski routes towards the bottom. Overall, the area offers over 1000m vertical.

Snow Even if it is largely non-glacial, the area is high enough to be confident of good snow for a long season.

System, Lift The major lifts are fast (gondolas and cable cars) but there are quite a few slow chairs and drag-lifts.

Sustenance There are three self-service restaurants including a large food court operation at Alpincenter, one table service (Gletschermühle) and one place (Gipfel, at the top) doing both.

More on the slopes

For beginners It makes more sense to start on friendly slopes at valley level.

For true blue skiers There's quite a bit to do here – you can get around much of the upper part of the area on blue runs,

and with good snow tackle easier reds.

For confident intermediates It's a good place to practise your carving, and venture on to freeride routes with the benefit of good snow. Red runs 2 and 11, both on skier's right, are the best pistes.

For experts The black pistes are a bit of a joke, but the several freeride routes are worthwhile, though most are quite short. The routes on skier's left of the central lifts are stiffer than those on skier's right. Much fuss is made over the Black Mamba piste; but it's just a normal (short) black.

There is plenty of easy off-piste to explore between and outside the pistes. There are off-piste routes going to points in the valley near the lift base. And long routes going north into the Mühlbachtal, ending near Niedernsill.

Fancy stuff There are several parks – Easy Park, Central Park (for intermediates and pros) and at the top of the area the small Glacier Park. There is a super-pipe, said to be Austria's biggest. The Eagle Line is a 1km funslope.

Kaprun

Kaprun is a widely spread village with a good range of accommodation. On one side is the chair-lift for Maiskogel, on the other an excellent nursery area, Lechnerberg (the two about 500m apart). The Kitzsteinhorn access lifts are 5km to the south. On the lower slopes of Maiskogel is a sled-on-rails coaster, Maisiflitzer. The Tauern Spa is a great asset – a huge aquatic centre 1km to the north, with various pools, saunas etc.

Ziller valley

Mayrhofen / Hintertux / Hochfügen-Hochzillertal / Zillertal Arena
Three major ski areas – and one of the world's best glaciers

The Zillertal is best known in Britain through the long-standing popularity of Mayrhofen, a resort with wide appeal, backed up by the snow guarantee of the Hintertux glacier slopes a bearable bus ride away up the valley.

But the valley has much more to offer than that. Its standard multi-day lift pass, the Zillertal Superskipass, also covers the slopes of Zillertal Arena, starting from Zell im Zillertal and stretching via Gerlos to Königsleiten, and Hochfügen-Hochzillertal, above Kaltenbach and Fügen. Altogether they claim to offer almost 180 lifts and about 500km of pistes.

All of these areas have a non-trivial feature distinguishing them from better-known areas a few miles east (Ski Juwel, SkiWelt, Kitzbühel, Saalbach) – altitude. The villages are low, in the standard Austrian way, but the skiing is almost all above the forest that blankets the steep valley sides, and the top heights are pretty high by Tirolean standards.

We describe the four main ski areas in detail, but give only brief descriptions of resorts other than Mayrhofen – it makes a great base for the valley. At certain times of year, of course, Hintertux makes more sense.

Buses between the resorts are covered by the lift pass – and so is the narrow-gauge railway that runs up the valley as far as Mayrhofen.

Mayrhofen

Mayrhofen / Finkenberg / Vorderlanersbach / Lanersbach

Mayrhofen is the major resort of the Zillertal, and much the best known in Britain. The village is lively and attractive, with the spacious neatness of an established summer resort.

Two mountains are accessible from the village, the larger Penken forming part of a sizeable area spreading up the valley to Lanersbach. Ahorn is an excellent additional resource: small but high, quiet, with efficient lifts – a great place to start, if you don't mind being segregated.

Set near the point where the road starts to climb from the flat valley floor towards Hintertux, Mayrhofen is also well placed as a base for full exploration of the territory covered by the valley pass.

The mountains in brief

Size A mid-sized area, if you include the awkwardly linked Eggalm slopes
Slopes Nearly all above the trees; a mix on Penken, easy slopes elsewhere
Snow No serious worries – and you can always fall back on Hintertux
System, Lift Pretty efficient; riding down may still be a problem at times
Sustenance One or two special places, and plenty of other options
For beginners Good slopes, but up the mountain – lift pass required
For true blue skiers Pretty good, considering the lie of the land
For the confident Lots to do, with a good range of reds and easy blacks
For experts One serious challenge on-piste, and quite a bit of off-piste
Fancy stuff A world-class park, and a funslope for the rest of us

Mayrhofen – the resort in brief

Convenience Not a strength; picking your spot can be tricky
Lodgings A couple of catered chalets, as well as the usual range
Bars and restaurants Throbbing bars are available at all hours
Off the slopes The good leisure centre is the highlight
For families Not ideal – the kids' areas aren't exactly handy

Pass notes	Key facts		Key ratings	
Day passes are available for the local slopes. For 2+ days, the Zillertal Superskipass is sold, covering the whole valley. There are no special payment arrangements for beginners, who need a full lift pass from day one.	Altitude	630m	Size	✱✱✱
	Range	630–2500m	Snow	✱✱✱
	Slopes (see text)	136km	Fast lifts	✱✱✱✱
	Where to stay, ideally		Mountain rest's	✱✱✱
	In central Mayrhofen, a walk from the main lifts.		Beginner	✱✱
			True blue	✱✱✱
	Websites		Confident	✱✱✱✱
	mayrhofen.at		Expert	✱✱✱
	mayrhofner-bergbahnen.com		Convenience	✱✱
	hintertuxergletscher.at		Families	✱✱
	zillertal.at		Village charm	✱✱✱

The mountains in detail

Mayrhofen has two local mountains, both accessible directly from the village. Much the larger is Penken-Horberg-Rastkogel, which we'll often refer to as Penken. Penken and Horberg are separated by a shallow, steep-sided valley; at the head of that valley is the link to the Rastkogel slopes, above the small village of Vorderlanersbach. From there you can progress by harmless ski route or gondola descent to Eggalm, above Lanersbach.

Penken is reached by a big gondola from the main street of Mayrhofen, and by two others, both 3km away. One is to the south-west, at the small village of Finkenberg. The other, going to the shallow valley between Penken and Horberg, goes up from a point north of Mayrhofen between Mühlbach and Schwendau. This is the main access point for drivers; don't plan on buying a lift pass here on a high-season Sunday.

There are no pistes from Penken to the valley – only a ski route to the Horberg lift base which we have never known to be open. So everyone has to ride down at the end of the day.

Size

The lift company claims 136km of slopes, properly measured, but this includes Ahorn. Christoph Schrahe reckons the figure is a bit high, but in any event this is a mid-sized area, scraping into the ✱✱✱ size category. This does assume you are happy to access Lanersbach's Eggalm slopes by ski route, gondola or bus up the valley – there is no piste link from Rastkogel; but the ski route is easy.

An undoubted attraction of Mayrhofen is that you are well placed here to ski Hintertux, Zillertal Arena (starting at Zell) and Hochfügen-Hochzillertal. One way or another, you should find enough to do.

Slopes

Penken is a classic intermediate mountain, with red runs all over the place, a decent sprinkling of blues and a few nominal black runs that are mostly just serious reds.

The infamous exception to that casual dismissal of the steeper stuff is piste 34, Harakiri, on the shady side of Penken; this is claimed to be Austria's steepest piste, although there are competing claims from other resorts. Read 'For experts'.

Virtually all the skiing is above the treeline, which is at about 1700m. There are exceptions: Lanersbach's Eggalm sector extends down through the trees to the valley, and its Eggalm Nord six-seater chair-lift is the one to head for on a bad-weather day. Ahorn has an excellent long piste down to its valley cable car station, recently re-classified black from red.

The defining characteristic of the skiing, arguably, is that most of the lifts and runs are quite short – verticals of around 400m are typical. Given good snow, you can put together longer descents on Eggalm.

There are three or four ski routes on the map. Here, as in so many resorts, the

SKI- & GLETSCHERWELT
ZILLERTAL
3000

status of ski routes is unclear. You can be confident that they are marked in some way, not exposed to avalanches, but not patrolled; but grooming is unpredictable. Read the introduction to the book for more on this. Route 75 linking the Rastkogel sector to the foot of Eggalm seems in every way like a piste, and is probably classified as a ski route because it is rather narrow.

Snow

You spend most of your day here skiing at around 2000m, which is high by the standards of the eastern Tirol and Salzburgerland, although no match for resorts further west such as Ischgl, Sölden and Obergurgl. But it is high enough to give reasonable confidence of good natural snow, unless there is a drought.

Snowmaking covers all the main pistes and is well used. In particular, even when the valley is turning green, the Ahorn valley run is thickly blanketed. Many slopes get quite a lot of sun, so conditions in late season are likely to be affected.

You have the additional security of the high and partly glacial slopes at Hintertux, described in this chapter – one of the best skiing glaciers in the Alps. If snow is in short supply, you won't be alone.

System, Lift

It's a generally impressive lift system – not quite challenging Ischgl and Saalbach in the top Austrian league, but with a good array of fast chairs including lots of six-seaters and several eight-seaters.

The resort has a long history of struggling to keep pace with demand for access from the village to the slopes. The latest gondola, installed in 2015, is a state-of-the-art three-cable affair carrying 2,880 people per hour up the hill in its 24-seat, Wi-Fi-equipped cabins and an even more impressive 3,840 per hour down the hill. This is to deal with the more concentrated crowds at the end of the day – achieved by herding a further eight people into each cabin, standing.

If at the absolute peak the new lift turns out to be a bit stretched, you still have the option of riding buses to use one of the other gondolas. As we write in 2017 the ancient Finkenberg four-seat gondola to mid-mountain is being replaced by a more powerful 10-seater. The one above is already an eight-seater.

Other highlights of the system include the oddity of Austria's largest cable car (carrying 160) accessing the limited, quiet slopes of Ahorn – probably accounted for by a typo on the order form.

The famously steep black piste Harakiri, with the return piste from Rastkogel on the ridge in the distance

Sustenance

The piste map is plastered with dozens of yellow symbols indicating mountain restaurants, which are clearly named. Rustic Alpine charm and table service are common, as usual in Austria.

For years the standout place has been Schneekarhütte, on Horberg. The beamed interior is well up to scratch, with log fires and the occasional sofa. Individual tables can be reserved, not only inside but on the terrace – rare in Austria. And there's great food, which is a world away from the standard sausage and chips – eg Flammkuchen, organic steaks, braised lamb.

In a radical and welcome departure from tourist office norms, the resort's website carries a review of the best places for Kaiserschmarrn. It names Schneekar as one of the top two, along with the smart Granatalm on Penken, crisply architect-designed (in wood) to replace the owners' more modest previous enterprise, Christa's Skialm. It has a spacious self-service and three cosier table-service stuben.

Among countless other worthwhile spots, an honorable mention goes to the modern, spacious Panorahma, also on Penken. Or, for a peaceful change of scene, seek out the secluded Gschösswandhaus, on its own little ski route below the Penkenbahn top station.

More on the slopes

For beginners

There are beginner lifts on gentle slopes both on Ahorn and at the top of the Penken gondola. Both have longer gentle blues easily accessible. You need a full lift pass for either. So the mountain works quite well – but you do need a lift pass.

For true blue skiers

Despite the generally quite steep nature of the terrain, the blue runs on the map are genuine blues and have been quite carefully arranged so that with a bit of planning you can get around most of the area. On Penken there are runs to the top of the main gondola and down into the high valley separating Penken from Horberg. Then there are runs on the Tappenalm and Schneekar chair-lifts. If you're feeling more confident, take a look at the reds on the sunny side of Penken, which are relatively gentle.

Back in that high valley, you can get to the big cable car to Rastkogel, which is a lovely open area of easy skiing. Many of the reds here are of blue gradient; sadly, advising which to avoid is complicated by the ludicrous Austrian habit of using one number for multiple runs.

Ahorn is worth a visit – high, sunny, quiet, gentle ... bliss.

For confident intermediates

It's a good mountain for keen intermediate skiers. You're unlikely to find yourself on Harakiri by accident – there are dramatic warnings at the top – and very little else is likely to cause distress.

The most interesting skiing is in the high valley between Penken and Horberg, and at Eggalm, which is quieter than Penken and offers proper red runs of up to 1000m vertical.

The reds at Rastkogel are at the easy end of the spectrum, but worth a look. The red run 66 back from Rastkogel to Penken is something else. In many resorts it would be classified black; what's more, it gets full sun, and in the afternoon gets crowded. All in all, late in the day it is pretty challenging. If in doubt, there is no shame in taking the short drag to the cable car station and riding down.

Don't miss the excellent fake black run from Ahorn to the valley.

For experts

The black pistes vary widely. The infamous Harakiri is certainly very steep – though if it reaches the claimed gradient of 78% (38°), it's not for very long. We've once found good snow on the run and enjoyed it a lot, but we've generally found the snow very hard, going on icy, which makes the run a serious challenge. If you fall, you will slide a long way. The best plan is to ride the Knorren chair beside the run to see whether others are managing to get an edge.

None of the other blacks come near that – in particular, run 33 just across the mountainside is barely of black gradient. Run 12 on Horberg is steep only at the very bottom. Run 45 is steep only at the very start. Both are sunny, 45 particularly so, which can affect things, of course. We've never tried run 56 down the 150er cable car from Wanglspitz – we've found the red enough of a handful.

The lovely valley run from Ahorn used to be red, and in our view should be still.

There is lots of off-piste terrain in and around the lift network, including quite a few routes from the high-points of the system, notably Wanglspitz and Horberg – and even more if you are prepared to do some hiking. From the top of

Mayrhofen is a pleasantly spacious, towny village with a life outside of skiing; the core is largely traffic-free

Rastkogel, for example, you can hike up to Horbergjoch for a 10km run via Pangert to Schwendau in the Zillertal.

Fancy stuff

The Vans Penken park, actually on the sunny lower slopes of Horberg, is claimed to be one of Europe's best, and certainly looks it, with dozens of metallic obstacles and close to a dozen kickers. There are several different sections to suit different levels of competence, including a separate kids' park. Twice a week there are photo shoot sessions when your tricks can be recorded for later download.

On Ahorn there is a funslope, 650m long, with waves and turns designed to be tackled by children and novices.

Mayrhofen – the resort

Mayrhofen's combination of towny polish and rustic setting is attractive. The village is well bypassed by the valley road, and the main street is pretty well traffic free – and lively in the evening.

Convenience

The core of the village, the pedestrian high street, is quite long. At the north end, you have the church, tourist office, bus/railway station (terminus of the valley narrow-gauge railway) and some long-established hotels; 700m away to the south is the Penken gondola, with its throbbing bars. The Ahorn cable car is a further 300m south. So there are some quite long walks, and picking your spot can be tricky.

Lodgings

There is the usual Austrian mix of lodgings, plus the rarity of a couple of mid-sized catered chalets. Inghams has one about in the middle of the high street, and Skiworld has one near the Ahorn cable car – but a bearable walk to the Penken gondola.

The top hotel in town is the 4-star S ElisabethHotel, in a good position between the high street and the bypass. If you want to be at the heart of the action, you want to be in the 4-star hotel Strass, next to the Penken gondola. If you don't, head to the other end of the high street and the Neuhaus or Neue Post. Alternatively, you might like to consider the hotel Sieghard in Hippach – read 'Bars and restaurants'.

If routine lodgings are no longer enough, check in to the White Lounge igloo village on the Ahorn.

Bars and restaurants

Given the numbers wanting to ride down, it's only natural that a bit of drinking should go on at the mountain stations at teatime. Then, there are two lively bars at the bottom of the Horberg gondola, while in Mayrhofen the Ice Bar in the hotel Strass gets rammed, as does the nearby Brück'n Stadl. There are countless other bars and clubs around the village.

There are plenty of places to eat. For satisfying Austrian food, look at Tiroler Stuben near the station and Wirtshaus zum Griena. But probably the best restaurant around is a few km down the valley in Hippach, the hotel Sieghard – two toques from the Gault-Millau guide.

Off the slopes

Erlebnisbad Mayrhofen is an impressive aquatic centre with various pools, flumes and other water features, plus sauna and other spa stuff.

If you ski the valley run from Ahorn, halfway down you'll pass the Gasthof Wiesenhof, and you have the chance to gauge what would be involved in hiking up with a toboggan in tow to then enjoy a rather more rapid 2.5km descent (vertical 420m). The hut stays open for meals in the evening, but the run is not floodlit. You can take a taxi halfway, they say.

There are quite a few cross-country trails in the valley, both near Mayrhofen and higher up around Lanersbach. And prepared paths amount to 80km, including walks up on Ahorn.

For families

A weakness of the resort is that it seems to lack convenient valley-level snow gardens. Different schools have their practice areas up on Ahorn or on Penken. But there is also a Kinderland practice area next to the Horberg gondola station, 3km away down the valley.

Alternatives to Mayrhofen

Finkenberg has another gondola into the Penken slopes, but not much else to recommend it unless you like the look of a particular hotel. Like Mayrhofen, it has no home run. Lanersbach and the almost merging Vorderlanersbach do have skiing to the valley, and good access to the slopes of Eggalm and Rastkogel. For a quiet time, worth considering.

Finkenberg 840m

Finkenberg is a curious spot. It is set at the point where the valley road climbs from the flat Ziller valley at about 650m towards Lanersbach at twice that altitude. The heart of the place really is the giant 5-star hotel Stock (they prefer to call it a resort), set where the road goes through double hairpin bends. The church is nearby, and other hotels and guest houses are dotted around, but It doesn't have much of a village feel.

The gondola station is 200m further up the hill. There is another pair of hairpins here, and another area of housing including more guest houses.

There is efficient access to Penken – the gondola was upgraded to a 10-seater in 2017. There are short blue runs at the very top, but they are on the steep side for complete beginners. The piste map no longer marks a ski route back to the village from the mid-station; but it always was of doubtful value – the slope faces south-east, and is rarely fit to be skied. It does of course now form an off-piste route home.

There is skating and curling near the gondola lift station, but we see no sign of any toboggan runs.

All in all, we see no great attraction in staying in Finkenberg unless you are set on 5-star luxury – Mayrhofen can offer only a 4-star S hotel in competition.

Vorderlanersbach 1300m

Vorderlanersbach is a bit more village-like, still set on the valley road but on more or less level ground with some open space where a stream passes through. Curiously, it is the base village for Rastkogel (reached by a gondola close to the centre) but has a piste only from Eggalm, above Lanersbach. If contemplating a stay here, read the earlier sections to figure out whether this would work for you.

You have a choice of one 3-star hotel and three 4-stars, of which the stylish 4-star S Tuxerhof looks the best bet, slightly off the main road and close to the gondola. But you might want to ask for a room remote from the HexenKessl bar across the street, which gets pretty lively and stays open late.

Lanersbach 1300m

Up the valley from Vorderlanersbach, houses and hotels are dotted along the road for about a mile before you reach the gondola station for Eggalm beyond which is downtown Lanersbach. In pole position across the main road from the lift is the 4-star Lansbacherhof.

But there are also options in the pretty heart of the village around the church, including the unusual Alpendorf Anno Dazumal ('Year Dot'), a 4-star hotel consisting of individual huts and chalets, with a charming central restaurant. Don't run away with the idea that this is a quiet backwater, though: also in the heart of the village is a lively après spot, the Kleine Tenne (sister to the Hohenhaus Tenne places at the lift bases in Hintertux and Schladming) – while across the street is the similarly boisterous Bergfriedalm.

Next to the village there is a gentle nursery slope served by the 350m Hinteranger button lift. There is a kids' practice area at the top of the Eggalm gondola, with moving carpets etc.

We understand there is skating and curling, but we see no sign of any toboggan runs.

A stay here makes sense in two circumstances: if you are happy to focus on skiing Eggalm and Rastkogel – getting to Penken on skis is quite a faff – or if you plan to spend as much time skiing Hintertux as skiing other areas.

Hintertux

The Hintertux glacier is one of the world's best, ranking alongside the Stubai glacier (which gets its own chapter a few pages back). There are lodgings at the lift base, and a short distance away is the small spa village of Hintertux itself.

   For most people, at most times of the year, staying in Mayrhofen makes more sense than staying here; but in the shoulder seasons, staying in Hintertux has clear appeal. The glacier is open 365 days a year, but the permanent snow is only a fraction of the area's winter size.

The mountains

The spine of the area is the Gletscherbus, a series of three big twin-cable gondolas rising from 1500m via Sommerbergalm (S-alm for short, 2100m) and Tuxer Fernerhaus (2660m) to Gefrorene Wand at 3250m – the high-point, despite the impression given by the piste map.

   At the top, there are drag-lifts on the glacier (which extends no further down than Tuxer Fernerhaus). There are pistes and ski routes down from there to S-alm and, to the right on the map, lifts and runs below Grosser Kaserer. From S-alm there are lifts on the right towards Tuxer Joch.

Size The resort claims 60km of pistes, but this appears to include ski routes. This is slightly less than the Stubaier Gletscher claims, and we're inclined to think it's about right. So: big for a glacier area, but only ✳ in the general scheme.

Slopes It's an area of three parts: the glacier, above Tuxer Fernerhaus, is treeless and gentle; the next chunk, above S-alm, is treeless but much steeper; and the final chunk, below S-alm, is steeper and partly wooded.

   The top to bottom vertical is 1750m, but it's not a continuous descent: you have to ride a short lift at S-alm. The biggest continuous descent, above that

Nothing to see but snow and rock, and the big Sommerbergalm lift/restaurant complex towards bottom left

lift, is about 1245m vertical. The longest descent is said to be the 7km from Tuxer Joch to the valley station.

Most of the runs on the middle section of the area are ski routes, which are prepared partly or not at all, and not patrolled. They are said to be free of crevasses, which is not surprising since they are below glacier level.

The long red run 1 on the right of the map, a groomed ski route with snowmaking in the past, is now a piste.

Snow Even if much of the skiing is on rock rather than ice, at these altitudes – essentially, all above 2100m – you can be confident of good snow. The slopes mainly face north, too, which helps.

System, Lift The access lifts are impressive, and you can spend time doing laps on the upper stages. Away from those lifts, it's a mixture, and less satisfactory. As usual on glaciers, there are some drag-lifts, but there are also some slow chair-lifts – the Lärmstange 2 and Tuxerjoch chairs are fast, but the mile-long Lärmstange is a slow double and the 1km-long Schlegeis on the back of the mountain is a slow triple.

Sustenance Some adequate spots. The ancient Spannagelhaus refuge was well revamped in 2013 in cool mountain style, but its menu is standard-issue dreary Austrian. Tuxer Ferner's Wirtshaus lacks atmosphere but its menu has wider

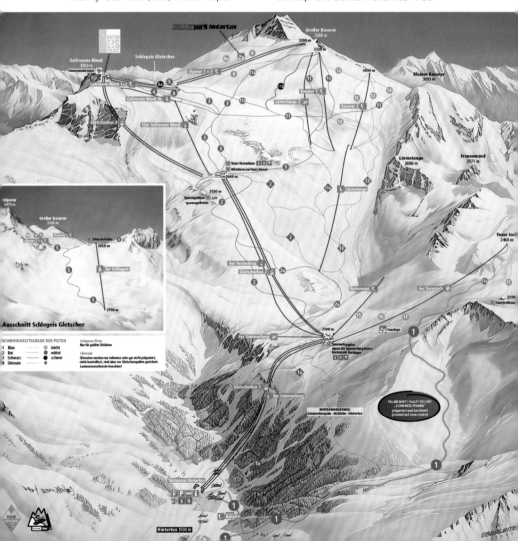

options (and the self-service bit is as good as it gets). The cosy Gletscherhütte at the top does decent table service, in parts of the place at least; good gröstl and gulaschsuppe.

More on the slopes

For beginners There is a 160m rope tow at the lift base. Why anyone would want to come up here to learn to ski on it, we can't imagine. After that, it's up (and down) the gondolas.

For true blue skiers The only slopes accessible to a non-confident skier are those at S-alm – a short run on the 500m Ramsmoos T-bar and a decent mile-long run from Tuxer Joch. So if you are forced to spend a day up here with your more confident chums, you will be able to do a bit of skiing. The higher blue runs, which are splendid, sadly involve red runs for access, and riding gondolas down to S-alm.

For confident intermediates It's a splendid area for keen intermediate skiers. The higher red runs are only just red in gradient, but the width and the snow are enjoyable. The middle section is much more rewarding though, provided you are happy on the ski routes which make up most of the runs; not that there is anything wrong with the piste, run 2, but it is the only piste.

The runs to the valley are excellent, too, and well worth doing early in the day before they get crowded and bumpy. Run 1a, which is still a ski route, is a lovely wooded run – not steep, but in many places narrow and gnarly, with highly variable snow conditions.

For experts The black pistes have short stiff pitches but the main amusement is going to be the mid-mountain ski routes and the large amounts of off-piste between the pistes and routes.

Venturing just outside the lift network, on skier's right is the long, snow-catching gully of Kleegrube; you can end this at S-alm or in good snow go on down to the valley lift station.

Fancy stuff In spring and autumn there's a serious Betterpark up on the glacier, with five lines. Presumably in winter the competition from Mayrhofen is too intense. There's a funslope on the lower slopes of Tuxer Joch, close to S-alm.

The resort

Hintertux is a tiny village – really just a cluster of substantial hotels – close to the head of the Tux valley. For skiing purposes it would be more appealing if it were actually at the head of the Tux valley; but the problem is solved – there are lodgings there too.

Convenience You can stay at the lift base, a short stagger from the lift station, or in Hintertux 1km away. If descending from the glacier on the piste, as opposed to the ski route, you can peel off to your left to ski to the village – so it can be ski-in even if it is a long way from being ski-out.

Nevertheless, our preference is for the lift base, where you have only a few yards to walk to the lift in the morning. The frequent ski-buses from lower down the valley – every 10 minutes at peak times – pick up in the village; but they may of course have quite a few people on board when they reach this point. The better village hotels will of course have their own shuttles.

Lodgings There are three 4-star hotels at the lift base. The 4-star Neuhintertux is close to the lifts and has a good spa. In the village you have wider options, including cheaper ones. In the village, the 4-star Badhotel Kirchler has its very own thermal spring. The 4-star Alpenhof has attractions: a very impressive spa, great kids' facilities and a toque from the Gault-Millau guide.

Bars and restaurants There's an umbrella bar at S-alm that gets busy in the afternoon. At the lift base, Hohenhaus Tenne is a famously lively place with several bars, DJs and sometimes live music (a formula replicated on a smaller scale in nearby Lanersbach, and a much bigger scale in Schladming). It incorporates a pizzeria.

Off the slopes There's a 3km floodlit toboggan run from Bichlalm – walk up or take a taxi at prescribed hours.

For families Near the lift base there is a kids' practice area, Flohpark, with moving carpet, carousel, rope-tow etc. And at S-alm, served by the Ramsmoos T-bar, there is a Kidsslope – a funslope for kids, with tunnels, waves and banked bends.

Hochfügen-Hochzillertal

Kaltenbach / Fügen / Hochfügen / Aschau

This area, more or less at the entrance to the Ziller valley, has an identity crisis. Pay attention at the back there: we will explain this only once.

Hochzillertal is the name used for the ski area above the valley village of Kaltenbach; this mountain is linked to another ski area called Hochfügen, centred on a high-altitude mini-resort satellite of Fügen that's also called Hochfügen, directly behind Hochzillertal (not next to it, as the piste map suggests). The two sectors are in separate ownership, have no shared identity and market themselves separately. The brand Ski-Optimal is sometimes used by Hochzillertal, but in a half-hearted fashion. Each sector runs its own website, and each produces its own map of the shared area. Could it be, perhaps, that the owners don't see eye to eye?

Meanwhile, the resorts of Kaltenbach and Fügen market themselves jointly under the catchy name Best of Zillertal, and call the combined ski area Hochfügen-Hochzillertal, no doubt annoying greatly the owners of Hochzillertal. To complicate matters further, Fügen has a separate home mountain, Spieljoch, that is in the same ownership as Hochzillertal.

The skiing is good and quite high, and the villages are pleasant places. If you want to stay here rather than in Mayrhofen, you could make a case for Fügen, or Hochfügen; but Kaltenbach makes the obvious base, at least until the owners of Hochzillertal realise their plan to build an impressive cross-valley link with Spieljoch (possibly by 2020).

Most of the skiing is above the treeline, and it gets up to 2375m where the two sectors meet

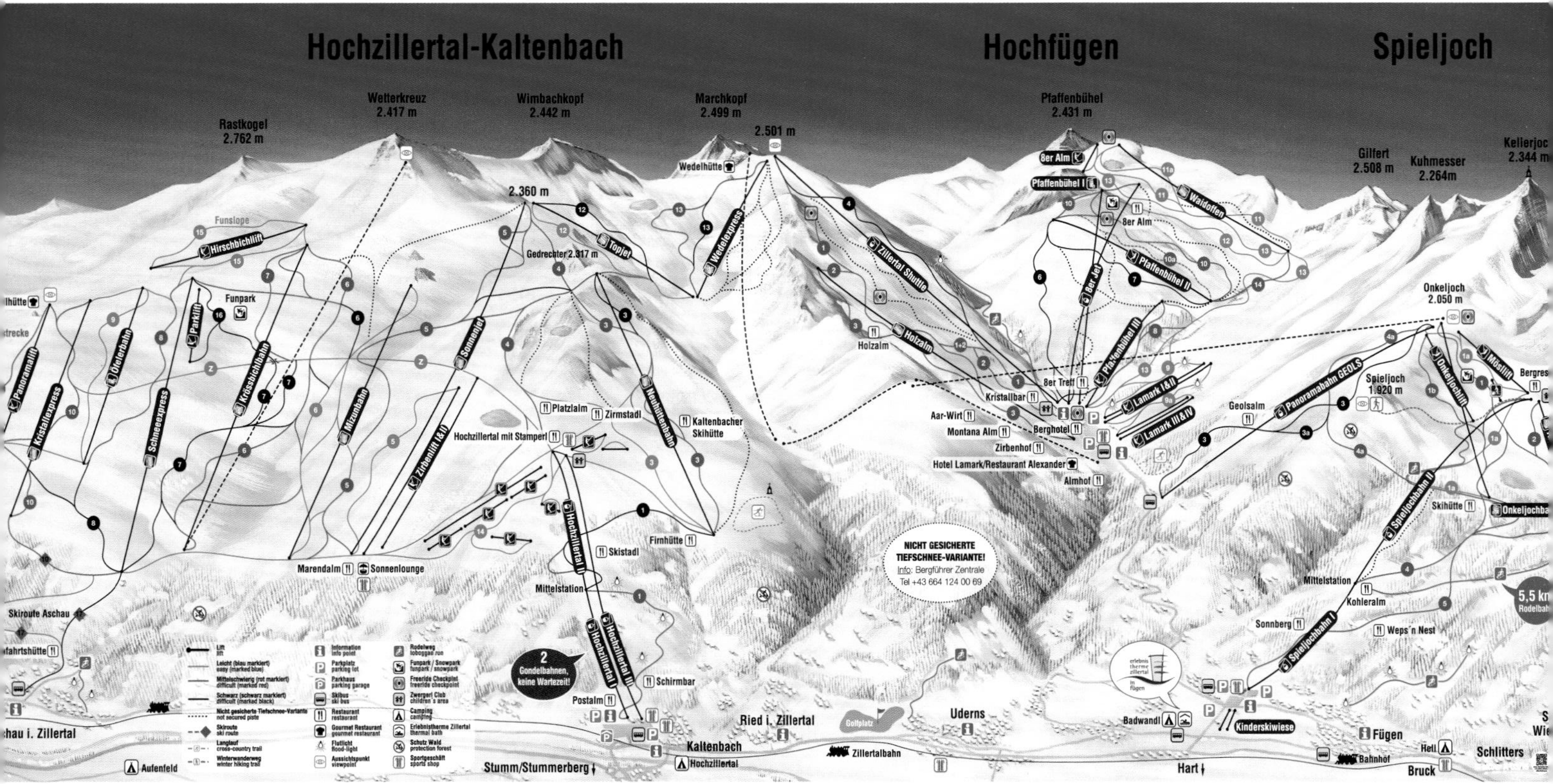
Hochzillertal-Kaltenbach
Hochfügen
Spieljoch
Rastkogel 2.762 m
Wetterkreuz 2.417 m
Wimbachkopf 2.442 m
Marchkopf 2.499 m
2.501 m
2.360 m
Wedelhütte
Pfaffenbühel 2.431 m
Gilfert 2.508 m
Kuhmesser 2.264m
Kellerjoc 2.344 m
Funslope
Hirschbichllift
Funpark
Parklift
Panoramalift
Kristallexpress
Ötelerbahn
Schneeexpress
Krössbichlbahn
Mizunbahn
Sonnenjet
Zirbenlift (I & II)
Gedrechter 2.317 m
Topjet
Wedelexpress
Zillertal Shuttle
Holzalm
Neuhüttenbahn
Kaltenbacher Skihütte
Platzalm
Zirmstadl
Hochzillertal mit Stamperl
Marendalm
Sonnenlounge
Skistadl
Firnhütte
Mittelstation
Hochzillertal I
Hochzillertal II
Hochzillertal III
2 Gondelbahnen, keine Wartezeit!
Postalm
Schirmbar
Skiroute Aschau
Aufenfeld
Stumm/Stummerberg
Kaltenbach
Hochzillertal
Ried i. Zillertal
Golfplatz
Zillertalbahn
Uderns
NICHT GESICHERTE TIEFSCHNEE-VARIANTE!
Info: Bergführer Zentrale
Tel +43 664 124 00 69
8er Alm
Pfaffenbühel I
Pfaffenbühel II
Pfaffenbühel III
Waidoffen
8er Jet
8er Treff
Kristallbar
Aar-Wirt
Montana Alm
Berghotel
Zirbenhof
Hotel Lamark/Restaurant Alexander
Almhof
Lamark I & II
Lamark III & IV
Geolsalm
Panoramabahn GEOLS
Spieljoch 1.920 m
Onkeljoch 2.050 m
Onkeljochlift
Möslift
Bergres
Skihütte
Spieljochbahn II
Spieljochbahn I
Mittelstation
Kohleralm
Sonnberg
Weps'n Nest
5,5 km
Badwandl
Kinderskiwiese
Fügen
Bahnhof
Hart
Heti
Schlitters
Bruck

The mountains

Hochzillertal consists mainly of an array of parallel chair-lifts and drags on the roughly east-facing open slopes above Kaltenbach and Aschau. Access is by twin gondolas from Kaltenbach, but there are also ski routes to Aschau.

On the back of the hill are short chair-lifts and runs in a shallow valley, at the far side of which is the link to Hochfügen. From the ridge, longer west-facing runs descend to the mini-resort, and from there lifts go off to access north-east facing runs from Pfaffenbühel.

Size

The area claims about 90km of slopes including a tiny amount of ski routes, and this seems not far off the real figure. So it's on the small side, and it's likely keen skiers based here will want to travel up the valley to some of the other resorts covered by the lift pass.

The planned link with Fügen's home slopes on Spieljoch, if and when it is built, will add another 20km or so.

Slopes

The skiing is pretty well all above the trees, and of reddish gradient, with blues cutting across the hill (though there are exceptions to this).

The piste maps cheerfully exaggerate altitudes, for example suggesting the ridge between the two sectors peaks at about 2500m when it's actually about 2375m – the high-point of the area. It's generally not an area for long runs – the lifts on the front of Hochzillertal have verticals of around 400m–500m; the runs down to Hochfügen are longer – up to 900m. And there is a run down to Kaltenbach, making a descent of 1800m vertical possible.

There are only a couple of ski routes at the bottom of the lift system, providing a way home to Aschau. But amazingly both areas have an entirely novel concept: 'not secured pistes'. In fact, this seems to be a misleading translation from the German, and they are not pistes but off-piste routes.

Snow

With practically all the skiing above 1500m, and most of the slopes facing north to east, snow should rarely be a problem. The runs down to Hochfügen from the ridge where the two sectors meet face slightly north of west, so they may be vulnerable on warm afternoons.

Hochfügen has half a dozen hotels and guest houses, some set on the piste from Hochzillertal

System, Lift

There are quite a few slow old lifts dotted around the area; most can be avoided, and the system works well in general, but slow lifts that might cause irritation include the quite short Topjet chair in the shallow valley between the two areas, the Öfeler double chair on the left of the Hochzillertal face and the Pfaffenbühel T-bars at Hochfügen.

Sustenance

This is not an area with a hut around every corner, but you certainly won't starve. There are lots clustered around the top of the Kaltenbach gondola and around Hochfügen, and a few others. All are marked and named on the map.

There are some excellent spots. Above Hochfügen, Holzalm is a welcoming woody chalet serving good food. Just on the Hochzillertal side of the linking ridge, Wedelhütte is a tiny smart hotel (not a mountain refuge) doing serious food with all the trimmings. At the far left of the piste map, Kristalhütte looks much the same.

More on the slopes

For beginners

Both sectors have quite good arrangements. Hochzillertal has a handful of gentle beginner lifts at the top of the gondolas, at over 1700m. Hochfügen has lifts right next to the 'village'; some are on the steep side, but there is a gentle covered moving carpet. Hochfügen is better equipped with longer blue runs to progress to.

For true blue skiers

There is skiing to do, but it's far from ideal. Starting from the Hochzillertal nursery slopes at the top of the gondola you can access long blue runs on a couple of lifts including the 1.7km Mizun fast chair. The short blue run at the far left of the map is at the tough end of the spectrum, and much like the adjacent reds.

At Hochfügen there is a high area of easy skiing on the 1km Waidoffen chair, with a genuine blue back to the village.

In principle, it is possible to move from the first of these to the second, by riding a gondola down to Hochfügen; but it doesn't work the other way round.

For confident intermediates

There's quite a lot to do and, although the runs are generally not long, there is some sensation of travel when moving between the sectors. The whole area is worth exploring, and you'll find many of the blacks quite approachable. There's more variety on the front face of Hochzillertal than the map might suggest.

The red and black runs on the Pfaffenbühel II drag-lift at Hochfügen are very short, but the longer black run 6 from that lift back to the village is good, and the runs down to Hochfügen from the linking ridge are long and testing.

For experts

There are black runs dotted around the whole area, and most just about merit the classification although it is usually on the basis of short pitches of black gradient. So there is quite a bit to do on-piste unless you insist on serious steeps.

The 'not secured pistes' shown as dotted lines on the map add up to a lot of skiing. As we've explained (read 'Slopes') they are basically off-piste. You might discuss the hazards of these runs with the experts in the Freeride Point, in the base station of the 8er Jet chair-lift.

Off piste routes outside the lift system include a good descent from the Waidoffen chair into the valley south of Hochfügen village, and one from the Neuhütten chair to Kaltenbach.

Hochfügen projects itself as a freeride hotspot, hosting extreme competitions. It runs free half-day off-piste guiding in small groups on weekends from early January, first come first served – a great scheme. You may be able to bag a place online. And it offers cat-skiing (not free!) for groups of two to six.

Fancy stuff

Hochfügen has a small (300m) park with 13 elements in three lines on the Lamark lift. There is a 900m funslope with the usual banked turns, rollers etc below the Waldoffen chair-lift. Hochzillertal has a slightly longer Betterpark, with beginner, medium and pro lines at the top of the SchneeExpress chair, served by its own drag-lift.

The resorts

Bear in mind that when Fügen's Spieljoch slopes are linked by lift to the main lift network, Fügen will become a more appealing base than it is now.

There are ski-buses between all the obvious points around the ski area, and bus and train services along the valley.

Kaltenbach 560m

Kaltenbach is a small valley village on which skiing has had a big impact, more to cope with the influx of car-borne day visitors than 'resident' tourists – there are four 4-star hotels, and two 3-stars. The 4-star hotel Post is in the core of the village, near the railway station, but a walkable distance from the lifts.

Fügen 545m

Fügen is a small town – although the largest in the valley, they say – with a pretty centre, and a gondola on the outskirts into the Spieljoch ski area, for the moment separate from the other sectors. There is a small, gentle nursery area at the lift base.

There are about 18 hotels and guest houses in and around the town, more 4-star than 3-star.

Erlebnis-Therme is a spa complex with various pools, flumes, and an outdoor hockey-size ice rink. There's a 3km toboggan run from the gasthaus Goglhof above the town, with a tractor and trailer arrangement to get you up the hill, open afternoon and evening.

Hochfügen 1470m

Hochfügen is a skiers' mini-resort, about 11km by road from Fügen, with a cluster of hotels mainly arranged up the slope above the road as you drive in – check out the photo on p182. The 4-star hotel Lamark has a ski-in ski-out location beside the piste from Hochzillertal. There is a 1.5km floodlit toboggan run; they say there's a hut at the top where you can have a beer after walking up; our advice is to check first.

Aschau 565m

Aschau is a valley village with no lifts in to the slopes but blue and black ski routes down from the southern extremity of Hochzillertal. Choose between the 4-star Familotel Aschauerhof, the 3-star hotel St Georg or various star-free guest houses. There's a short toboggan run, reached on foot. Buses and trains run to the lifts at Kaltenbach.

Kaltenbach has a bit of industry – although one of the large buildings near the lift base is a parking garage

Zillertal Arena

Zell im Zillertal / Gerlos / Königsleiten / Hochkrimml

This is an unusual area, with small areas above its four resorts linked by chains of lifts to form a thin but very long network, spread above the road over the 1531m-high Gerlospass road. The resorts vary widely in style and appeal. Gerlos has the obvious advantage of pole position.

The mountains

Two gondolas starting a mile from central Zell go up to two points in its home slopes, one of them the mid-mountain focus of Rosenalm. Above there, lifts spread across an open mountainside to Arena Stadl, from which point a chain of four lifts/runs, all above 2000m, make the link to the top of the Gerlos slopes.

Gerlos also has two gondolas into its slopes, one going to its mid-mountain focus of Arena Center. From there a less elevated chain of four lifts/runs links to the top of the Königsleiten slopes. There is a gondola into these slopes from the village, and another from the roadside at Gerlospass, where an eight-seater chair-lift goes up into the Hochkrimml slopes on the south side of the Gerlospass road.

Size

The area claims 143km of pistes, and this appears to be roughly accurate, making this a ✳✳✳ mid-sized area.

Slopes

Most of the slopes are above the trees, with exceptions in each sector. And most are of red-run gradient, with blue runs cutting across the hill — except at Arena Center and Hochkrimml's Plattenkogel, which have some fall-line blue skiing.

With several high-points over 2200m, it's possible to put together some good long descents. The descent to the valley from Zell's Übergangsjoch is claimed to be the biggest in Austria at 1930m vertical. We make it 1920m, but that probably qualifies.

A lot of the skiing is above the treeline, with the Zell–Gerlos link reaching 2500m – the area high-point

Snow

The skiing goes high by local standards, and apart from Zell the resorts are high too. The big concern later in the season is orientation: most of the slopes are sunny, and some very sunny. Plattenkogel is an admirably shady exception, facing due north and not east as the piste map might lead you to think.

System, Lift

The system is generally impressive. The access gondolas are eight-seaters, except the 10-seater Dorfbahn out of Gerlos. The upper slopes are festooned with six-seat chair-lifts, but there are some slow quads and some doubles. Helpfully, most of the fast chairs have some variant on 'Xpress' in the name. The main weaknesses are the slow and long chairs on both flanks of Isskogel, between Zell and Gerlos, and at Larmach Alm at Königsleiten. Drag-lifts are confined to harmless positions.

According to the Zillertal website, the Zell lifts run until 4.30pm – unusual in Austria, and very welcome.

Sustenance

You might want to take emergency provisions with you on the hut-free link from Zell to Gerlos, but elsewhere there are adequate numbers of restaurants, all marked and named on the map.

At Zell, head to Kreuzwiesenalm for gröstl or krapfen (Austrian Cornish pasties). Above Gerlos, Seppi's is the place, complete with wood-fired pizza oven. At Königsleiten, Larmach Alm is a very civilised spot with armchairs and open fires; grilled chicken is the speciality.

More on the slopes

For beginners

Zell has extensive nursery slopes at Rosenalm (1744m), reached by gondola. What it doesn't have is any way to progress from there. Gerlos has a quite gentle slope next to the village with a 300m drag-lift, plus other gentle slopes up at Arena Center, including a long run from Isskogel. Königsleiten has several slopes at village level, but no longer runs suitable for progression. Hochkrimml had beginner lifts at two of its slightly separated lift bases, and plenty of long runs to progress to.

For true blue skiers

Although Gerlos has some nice blue skiing that might satisfy a beginner with no great ambition to get around the mountain, even the most apprehensive intermediate wouldn't want to be confined to that. Hochkrimml's Plattenkogel is essentially a blue mountain, but for any more adventurous skiers in your party it is probably too much out on a limb.

For confident intermediates

There's a lot of satisfying skiing for a keen intermediate at Zell and Königsleiten, with some decent long runs even if snow low down isn't good enough for Austria's biggest descent to be tackled. The skiing on the long, high link between Zell and Gerlos is a bit mixed – some parts quite interesting, others a bit featureless.

But our main reservation about the area is the time it takes to travel between Zell and Königsleiten if you are starting from one and wanting to spend some time skiing at the other. Of course, there are buses, reasonably frequent.

For experts

There are black runs dotted around, almost as if each resort thought they should have one on the map. None is seriously steep, but they are worth a look.

The one at Zell is the final 700m vertical section of the famously long descent; the main challenge it presents is snow conditions – it's low and faces west. The runs in the woods at Gerlos have more black bits to them, and run 36 to the link with Königsleiten curls nicely away from the sun for most of its length. The ones on the Falschbach gondola at the top of Königsleiten are certainly steeper than the nearby reds, but barely black.

As you might expect, given the layout of the area, there is quite a lot of off-piste to be done, for example from Isskogel and Übergangsjoch.

Fancy stuff

Zell has its extensive Action Park (with air bag in the early season) conveniently located at the top of the Karspitz gondola, served by the Kreuzwiesn six-seater chair. Gerlos has its three-line Snowpark on the Vorkogel drag at mid-mountain. In the valley between Gerlos and Königsleiten is a 100m half-pipe. Hochkrimml has a small fun park and funcross for kids.

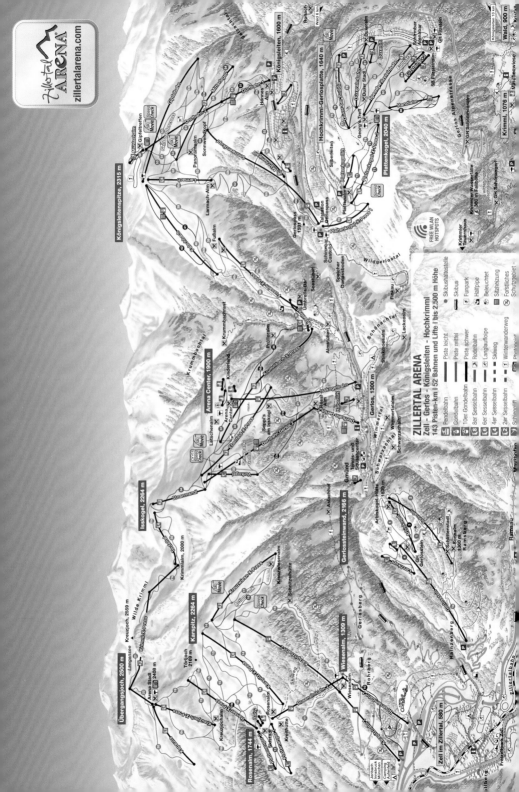

The resorts

If your plan is to make good use of the valley lift pass but you fancy spending most of your time on the Arena slopes, Zell might be the place to stay. For a solid week skiing the Arena area, Gerlos in the centre of things probably makes the best sense.

There are local buses, and a Zell–Königsleiten service, not super-frequent but adequate.

There are, as usual, mid-mountain restaurants in each sector that get lively in the afternoons, and popular bars at the lift bases.

All the 4-star hotels recommended below have swimming pools.

Zell im Zillertal 580m

Zell is a proper little town with a life outside skiing, but is no less pleasant for that. The town is a mile or so from its lift base, but the 4-star Sonnenhof is only a short walk away.

At the lift base is the Ziller valley's only sled-on-rails coaster, 1.5km long. On the little local ski hill of Gerlossteinwand there is a 7km toboggan run – longest in the valley, they say, and floodlit (until 1am!); gondola access.

Gerlos 1250m

Gerlos isn't really a village, more a row of handsome 4-star hotels lining the Gerlospass road. The 4-star S hotel Platzer is handy for both the village slope and the more modern gondola with heated seats. There are good walks up the hillsides to rustic huts, and cross-country loops towards the pass and in the quiet Schönachtal.

Königsleiten 1600m

Königsleiten is an unusual resort – a sprawl of small chalets across a wide area, on a sunny, partly wooded shelf, with a long nursery slope in the middle. It does have something like a village centre not far away, around the church and tourist office. The 4-star Alpenwelt is next to the gondola station and just above the nursery slope. There are walks at village level, and unusually high cross-country at the top of the gondola.

Hochkrimml 1640m

Another unusual resort – three little estates of chalets dotted along the quiet road that links the lift bases. There is only one hotel – the stylish 3-star S Filzstein. A cross-country trail runs parallel to the road. There is a short toboggan run.

Zell is the main town in the Ziller valley, and sits well away from the ski slopes and lift station, off to the left

Published in the UK by
Guide Editors

Editor **Chris Gill**
Consultant editor **Dave Watts**
Editorial assistant **Mandy Crook**
Design and production **Graham Wells**
Ad manager **Dave Ashmore**

Printed in the UK
by Kingsdown Printing

ISBN-13: 978-1-9997708-0-8

A CIP catalogue entry for this book is
available from the British Library.

Trade orders to:
The Travel Alliance
5 Riverside Court
Lower Bristol Road
Bath BA2 3DZ

T 01225 406440
E kholmes@pelotongrey.com

**Individual copies of the book can be
bought at a discount price from:
www.wheretoskiandsnowboard.com**

This first edition published 2017

Enquiries and feedback to:
publisher@wheretoski.uk

Map credits

Photo credits

The copyright in photos listed here belongs to the photographers or entities credited below. Other photos are the copyright of Chris Gill.

page	chapter	
4	Foreword	Michael Werlberger
17	Choosing	Andreas Tischler
19	Choosing	Alexander Lohmann / Oetztal Tourismus
30	Arlberg	Göran Assner
38	Arlberg	Sepp Mallaun / Lech-Zürs Tourismus
42	Arlberg	Dietmar Walser
49	Gastein valley	Gasteinertal Tourismus
54	Hochkönig	Hochkönig Tourismus
61	Ischgl	Albin Niederstrasser / TVB Paznaun-Ischgl
63	Ischgl	TVB Paznaun-Ischgl
72	Kitzbühel	Michael Werlberger
78	Montafon valley	Silvretta Montafon
80	Montafon valley	Patrick Säly / Montafon Tourismus
81	Montafon valley	Patrick Säly / Montafon Tourismus
86	Obertauern	TVB Obertauern
90	Ötz valley	Isidor Nösig / Oetztal Tourismus
100	Ötz valley	Alexander Lohmann / Oetztal Tourismus
102	Ötz valley	Philipp Horak / Oetztal Tourismus
105	Saalbach	Saalbach / Christian Wöckinger
109	Saalbach	Saalbach.com
111	Saalbach	Saalbach.com
118	Salz. Sportwelt	Erwin Trampitsch
120	Salz. Sportwelt	Christian Fischbacher
126	Salz. Sportwelt	Erwin Trampitsch
131	Schladming	Fotograf Hauser Kaibling
133	Schladming	Schladming-Dachstein / Raffalt
138	Serfaus-Fiss-Ladis	Andreas Kirschner / Serfaus-Fiss-Ladis
140	Serfaus-Fiss-Ladis	Andreas Kirschner / Serfaus-Fiss-Ladis
145	Ski Juwel	Simon Oberleitner / Ski Juwel
146	Ski Juwel	Alpbachtal Tourist Board
149	SkiWelt	Tim Marcour / SkiWelt
152	SkiWelt	Kurt Tropper
154	SkiWelt	Simon Oberleitner
158	Stubai Gletscher	TVB Stubai Tirol
160	Stubai Gletscher	TVB Stubai Tirol
164	Zell am See	Christian Mairitsch
166	Zell am See	Gletscherbahn Kaprun AG / Zell am See-Kaprun Tourismus
172	Ziller valley	Frank Bauer
174	Ziller valley	Laurin Moser
177	Ziller valley	MediaLounge / Hintertuxer Gletscher
180	Ziller valley	Wörgötter
182	Ziller valley	Wörgötter
184	Ziller valley	Wörgötter
185	Ziller valley	Hannes Sautner / Zillertal Arena
188	Ziller valley	Franz Schiestl / Zillertal Arena

Resort / Chapter Index

For minor resorts, the page reference takes you to the start of the chapter, not to the precise page on which the resort is described

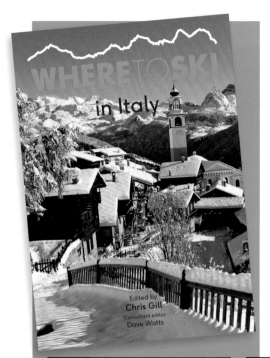

Edited by
Chris Gill
Consultant editor
Dave Watts

We hope you like *Where to Ski in Austria*. If you do, maybe you should get hold of *Where to Ski in Italy*, also published in autumn 2017. Like this book, it covers all the resorts you're likely to be interested in, and it covers them in just the same thorough, uncompromising way.

You can buy both books at discount prices through our website at wheretoskiandsnowboard.com – and the resort pages of the site are updated annually, so it's a good way to keep track of the ever-growing number of ski area links etc.

In 2018 we plan to publish Where to Ski in France and Where to Ski in Switzerland. A book on North America will follow those. If you'd like to keep up to date with these publishing plans – and be among the first to know about discount pricing offers – sign up for our email newsletter on the website.